Anarchist Perspectives for Social Work

Anarchist Perspectives for Social Work

Disrupting Oppressive Systems

ALEXANDER W. SAWATSKY

OXFORD
UNIVERSITY PRESS

Oxford University Press is a department of the University of Oxford. It furthers
the University's objective of excellence in research, scholarship, and education
by publishing worldwide. Oxford is a registered trade mark of Oxford University
Press in the UK and certain other countries.

Published in the United States of America by Oxford University Press
198 Madison Avenue, New York, NY 10016, United States of America.

© Oxford University Press 2024

All rights reserved. No part of this publication may be reproduced, stored in
a retrieval system, or transmitted, in any form or by any means, without the
prior permission in writing of Oxford University Press, or as expressly permitted
by law, by license, or under terms agreed with the appropriate reproduction
rights organization. Inquiries concerning reproduction outside the scope of the
above should be sent to the Rights Department, Oxford University Press, at the
address above.

You must not circulate this work in any other form
and you must impose this same condition on any acquirer.

Library of Congress Cataloging-in-Publication Data
Names: Sawatsky, Alexander William, author.
Title: Anarchist perspectives for social work : disrupting oppressive systems /
Alexander William Sawatsky.
Description: New York, NY : Oxford University Press, [2024] |
Includes bibliographical references and index.
Identifiers: LCCN 2023056777 (print) | LCCN 2023056778 (ebook) |
ISBN 9780197750469 (hardback) | ISBN 9780197750483 (epub) |
ISBN 9780197750490
Subjects: LCSH: Social service—Practice. | Anarchism.
Classification: LCC HV10.5 .S29 2024 (print) | LCC HV10.5 (ebook) |
DDC 361.3—dc23/eng/20231229
LC record available at https://lccn.loc.gov/2023056777
LC ebook record available at https://lccn.loc.gov/2023056778

DOI: 10.1093/oso/9780197750469.001.0001

Printed by Integrated Books International, United States of America

While there are too many to mention that have helped me grow and develop into who I am today, I want to thank my parents, Walter & Margaret, for instilling my love of learning and belief in social justice. My partner Wendi, for her wisdom and for her unending support, love, and belief in me, especially when I struggled to do so myself. My children, Marianne and Lukas, who continue to challenge me and give me reason to believe that a better world is indeed possible. Thank you from the bottom of my heart.

Contents

1. Anarchism and social work? An introduction — 1
2. Comments on the welfare state and social work: An anti-state perspective — 16
3. Supported employment: Wage slavery entrenched in recovery — 36
4. Green anarcho-social work: Social ecology, the social world, and nature — 56
5. Crime, social work, and anarchism: Seeking to abolish the carceral state — 79
6. Education, social work, and anti-capitalism: A theoretical exposition of teaching social work differently — 114
7. Mutual aid and the way forward: Ideas and implications for social work practice — 138
8. Wither social work? Reflections on the end of social work (and a world that needs it) — 181

Index — 221

1
Anarchism and social work?
An introduction

> By undermining voluntary associations and the practice of mutual aid, it eventually turns society into a lonely crowd buttressed by the social worker and policeman. (Marshall, 2010, p. 24)

This book is being written during a historic moment. I had found myself planning to write about this topic of anarchism[1] and its application to social work based in part on my own misgivings about what I believed to be the root of the problem of the social work paradox. The very circumstances that social work is called to respond to are the result of our current status quo. The quote above by anarchist historian Peter Marshall, serves to illustrate the problem. Is this profession an artifact of a broken social world? Or is it, like Antifa, dispersing when its essential function has been accomplished (Bray, 2017)?

Initially I thought I was responding out of a need to expand the analysis of social problems from an anarchist perspective. I was assuming this would be in connection to the leviathan of capital dressed in neoliberal garb. I could not have anticipated where we are now. We have a global pandemic that has challenged every country and exposed the contradictions of capitalism. Public health colliding with private health care, the consequences of poverty on the resiliency of communities, and the question of what is essential for economies to function are issues that are front and center now. Social work has long been confronting the issues located in the social world, arguing for meaningful change at systemic levels. Narratives that blame individuals for their misfortunes are not effective at addressing our current health crisis.

---

[1] The reader will notice anarchism and associated derivations to be uncapitalized (unless at the beginning of a sentence). This is intentional and a common feature found in anarchist writings.

A common thread when looking at the history of movements, of moments of social unrest and change, is how they seem to emerge from nowhere. It is usually the people most impacted by oppression, not their oppressors or the intellectual elites who are sympathetic to their plight that engage in the direct action necessary for change to occur. It would be a mistake, however, to assume that there were no prior conditions that could have predicted this current period of social unrest. To lay the current situation at the feet of the pandemic is myopic at best. Social work has been a part of raising the alarm about capitalism and the social world (Hick & Stokes, 2016; Mullaly, 2007). One unique characteristic is social work's focus on the person in the social environment. In other words, individual plight is impacted or influenced by the social world. Social problems are the result of disparate factors, including decisions made at all levels of governance. If societies are led to believe that poverty, for example, is the result of personal choices, any kind of welfare policy will have moralistic and punitive aspects. How this gets internalized by those dispossessed in society is the final violence of oppression (Hick & Stokes, 2016; Mullaly & West, 2018).

I will echo Catrina Brown's (2021) position that this is an effort to add or extend the growing work done in the area of critical social work. There is no unifying theory, but the multiple intersectional encounters seek to find ways to articulate oppression as well as theories of resistance. It is important to note that this is only the beginning of an attempt to reconcile what, at first glance, seems to be two disparate ideological/philosophical approaches. Furthermore, the idea that what social work approaches, such as Structural (Mullaly, 2007), Anti-oppressive (Brown & Strega, 2015; Martin, 2003a), and Anti-privilege (Mullaly & West, 2018) have shown is that there is no need to ascribe a monolithic concept to "social work." This is true in anarchism as well (see Baillargeon, 2013; Kinna, 2009; Marshall, 2010).

Social work theory

The changing landscape of social work theory has always been influenced by epistemologies and ontologies of other fields of knowledge. Early approaches would seek to address problems for the individual from a psychodynamic or functional lens (Payne, 2005). Behavioral approaches continued to reflect the influence of the field of psychology. As the environment became more of a focus—with both dire concerns about nature and contamination influencing a person in an environmental focus (Hick & Stokes, 2016) so too did social theories during a period of civil disobedience and upheaval (Murray & Hick, 2010, p. 4). Political structures and corresponding economic conditions further influence the evolving theories of social work practice. With families and communities becoming the target for intervention, ideas of helping shifted to consider something greater than the individual. In effect, feminist social work illustrates it best when a claim of the personal being political would mean that if women are more likely depressed than men, it isn't genetic but the conditions of living in an androcentric world that make it so (e.g. Martin, 2003b).

With the ascendance of neoliberal influences, evidence-based practice has become common in North American social work. The individual and their problems are once again the main object of intervention. Clinical social work is frequently influenced by theories that focus on how to help the individual improve their functioning in the environment (see strength based, solution focused, motivational interviewing, etc.). The ideas augured by the application of Marxist critiques of society in the 1960s and 1970s have not disappeared, however. They remain in the work of approaches such as Structural Social Work and Critical Social Work practices (Mullaly, 2007). Most recently, there has been a greater interest in approaches such as Anti-oppressive Practice that seeks to extend the work of such practices that remind that the environment is not neutral and that multiple intersections of oppression are realities for many who encounter social work in real life (Hick & Stokes, 2016; Mullaly & West, 2018).

The political context of the now

Historians will need to decide if 2016 was a moment for the emergence of another way or approach to thinking about social problems and their possible resolution. With the Trump presidency, it became apparent that a growing dissatisfaction with the status quo was emerging. A Marxian perspective would suggest that growing awareness of dispossession by the proletariat will lead to class war. Critical theory, a constellation of re-interpretations of Marx, posited the notion of some force distracting or pacifying society, so it is not able to reach an epiphany for its liberation (see Agger, 2006). Debord goes as far as describing this phenomenon as "the spectacle" (1998) that has us all unable to clearly see the way we are all being exploited and oppressed by capitalism. In this current moment, a hollowed-out welfare state is no longer able to disguise the growing discontent of a society that has not managed to address a growing inequality, both socially and financially. The growing atomization of an individualistic approach to social organization has resulted in the polarization of political ideologies with attendant expressions of right-wing extremism as capital seeks to protect itself in fascist tendencies (Gelderloos, 2007; Rappaport, 2019).

While postmodern theories would caution the idea of the great man theory, the strongman is emerging to take the reins of democracies. With these worrisome trends, there is a growing interest in exploring alternatives to capitalism. The protests against the World Trade Organization (WTO) meetings in 1999 in Seattle is seen as an illustration of mobilization by diverse groups coming together to address a shared nemesis—the neoliberal globalizing elites. A "new anarchism" can be found in these movements (Graeber, 2013). "Anti-oppressive practice" is a broad approach to social problems and their remedy that echoes this postmodern turn. There is room for many anti-oppressive approaches, including anti-capitalist movements that embrace anarchist ideas (Brown & Strega, 2015, p. 8).

Given the existence of the welfare state and the role of social work within, it has become common practice to include knowledge from economic theories. Hick (2013), for example, frames welfare in the context of Keynesian market approaches. Political theory is another area essential to understanding policy development (see, for example, Lightman & Lightman, 2017), as in a representative democracy, political ideology shapes how those who are economically disadvantaged or socioeconomically marginalized are understood and treated. Anarchist theory is both interested in addressing the issue of governance (and self-governance) as well as critiquing the very idea of a free market capitalist economic model in the first place. A brief note on the use of capitalism and neoliberalism: These terms may at times be used interchangeably to reflect the fact that the neoliberal turn is really just the most current expression of capitalism. Given that anarchist ideas are based on a fundamental rejection of capitalism, it stands to reason that the term "capitalism" will tend to be the more common one employed throughout. The reader can expect the reference to neoliberalism to be deliberate in illustrating how capitalism is operating in the world today.

If we reject the "invisible hand" theory of classical liberal economics, we need to do the same with politics. A representative democracy does not have an essential good beyond the collection of individuals involved in governance.

Too frequently, it is a tyranny of the majority (Wolff, 1998) which is tacitly accepted by all parties as in their best interest. Even modern social work writers acknowledge the fallacy of pluralism in the notion that each person's voice has equal weight and merit (Hick, 2013; Mullaly & West, 2018). It is obvious how economic policies favor the wealthy few.

One way that real change can be stifled is when we are convinced that "There Is No Alternative" (TINA), as Margaret Thatcher famously declared regarding free market capitalism (Malleson, 2016). If we believe that capitalism is the only viable reality, our responses to oppression and other forms of disenfranchisement are restricted to tinkering with existing systems, and we are back to the original problem. Oppressors cannot resolve oppression as systems cannot be revised to address issues related to having systems in the first place. What has drawn me to anarchism in general has been the stubborn insistence that, as stated above, "A better world is possible." This requires both the critical deconstruction of worldviews that disempower most people on this planet as well as the insistence that there is hope for ways of being that maximize the best for all.

We are all products of our time. Aside from the aforementioned Trumpian concerns, global pandemic, and civil unrest, there has been a standoff where the Wet'suwet'en protests illustrate the very issues related to unfettered capital expansion-corporations using the law as a cudgel to legitimize the exploitation of land for profit. As social workers, we are likely to be working with Indigenous peoples here on Turtle Island. Their battle for defending the First Nations that they are, while confronting a legacy of horror through genocidal laws, extend back to the original notions of property and ownership. A famous axiom of anarchist thought is that property is theft (Marshall, 2010, p. 239) or as Proudhon (2022) initially coined it, "Property is robbery!" (p. 12). It is the idea that anyone who seeks to possess (in this case, land) is taking away from the commons, from everyone else. An extension of this view is that the enforcement of laws is about entrenching the legitimacy of ownership and discouraging any reflection on the rationality of concepts related to possession, such as the accumulation of capital. The blocking of pipelines is as much about sovereignty as it is about saving the environment itself from further calamity. The strategy, from an anarchist perspective, is direct action while ecological recovery is an imperative of this philosophy (Bookchin, 2004). Capitalisms' infinite appetite for profit requires production beyond rational need. Anarchism would see utility and need as the boundaries of production, not profit.

A critique of capitalism is essential for social work. If the intention is to truly be a helping profession for those pushed to the margins of society, we should be developing methods of critique and ways to challenge the hegemony of hierarchies, of capitalism. This is the toxic environment that has resulted in the harm we are confronted with on a daily basis. This book is making the case that there are alternatives. What will be a common recitation throughout this book is a popular anarchist idea, "A better world is possible."

> ...how could a raggedy band of freedom fighters in South Africa resist such a forceful global tide? ... was the message being peddled by the lawyers, economists and social workers who made up the rapidly expanding "transition" industry—... who hop from war-torn country to crisis-racked city, regaling overwhelmed new politicians with the latest best practice. (Klein, 2007, p. 274)

The quote refers to the process by which disaster capitalism expands its global grip of dominance. There are several observations that make sense here. For one, it illustrates the ongoing challenge for social work. I cannot know what the motivations are, but I could understand the siren song for individual social workers. We are wanting to maximize our effectiveness in doing good in the world. Partnering with international efforts to "help" that are well funded and have the support of the international community is tempting. However, there is a history of social work being the enablers of practices and ideas that are anything but benign (e.g. Blackstock, 2009).

Around the world, protests are erupting, and the focus is on how agents of the state enforce law and order, exposing what has been known before—racism is systemic and real. Recent calls for social workers to take over for police are the second reason for Naomi Klein's quote above. It may be tempting to step into the fray, both to legitimize the helping profession and to show how a more empathetic approach to social problems could be the solution. However, again, concerns raised about the deadening effect of responding to surface issues (as opposed to effecting real change) need to be considered. In fact, theories that challenge the assumptions of authority as a construct can be used to help understand better how to apply anti-oppressive approaches.

> Where the main support for old anarchist movement came from peasants and artisans, the new anarchists were principally disaffected middle-class

intellectuals, especially teachers, social workers and students. (Marshall, 2010, p. 542)

What the above quotations have in common are glimpses of the way social work is perceived and understood. The profession could be seen as facilitators of the status quo by participating in normalizing a neoliberal worldview while providing relief and welfare reform. However, a new anarchism seems to be in part driven by "social workers and students" suggesting a new and growing interest by this discipline. This needs to be balanced with concerns about authorities, be they political or intellectual. I have long made the case in class that my concern is that the role of community is increasingly being outsourced to the "experts" of social work. Furthermore, when approaches like Critical Theory, despite their merits, dismiss theory that promotes a "revolutionary expediency that oppresses others in the short term" (Agger, 1999 as cited by Mullaly & West, 2018, p. 87), further discourse is needed. While anarchism certainly would applaud dismissal of any vanguard party invariably recreating oppression, this could imply support for incrementalism within the existing systems that simply reproduce or reinforce the status quo by engaging in liberal parliamentary reform. I would want the influence of anarchist ideas to challenge such assumptions. Without doing so, I fear we reproduce the charge leveled against theory, that it is essentially toothless in improving real material conditions.

The main point I want to make here however is that social work, like anarchism, is not easily labeled nor understood. The challenge here is to draw connections while highlighting divergencies for both theories and their approaches. Finally, I will make the case that they can coexist when imagining current anti-oppressive approaches, especially those that eschew hierarchies and share anti-capitalist sentiment.

As I begin to write about the ways that I can see anarchism and social work together, it is perfectly legitimate to examine how my own work reflects these ideas. My own growth within the body of work of anarchist thought is quite recent. I think this is an important point to raise at the outset. Therefore, I cannot impress the reader with courageous acts of resistance to compel them to consider the challenging work of anarchism let alone how it could apply to social work.

There are several things that I believe are important about the fact that I am a novice to this. For one, now that I am learning about anarchism, I am balancing my regret at having waited so long with my growing enthusiasm about the potential for a better world that this literature offers. Taking a step back, I reflect on why I delayed. I recall in my early days in college, feeling an anger at the world and its expectations. The generic career and future that, if privileged enough to have access to, was all there seemed to be. I remember thinking that government and all forms of authority are just elaborate devices that ensure compliance to a gray existence. Why did I not pursue this line of thought?

I have an idea why this was, and perhaps it is the reason for allowing myself to let go of the regrets. Anarchist ideas seemed to be reactionary and juvenile expressions to me. As a social worker, I even had the language for this: children and youth engaging in individuation (Bell & Bell, 2009; Chapman & Withers, 2019, p. 173) in order to establish more firmly their own personalities, morals, and values. Fancy language to dismiss resistance and critical exploration of norms that validate a hegemony of capitalist modern life.

In my time in Canada, I have had the opportunity to explore critical social work as well as the associated ideas and literature. This has empowered me to reexamine my own relationship to authority and hierarchy. As I write this, I can recall the thrill of returning to anarchism while reading Swift's *S.O.S. Alternatives to Capitalism* (2014) after attending a national conference for social work educators in 2016. Here are the ideas that help challenge a critical assumption, that there is no alternative. Holding to existing models of economic exchange and state-centered solutions is based on such an assumption.

This book tries to answer a challenging problem. Can a helping profession, such as social work, reconcile with antiauthoritarian, anti-hierarchical ideas such as anarchism? Perhaps some readers would want to question the premise in the first place. While the next chapter will delve into this more fully, I would remind as above, that there has been a tendency since the 1960s for social work to question its role within a system that reifies oppressive social conditions, including from Marxist perspectives. Anarchist thought found its renaissance around this as well at the beginning of the 70s (see Marshall, 2010, p. 602), and it is my contention that this diverse field of thought/praxis can extend current approaches that question the relationship between social work, the state, and those oppressed by the status quo.

Put another way, the discipline of social work has sought to work through a history that has reinforced assumptions about social problems that have validated social relations and ideas about capitalism. This has caused harm to those we claim to help. Mullaly and West (2018) describe progressive approaches that intend to step outside of hegemony and question the nature of these relations. While the welfare state has been criticized for the way it reduces the tensions and contradictions of capitalism, there is an implicit assumption. Perhaps it is further proof that we are not able to step fully outside hegemony in that we remain convinced that a version of the state is necessary. That society is unable to function without regulatory authority. By this token, we remain locked in a worldview where the only contention is a form of governance.

Anarchism is, broadly speaking, a diverse school of philosophical thought, theory of economic relations, and political ideology, to name a few of the branches here. To be clear, I want to make this point at the outset—I am not an authority (pardon the pun) on the subject, nor would I claim to be. This is anathema to the idea of anarchism itself. The point of this book is to stimulate thought and discussion for ways to think of anarchism for social work. This book is not intended to be complete as is illustrated by the chapters within. A few branches of social work (ideas, approaches) are explored, and I hope this will stimulate further interest in the topic. I make a key assumption that a discipline such as social work has a function outside of its origins. It need not be seen only as an essential feature of liberal or now neoliberal societies. As such, the ideas of anarchism, that challenge hierarchies and existing authoritarian tendencies found in such constructs of the state, can be considered.

During this difficult time of both increasing neoliberal world domination and with it the increasing gap between the wealthy and the poor, it may be tempting to become cynical, to engage in practice that can only reduce harm. If anything, this book is intended to be a hopeful message. In my prior occupation, I used to tell new staff during orientation that their job was to make themselves redundant. I have taken this idea into the classroom as well. It is my belief that anarchism's focus is to destroy any vestige of authority and hierarchy, such as the state, and the exploitative economic relations which share a similar point of view. Without the instruments of oppression, there would not be any inequity or related social problems requiring intervention.

It is my intention for the following chapters to encourage you to join me as I am encountering new ways of viewing the world as well as how to engage with social problems that incorporate anarchist thought. It is my hope that, in the spirit of anarchism, I do not lead the reader but join you in exploring this rich area of ideas toward a shared goal of realizing that a better world is indeed possible. The following chapters will then look at various current aspects of social work and seek to find how anarchist concepts and approaches can add or build on these. I again want to note that I am not claiming that these attempts at incorporation are exclusive. If this leads to further discussion about possibilities, I would be satisfied.

Anarchism holds the view that all forms of the state, whether of monarchial, oligarchical, democratic, or socialist orientations, are harmful to society. As will be elaborated in the following chapters, anarchism opposes hierarchies of every iteration. This is primarily based on the philosophical premise that true equality is at odds with any attempts to establish systems of rule. The very idea that someone needs to shepherd society implies a dim view of the human condition. This notion suggests we are unable to manage our own affairs and to cooperatively act in collective or mutual best interests. In fact, history has shown ample examples of autonomous anarchist responses by peasantry and other sections of society frequently considered unable to manage their own affairs without state intervention.

An interesting question is being asked by anarchism. What if the way we think about society and the state is the inverse of what is really going on? If liberal notions of a state to protect us from our barbarous natures is in fact incorrect? Anarchism questions ideas that support a status quo of state authority for our own good. In effect, the question becomes, what if the state exists to defend inequality and wealth disparity and creates, not eliminates, poverty and crime? What if capitalism is not an opponent of the state but an intrinsic feature of economic relations within a society that is organized in this way? How would this change our perspective of the world and the nature of social problems?

First, this book will look more broadly to current progressive approaches to social work such as anti-oppressive practice, for example, to locate places where anarchism can help extend the work being done here. This is followed by an exploration of common ideas in this field that encourage the imagining of an anarchist social work orientation. It is offered at the outset to view the remaining chapters as invitations to new ways of identifying social problems, their causes, and hopefully their resolution.

As Chapter 2 (related to welfare states) will explore, anarchism offers an alternative explanation to today's worrisome neoliberal trends. Marx assumed that the state will always reflect economic relations as a reactive device or put another way, the political expression of that dominance (Knuttila, 1992). In our present time, hence dependent entirely on capitalism, anarchism offers a more complex understanding of the relationship that better explains current conditions. The state has self-interest and will seek to ensure its own preservation. In effect, it will make decisions at odds with capitalist interests if the long view ensures its survival. In fact, some writers (Carter, 2013) make the case that it will go as far as allowing revolutions to take place in order to reconstitute itself with economic models that are more appropriate or useful to its current state. Such a view helps explain how past revolutions only reset classes, reinstating similar hierarchical relations post monarchy.

Neoliberalism then, is not the destruction of the state but a reshaping that serves the interests of the state to remain relevant and in power by adapting free market approaches to governance. Put another way, third party provision of services via privatization of essential services by the government has a political benefit. By outsourcing, government engages in the same practice of externalizing risks (Lightman & Lightman, 2017). If it goes wrong, they can blame the private service provider, cancel contracts, and move on to the next option as they only administered funds. Voters cannot accuse government of failing to act, as they can pass the blame on to the provider.

In Chapter 3 (on supported employment) the specific construct and features of the welfare system from a mental health perspective are explored. While other examples exist such as vocational rehabilitation, job training centers and so on, social workers in the field of mental health will be familiar with expectations around supported employment. Anarchism here is intended to assist in providing a critique about the problematic assumptions by society due to the state's view of all of us as only having value if contributing to the accumulation of capital. The anarchist literature on work questions this construct, to begin with, as part of a larger hegemony. Pointing to a past where work and leisure time were less distinct, it is suggested that we reconsider our understanding of these things.

Research on social work in mental health is used to illustrate the implicit assumptions around recovery being related to ability to work for a local mental health institution in Canada prior to deinstitutionalization. The concern about normalizing work as a condition of living is examined given how work for the sake of work increases stress and worsens mental health. The reader is asked to consider how this is not only our responsibility—to consider how work is a harmful idea for recovery and hence to those we claim to serve—but how to extend this concern. Any population that is deemed unable to work will fall under the same spell of internalizing these destructive definitions of the human condition. Finally, we ourselves, and the society we live in, are encouraged to reconsider the way we think about work and our worth as members of said society.

Chapter 4 (on green social work) seeks to connect with a long-standing concern about the environment in anarchism. As will be discussed more fully, anarchist thought has raised the alarm about industrialization and the advance of capitalism. In essence, this lines up with the larger logic that if land is property, it can be commodified, abused, and exploited without consideration. Rather than seeking to shame or instigate an "ethical" capitalism, anarchism would seek to eliminate the ownership of things. Put another way, the concept of ownership is challenged as fiction. Anarchist writings exist that seek to imagine alternative ways of relating to each other and the natural world that would go beyond incremental adjustments to a system of relations requiring ongoing exploitation to exist.

Structural social work has critiqued the role of the social worker as an agent of social control (Payne, 2005; Mullaly, 2007). I have found that it is difficult but necessary to consider how the power and authority given to social workers can serve the state and its oppressive structure. Chapter 5 is intended to challenge myself and the reader to confront the problematic assumptions about crime, policing and incarceration that serve to legitimize a system that has harmed those social work professes to want to be helpful to. The ways in which social work has been involved in the carceral system are examined while reflecting on how abolitionist and anarchist criminological theories could influence a new way of helping those most impacted by the justice system.

A challenge for social work can be how to teach this discipline in the first place. As social work emerged as a body of knowledge along with requisite degrees, it must confront ideas about pedagogy. If social work seeks to be on the side of those who are oppressed, how do you teach that without replicating the same in the classroom? Foucault (Foucault & Blanchot, 1987, pp. 80–81), after all, identified one place of power over others to be the totalizing experience of the classroom. This is a similar conundrum that anarchism has faced. After all, if authority is rejected, what role does a teacher play? Chapter 6 (on social work education) seeks to explore critical pedagogy along with attempts by anarchism to resolve a seeming paradox in education.

Social work can be understood as emphasizing a social world where individuals are connected to each other and the communities that they inhabit. Shulman (2016) emphasizes the notion of mutual aid as a key factor in group work. Chapter 7 seeks to engage with the potential of this concept for social work practice. Given it's focus in anarchist literature, this concept is explored as a way to consider how the flourishing of mutual aid could lead to new ways for social workers to be involved in fostering healthier groups and communities.

Finally, this book will ask the question of how social work can become irrelevant. It may be tempting to see the profession as having job security, given the ills of this world and the need to attend to these. Chapter 8 will call this into question, to challenge the reader to consider how social work could contribute to real change that makes the profession obsolete-at least in its current form and function. It would be foolish to assume that this book is a complete review of both anarchism and social work. Therefore, further topics for future discussion will be included in this concluding chapter for the reader to consider.

In summary, the purpose of this book is to challenge previously held assumptions about the world we live in and ideas that may have been dismissed, at best, as juvenile and, at worst, as chaotic and dangerous. For many, anarchism has been represented by such imagery as the Sex Pistols and terrorist bombings or other acts of violence and discord. It is my hope that by the end of this book you have had the opportunity to reconsider. We live during a moment in our collective history similar to others, where many voices gained an audience. As history has shown, this has unfortunately led to periods of greater unrest, war, and death. Among the demagoguery, jingoist rhetoric and fascist tendencies to protect capital, other voices have contributed their ideas for a better world. Rather than engage in a competition for power, anarchism advances a view about the human condition that—all things being equal—we will choose peaceful coexistence over domination, oppression, and dispossession. It is my hope that the following chapters will engage and inspire social work to find ways to incorporate anarchism into their approaches. Perhaps we can envision a nonhierarchical social work practice—a ghost in the machine—to continue to help but always engaging with the project of seeking the destruction of all hierarchies, powers, and authority.

References

Agger, B. (2006). *Critical social theories: An introduction* (2nd ed.). Paradigm Publishers.

Baillargeon, N. (2013). *Order without power: An introduction to anarchism: History and current challenges*. Seven Stories Press.

Bell, L. G., & Bell, D. C. (2009). Effects of family connection and family individuation. *Attachment & Human Development, 11*(5), 471–490. https://doi.org/10.1080/14616730903132263

Blackstock, C. (2009). The occasional evil of angels: Learning from the experiences of Aboriginal peoples and social work. *First Peoples Child & Family Review, 4*(1), 28–37. https://fpcfr.com/index.php/FPCFR/article/view/74

Bookchin, M. (2004). Ecology and revolutionary thought. In M. Bookchin (Ed.), *Post-scarcity anarchism* (pp. 19–40). AK Press.

Bray, M., (2017). *Antifa: The anti-fascist handbook*. Melville House Publishing.

Brown, C. (2021). Critical clinical social work and the neoliberal constraints on social justice in mental health. *Research on Social Work Practice, 31*(6), 644–652. https://doi.org/10.1177/1049731520984531

Brown, L., & Strega, S. (2015). *Research as resistance: Revisiting critical, Indigenous, and anti-oppressive approaches* (2nd ed.). Canadian Scholars Press.

Carter, A. (2013). The logic of state power. In R. Graham (Ed.), *Anarchism: A documentary history of libertarian ideas. Vol 3: The new anarchism (1974–2012)* (pp. 119–129). Black Rose Books.

Chapman, C., & Withers, A. J. (2019). *A violent history of benevolence: Interlocking oppression in the moral economies of social working*. University of Toronto Press.

Debord, G. (1998). *Comments on the society of the spectacle*. Verso Books.

Foucault, M., & Blanchot, M. (1987). *Foucault Blanchot*. Zone Books.

Gelderloos, P. (2007). Fascists are the tools of the state. https://theanarchistlibrary.org/library/peter-gelderloos-fascists-are-the-tools-of-the-state

Graeber, D. (2013). The new anarchists. In R. Graham (Ed.), *Anarchism: A documentary history of libertarian ideas: Vol 3: The new anarchism (1974–2012)* (pp. 1–11). Black Rose Books.

Hick, S. (2013). *Social welfare in Canada: Understanding income security* (3rd ed.). Thompson Educational Publishing.

Hick, S., & Stokes, J. (2016). *Social work in Canada: An introduction* (4th ed.). Thompson Educational Publishing.

Kinna, R. (2009). *Anarchism: A beginner's guide* (2nd ed.). One World Publications.

Klein, N. (2007). *The shock doctrine: The rise of disaster capitalism*. Alfred A. Knopf Canada.

Knuttila, M. (1992). *State theories: From liberalism to the challenge of feminism* (2nd ed.). Fernwood Publishing.

Lightman, E., & Lightman, N. (2017). *Social policy in Canada* (2nd ed.). Oxford University Press.

Malleson, T. (2016). *All fired up about capitalism*. Between the Lines.

Marshall, P. (2010). *Demanding the impossible: A history of anarchism*. PM Press.

Martin, J. (2003a). Historical development of critical social work practice. In J. Allan, B. Pease, & L. Briskman (Eds.), *Critical social work: An introduction to theories and practices* (pp. 17–31). Allen & Unwin.

Martin, J. (2003b). Mental health: Rethinking practices with women. In J. Allan, B. Pease, & L. Briskman (Eds.), *Critical social work: An introduction to theories and practices* (pp. 155–169). Allen & Unwin.

Mullaly, B. (2007). *The new structural social work*. Oxford University Press.

Mullaly, B., & West, J. (2018). *Challenging oppression and confronting privilege: A critical approach to anti-oppressive and anti-privilege theory and practice*. Oxford University Press.

Murray, K. M., & Hick, S. F. (2010). Structural social work: Theory and process. In S. Hick, H. I. Peters, T. Corner, & T. London (Eds.), *Structural social work in action: Examples from practice* (pp. 3–21). Canadian Scholars' Press.

Payne, M. (2005). *Modern social work theory* (3rd ed.). Lyceum Books.
Proudhon, J. P. (2022). *What is property?* (B. Tucker, Trans.). Critical Editions. (Original work published 1876.)
Rappaport, C. (2019). Fascism. In S. Faure (Ed.), *The anarchist encyclopedia abridged* (M. Abidore, Trans.) (pp. 91–94). AK Press.
Shulman, L. (2016). *The skills of helping individuals, families, groups and communities* (8th ed.). Brooks/Cole.
Swift, R. (2014). *S.O.S. alternatives to capitalism*. Between the Lines.
Wolff, R. P. (1998). *In defense of anarchism*. University of California Press.

Chapter questions

1. This chapter introduced the concept that the book offers the "idea" as an invitation to explore. What do you think? Would you prefer certainty over exploration when learning new ideas? Why or why not?
2. The chapter argues that there is no authority or hierarchy that does not lead toward oppression. Do you agree? Can you think of an example where this is not the case?
3. The introduction chapter outlines the remaining topics for this book. If you were writing this book, would you change any chapter topics? Why or why not? What would you find missing?

2
Comments on the welfare state and social work

An anti-state perspective

What responsibilities does the state have to society? Is the state a reflection of society's values, a response to how it is constituted? Are states the natural expression of the spirit of a society or does the economic structure determine its nature instead? These are common questions about the purpose and function of the state.

When I think about teaching Introduction to Social Work Practice, I am tempted to begin in the following way: "Our world, as comprised within the state and its current expression as the welfare state, is the product of our social relations (gender, age, race, and so on) as developed by evolving notions of wealth accumulation, property, and value. The state is an expression of violence that upholds a representation of a world that legitimates inequity and injustice, and its policies and laws serve to normalize them. These are the bars of our prison cells. Now that we can see them, we can plot our jailbreak together." In the same way, the reader is encouraged to see this chapter as helping to gain sight of the proverbial prison bars of the state.

Critical social work theories have long been questioning the state's purpose, claiming from Marxist perspectives that its motives are not benign (e.g. Martin, 2003). While current social work approaches engage with ways in which oppression and privilege intersect to maintain power (Mullaly & West, 2018), the assumptions regarding an essential state in relation to society remains unchallenged. Curriculum in Canada, for example, seeks to ensure students are aware of how welfare states operate (e.g. Chappell, 2010; Hick, 2013). It is a reasonable approach given how the places where social workers frequently operate are directly impacted by the welfare state and its policies.

This chapter seeks to engage with how social work sees its relationship with the state in light of welfare and how this validates the idea that capitalism and its corresponding state apparatus are legitimate. By exploring anarchist concerns about the state, the position is taken that this is problematic and contributes to the hegemony of neoliberalism which ultimately inhibits social work in achieving its goal of helping those at the margins of society.

The following will be a summary of historical currents in social work in relation to the development of the welfare state. Further, a brief primer on liberal thought and how this has been responsible for the origin and development of the state is introduced. Anarchist theories of the state will be presented and conclude with thoughts as to how this can influence social work's own relations to the state. It is the intention that readers will be inspired to consider new ways of thinking about collective action, mutual aid, and resistance to authority as goals for societal welfare.

Social work and the welfare state

The emergence of the modern state coincides with social work's origins (Jennissen & Lundy, 2011). Poor laws sought to control marginalized peoples with narrow definitions of who deserved welfare, while the remaining would be forced to attend workhouses (Hick & Stokes, 2016). Toward the end of the 19th century, the approaches of Charity Organization Societies (COS) and the settlement house movements were attempts to address the growing awareness that the environment itself, under industrialization with its dense urban population growth, required a more direct intervention against poverty. Over the course of the 19th century, a shift away from churches as the primary driver for social organizing and poverty relief included the development of the social gospel movement (Hick & Stokes, 2016). This meant that more affluent women would seek to target a fallen society rather than the sinful individual. It was up to them to go as friendly visitors into the homes of the poor to lift them out of their circumstance by being models of the good life to which they could aspire.

The efforts at addressing poverty at the end of the 19th century via COS and settlement houses produced divergent approaches to social problems and ultimately to social work itself and its role in relation to the state (Lane et al., 2018). The settlement house movement was more oriented toward environmental factors, community and labor organizing. Leaders of this movement, such as Jane Adams, believed in living with people in dire straits and organizing from the bottom up. In fact, she supported the Marxist scholar W. E. B. Dubois and his activism; was a founding member of the National Association for the Advancement of Colored People (NAACP) (Jennissen & Lundy, 2011); and seconded the nomination of Teddy Roosevelt as a third-party candidate in 1912 (Lane et al., 2018). The COS under Mary Richmond preferred case work approaches which focused on individual failings and working within the existing systems, leading to the first social work training program in 1898 (Tannenbaum & Reisch, 2001). It is apparent that, over time, the former approach won out as the foundation for modern day social work education and practice.

The civil rights movement of the 60s revived interest considering the environment and associated social conditions being fundamental to addressing welfare. By the 1970s Marxist critiques of North American and British social work as being servants of the state, as social control agents in charge of a narcotic welfare system (Martin, 2003) were being made. In effect, the contradictions of capital were being ameliorated by well-intentioned social workers. The actual structure that is the cause of suffering in poverty and related oppressions never gets addressed. In effect, a Marxist analysis of the welfare state ultimately paved the way for a Marxist theory of social work. Individual approaches, such as psychodynamic theory, were dismissed as reducing problems in family relationships but neglecting the larger societal sphere of influence and problems (Prilleltensky, 1994). Regarding the welfare state, it was viewed as being in a condition of profound crisis and that other theories and ideologies had failed to adequately explain the continued poverty, exploitation, and deprivation that were evidence of this crisis (Martin 2003).

Due in part to the financial crisis and subsequent austerity reforms of the 70s, severe cutbacks in welfare expenses and a formalization of the social work discipline resulted in the state becoming the employer (Martin 2003). Such a shift no longer provided social workers with the independence to question or challenge as effectively. This was exacerbated by increased governmental bureaucracy (Hick & Stokes, 2016). Social workers were becoming increasingly frustrated in their efforts to integrate theory and practice. Academics were developing feminist and Marxist social work approaches in theory, but this didn't translate to social work in practice. Social workers were now working in a context of demands for greater productivity (Martin, 2003). Most efforts at social reform floundered by the middle of the 1970s (Tannenbaum & Reisch,

2001). Today the concern is that a social work curriculum that is reductive to only clinical training has resulted in graduates with little knowledge about politics or the role social work has in policy making (Miller et al., 2017).

In terms of welfare, neoliberal ideology has effectively shifted responsibility for social problems since the 1980s to the individual as actor and is reflected in the paternalistic policies designed to compel desired behaviors in recipients (Toft, 2020). Furthermore, there has been an alarming increase in the incarcerations rates for people of color in the United States during this time. The privatization and hence commodification of carceral practice reflects the culmination of market-based solutions to social problems and the state's response.

The last two decades of the 20th century saw changes in how the state performed its role or mandate by moving toward a business model. In fact, the relationship between government and the economy increasingly saw solutions that privileged the business sector. Subpar benefits are intended to encourage people to accept low-paying jobs (Toft, 2020).

Social work has reflected these changes as increasingly concerns have been raised about how the discipline has adopted ideas about efficiency and effectiveness (Brown, 2016; Toft, 2020). What this means in practice is that neoliberalism recasts political problems as administrative ones based on efficiency and effectiveness. Certainly, if outcomes for practice are predicated on outcomes that are evidence-based (e.g. evidence-based practice) it is of concern that training is preferred over the cultivation of critical thought. In effect, the neoliberal influence has been felt in education (Brown, 2016; Toft, 2020), hence one could expect that social workers remain focused on individual and group problems while contextual or structural factors remain underemphasized or largely ignored.

While there has been a history of social work in politics (Lane et al., 2018; Toft, 2020), this has not arrested the shift of the welfare state becoming increasingly austere in its fiscal administration of resources due to devolution and neoliberal policies. Recently there has been an interest in leveraging ideas of public health and, more specifically, social determinants of health (SDOH) to challenge these trends (Cederbaum et al., 2018; Miller et al., 2017). Ultimately, the welfare state is beholden to the political parties that manage them. In North America this has tended to be represented from a democratic/liberal orientation or a republican/conservative position. The latter generally holds that capitalism is good and should not be interfered with. The former might agree but would formulate conditions to regulate capitalism in order to ensure its excesses do less harm (Hick, 2013). It would seem to be the case that social work has taken the path of a profession that leads to allegiance with the state, but this need not be the case.

Foucault (Macias, 2015) described how the state has leveraged power over our bodies and minds and how that discourse has legitimized this power. We have internalized assumptions about humanity and the need for it to be controlled for its own best interests. Given the increasing concerns about the power of the state in our lives, as well as how the welfare state has impacted the development of social work more specifically, the following will be a summary of thought related to how the state has emerged in the first place.

Theories of the state

Monarchies are precursors to the modern state. Knuttila (1992) identifies the emergence of liberal thought coming from the struggles between the mercantile class and monarchies eventually leading to industrial capitalism. During the period of mercantilism, the concept of utilitarianism emerges (Gouldner, 1970). Within the feudal state, relations were clear. The aristocracy owned everything, vassals worked and hence provided all value. The challenge lies in how to view a rising middle class. This group of merchants did not have the power of monarchies but had a status above the average vassal. The middle class defends its existence along the "utility" it can provide. In exchange, the state was needed to protect this class. Merchants would pay taxes and offer other financial support to the state. In exchange, the state would standardize currency, enforce trade regulations and practices as well as ensure law and order prevailed (Knuttila, 1992, p. 10).

According to Gouldner (1970) utility becomes the defining characteristic of this class. Ultimately this becomes the factor by which all other classes are judged. In effect, the aristocracy is seen as not having any utility as they do not produce anything: they go on fox hunts and consume the appropriated wealth generated by the other classes. Revolution is hence the fulfilment of the judgment made on this class. They have no utility. The new ruling class, now the bourgeoisie, had permeable boundaries. Its values were accessible to all other classes for incorporation which, according to Cesar Grana (cited in Knuttila, 1992, p. 64), made it "the first true democratic culture."

However, the emergent idea of utilitarianism extending a kind of universalism did not actually celebrate the individual but facilitated a generic view of the same (Gouldner, 1970). In effect, the individual's unique attributes are ignored in favor of a comparative value of how this translates into usefulness or utility. Hence emerges an impersonal and atomistic conceptualization of individual rights under the state.

Liberal philosophers such as Locke and Hobbes help establish a fundamental notion of the role of the state. Liberalism emerges as a body of thought that seeks to articulate a necessity for the state to prevent chaos (Hobbes) and mediating enlightened and rational self-interest via a sovereign (Locke), which Knuttila (1992) identifies as being connected to the marketplace in that it is intended to protect property.

Put another way, Locke is understood as having developed the idea that rights of property are directly connected to "that which we can use productively" (Harrison, 1983, p. 38). Hence liberal theory as presented by early writers, such as Locke, makes it clear that the state exists to protect property and all the other trappings of capitalism (Knuttila, 1992).

This idea of utility reaches its apex in industrial capitalism. The industrial capitalist class saw, in the use of new technologies applied to the process of production, a way to increase the accumulation of capital as labor costs would be reduced (Knuttila, 1992). In effect, as trade and mercantilism decline with industrial capitalism, a new relationship to wealth accumulation as well as to the state emerges. Society must be guarded against its own worst natures by a state that can ensure order, civility, and safety and facilitate progress flourishing in a civil society.

Liberal models of governance, then, at least in the classical sense, are about how rule is best achieved—by a hierarchy of legislative organization that may have limited terms, or be somehow removed from office at the pleasure of the population which likely is constituted of propertied or, in the case of John Stuart Mills (Knuttila, 1992, p. 25), of the educated. Ultimately, the government is to act in the best interest of civil society to the maximization of happiness for the greatest number of its citizens—a hallmark of utilitarian thought. In fact, Gouldner (1970) notes that the focus on utility is enshrined in the French "Declaration of the Rights of Man and of the Citizen" and hence utility is found to be a moral value of the middle class. A shift in social relations occurred where reciprocity becomes the principle of exchange. In effect, interactions were evaluated on the benefits and the utility they provided. Rights were viewed in the context of what useful contribution they (the individual) could provide to others. Notions of charity were now replaced by an obligation based on reciprocity. Giving is based on what one has received before. Hence, if one gives generously, it is with the self interested expectation that this will be returned in the future (p. 72).

This is further reflected in the utility of the state. If the state is unable to be of benefit to the people (to ensure its mandate of regulation, protection, etc.) then one is not obligated to be loyal to the state in return. This defined the underlying conceptualization of the welfare state. "In effect, the state's contribution to the well-being of individuals became the standard of its political legitimacy . . . In short, bourgeois utilitarianism was consistent with the assumptions of the Welfare State to whose development it contributed." (Gouldner, 1970, p. 73). This has further implications as to the behavior of the welfare state. Beyond a utilitarian view of the human condition, the state is slow to react as the middle class is reluctant to invest proactively and will only pay more taxes for existing problems.

In light of this analysis of the emergence of liberalism and the welfare state, it becomes easier to understand the residual policies embodied in the poor laws that seek to define relief. Not only do they portray the reductive view of the human condition as utilitarian but they also perpetuate a dim view of society needing protection from its own worst features. We need to be governed in order to prevent chaos and greed from dominating.

Anarchist/libertarian thoughts about the state

There seems to be a fork in the path where liberal and libertarian thought diverge from each other. Notions of freedom are defined differently. At this time, it is important to note that libertarianism is a term that can be misunderstood. In North America, this term usually refers to a vision of society that is extremely individualistic—at times it is even confused with the misleading term "anarcho-capitalist." Outside of this geography, the term is broader and applies to anarchism more generally. There are various perspectives and critiques of the term libertarianism (e.g. Kinna, 2009). Peter Marshall (2010) makes the point that no "pure anarchism" has ever existed, no matter how much some will gaze into the past, to preindustrial societies, for proof. At best, libertarian approaches may have existed in some societies where sanctions such as invoking superstition or supernatural authority to control antisocial behavior were present. Robert Graham's work on anarchism is subtitled "A Documentary History of Libertarian Ideas" (2009, 2013). In effect, he is acknowledging how apparent it is that anarchism shares some ideas with liberal philosophy. What is important to note, however, is that anarchism does not share notions of a state, let alone a welfare state.

While Marshall (2010) claims that looking into the past for an ideal example of anarchism is foolish, he does concur with prior authors of the emergence of the state as coinciding with the accumulation of wealth and a capitalist orientation. In fact, the state and empire are not synonymous. The great empires of the past (Roman, Greek) were vast constellations that did not impact daily life of those inside its boundaries until the emergence of wealth. "It was only when a society was able to produce a surplus which could be appropriated by a few that private property and class relations developed" (Marshall, 2010, pp. 17–18). The main critique of the state is that it is an artificial (super) structure, and it is only an instrument that supports oppressive conditions. Strategies such as appealing to patriotism and ideas of democracy are viewed as questionable and inevitably manufacture consent for the ruling minority. Essentially, the state will use "its monopoly of force, through the army and police, to defend itself against foreign invasion and internal dissension" (p. 18).

Expanding Gouldner's (1970) assertion about the reason that welfare states tend to react rather than proactively address social problems, Marshall (2010) refers to an early anarchist thinker, William Godwin. It was his view that the state in effect halts the motion of society to be creative. In other words, the state, by definition, will be conservative to render social relations static as well as to maintain inequity in terms of property. This is pernicious, as anarchist writer Murray Bookchin (cited in Marshall, 2010, p. 605) describes how the state becomes internalized as a state of mind. We are unaware of how we all organize reality according to the structure of the state and its assumed necessity for mediating all social relations. The state no longer needs violence since the psychological is more effective: we are in sheer awe of the all-seeing power of the state, rendered to feel helpless and powerless (Kinna, 2009). Alan Ritter (2013) makes the case that even the way our physical living arrangements have been developed ensures that neighbors become more suspicious of each other and directly leads to an undermining of any true sense of community.

Anarchists not only question the legitimacy of the state but also whether government of any kind should exist in the first place. As stated earlier, when the individual is seen by the state as a generic subject, real individuality and freedom are absent. Philosophical anarchist Robert Wolf (1998) makes this clear when interrogating our ideas about a liberal democracy. In a representative democracy there is almost a mystical belief in the process of voting that the majority rule will be somehow fairer. Referring to a tyranny of the majority, Wolf (1998) argues that the mythical belief that one is not losing one's freedom under a majority rule, keeps everyone docile and ignorant of the status quo. By submitting to the collective will of a majority, a permanent minority will have no alternative but resistance to such forms of governance.

Marshall (2010) would remind of Godwin's words regarding voting. Truth cannot be discovered by casting a vote and is offensive to any appeals to reason or justice. Furthermore, the welfare state is a harmful structure that, in the guise of benevolence, regulates and restricts the lives of those unfortunate to be under its dominance. "It singularly fails to make people happy, and by offering a spurious security it undermines the practice of mutual aid. It tends to be wasteful by not directing resources to those most in need" (p. 24).

In contrast to Marxist critique, anarchism does not propose a new state and, in fact, sees any such attempts, either via revolution or reform (e.g. parliamentary intervention) as reproducing oppression. Furthermore, where Marxist thought valorized the working class, anarchism is more dynamic in the application of class concepts, even expressing belief in the unemployed, the discarded groups of society as the locus for change (Kinna, 2009). In fact, the critique is made that Marxism fails to explore the problem of nationalism due to its focus primarily on the economy (Carter, 2013). Nationalism has benefits for the state and can almost be described as the establishment of a super class which then can be moved to oppress others. The state would profit from such a construction where, "oppressing a foreign group could reduce the need for coercion with the national community. It offers the prospect of increased wealth for all nationals as long as it can be extracted from foreigners" (p. 121).

The state is not only problematic for what it represents and whom it defends but also how it maintains its authority. Godwin for example, believed that all laws seeking to punish are an admission of failure by the state (Marshall, 2010). Its project cannot be defended hence laws are enacted to maintain its authority. Given that crimes are the product of their context, people who commit these are a product of said environment and punishing them is illogical. Alan Ritter (2013) captures a similar sentiment in that he sees not only the distance or remote nature of authority but also its tendency via laws to treat citizens as "abstract strangers" (p. 118).

The argument that the state is organized violence is well understood when looking at critiques of the agents of control, such as law enforcement.

Assumptions of the need for the state involve a concept of society as needing an arbiter or control agent to maintain the peace amongst a dense, diverse population (Barclay, 2013). This would be a dim view of the human condition and misses an important point: "The vast majority of people do not kill and maim because of the presence of the police, but because they have been trained that killing is a 'mortal sin'" (p. 107). Even well-intentioned politicians will be caught up in the preservation of the state as primary directive, which requires its defense and the enforcement of laws let alone the failed equivalency of saving automobile and oil companies "for the public welfare." Ultimately, domination produces integration and order, but the price is through force not cooperation or autonomy.

Jeff Ferrell in his work, "Against the law: Anarchist criminology" (1998) offers an intriguing glimpse as to how laws can be understood from this unique philosophy and approach. Crime is seen here as a direct result of the centralized authority of the state. It is the application of state authority and its centralized administration that ruptures and destroys community—in fact, increasing antisocial behavior and crime. The application of laws then, in response, further damage and abuse those at the margins of society even further with their discriminatory and oppressive quality. Hence, breaking the law always has a political dimension. Godwin presages notions of consciousness raising (Marshall, 2010) found in structural social work (e.g. Mullaly, 2007). Godwin would argue that the conditions that produce crime need direct addressing, as they relate to the accumulation of wealth and its resultant dispossession for the have-nots and stressed the importance of education in helping people to see beyond their own condition and so on (Marshall, 2010).

In other words, looking for the kernel of repressed aspects of human dignity and self-determination in acts of crime is the purpose of anarchist criminology. Violating the laws of the state is hence understood in how legal authority damages the social, resulting in said antisocial acts in the first place. According to Ferrell (2013), an anarchist critique of the law "serves to remind us that human relations and human diversity matter—and that . . . they matter more than the turgid authority of regulation and law" (p. 134).

Another pernicious aspect of the state is its appeal to national interests. A state will hold that its boundaries signify a territory where all within ought to identify collectively. As can be seen in the splintering of nations post-cold war Soviet Union, such boundaries can be challenged. Anarchists have argued that the nation is a product of the state and not vice versa. Communities are natural. The pressing of diverse communities, frequently by violence, into some national framework is the product of the state to get generic citizens and hence acquiescence to the superstructure of the state (Marshall, 2010).

Invariably, the state is the reason for violence including the waging of wars for national interests and the expansion of said nation states' boundaries. Leo Tolstoy, while avoiding identification as an anarchist given its association with violence (Marshall, 2010), but a supporter of a Christian anarchism, argued that patriotism is an evil that ties people to an imaginary fatherland and sets them up to be enemies of each other to serve their respective governments.

War is a direct condition of the existence of a state. War and the state evolved together rather than war or conquest preceding the state (Barclay, 2013). In effect, they feed each other as no state can hope to survive without some military support. Barclay asserts "no state can expect to achieve importance and prestige unless it does have a good army and pursues the road to dominance" (p. 106).

Voline (2019), the Russian anarchist who had been actively involved in the Soviet revolution describes the state as a fiction and a fetish that is valorized as the most important of social organizations. He believed that, due to conflicting claims based on ideology of the speaker, the origins of the state are largely unknown. Hence, if the historic role of the state is in dispute, as are its origins or even its reality, there is little strength to the argument that one ought to venerate or obey it in any way. He inverts the accusation regarding utopia by pointing out that for centuries people have fought and died for a fiction and have ignored reality in preference for chasing ghosts.

Other anarchist voices make strange, for lack of a better analogy, ideas taken for granted about the nature of the state. According to David Graeber (2018), the economy and politics should not be seen as separate concepts but intimately connected.

> because the goods are extracted through political means and distributed for political purposes. In fact, it was only with the first stirrings of industrial capitalism that anyone started talking about "the economy" as an autonomous sphere of human activity in the first place. (p. 176)

Alan Carter (2013) cautions against being reductive about the relationship between the economy and the state. He makes the case that the state is not simply an agent of capital. It has its own desires for maintaining power gained through its authority. After all, "being in control of the instruments of coercion, the state would be in a position both to protect and to further its own interests" (p. 122).

Carter refers to what he calls the "state-primacy theory" to unpack the idea that the revolutionary concept is inverted, and the state will seek to continue existence beyond each reset by employing the economic models most suitable to its preservation. In effect, the revolution begins with the state "ceasing to stabilize the current relations of production and choosing, instead, to stabilize new ones that are functional for it" (p. 123). Hence, to assume that only the economic sphere is of importance in a salient critique of the state is missing this important consideration. Self-preservation for the state is its aim; there are no other arguments for its purpose.

Carter's (2013) idea deserves further consideration in how he argues for an anarchist versus Marxist critique of the state. The state requires inegalitarian economic relations to have a purpose—to protect the interests of whichever ruling class has power and wealth. According to his analysis, the state does not need to represent a particular political ideology. For example, the Russian revolution sought to bring about egalitarian economic relations via Marxist thought, but "the Bolshevik state replaced the factory committees with inegalitarian 'one-man' management" (p. 128). Lenin's own justification was based on the idea that the state needed a strong economy to have national defense (i.e. military), thus proving the theory that a state will embrace economic relations that will help it sustain itself—in effect, capitalism as the profit motive is needed to allocate capital for the preservation of the state. This has important implications to how one can conceive of a welfare state. If its existence serves the purpose of maintaining power and authority, appeals to a higher ethical principle will fail and only serve to obscure what is really going on.

While history is vague—anarchists would agree that the emergence of the state coincides with the end of economic and social equality and the genesis of ideas like private property. Voline (2019) asserts "the state always and everywhere was a social system that definitively established, legalized, and defended inequality, property, and the exploitation of the laboring masses" (p. 191). Any thought of reform, including what Voline described as ideas from bourgeoisie sociology, is a troubling perspective of seeing society in a mechanistic fashion. The state is the construction by the original victors who established a system that reinforces and validates, "a system of human coexistence based on the exploitation of the laboring masses" (p. 194). This system was initially presented as beyond human free will by imbuing it with supernatural qualities, such as divine right. Hence the state is not neutral, nor can it bring about liberation or empowerment, because it is forever connected as a project to reinforce exploitation. Anticipating later notions of the complex interaction between the state and neoliberal hegemony, Voline categorically claimed that to oppose capitalism means opposing the state. He describes both as two heads of the same monster. In other words, the relations between the two—capital and state—are complex and intertwined with each other.

Anarchist anthropologist Harold Barclay sees the process of industrialization as having conditioned workers to become less creative and duller, submitting to a daily schedule of long and monotonous work (2013). The distribution of wealth via taxation is out of the control of individuals who end up contributing to the funding of a vast bureaucracy and military to defend national interests. He notes that, as recently as the 19th century, most of the redistribution of wealth primarily went to royal families and militaries and that a recent lesson is that the welfare state and its redistribution to the common folk has been strategic: it is less expensive to keep us calm with some scraps than to use force in order to avoid revolution.

I'm always reminded of the challenge of phenomenological or humanist ethics struggles to resolve the seeming paradox between the individual and the collective. How can a Rogerian facilitation of the individual be complete without infringing on other's empowerment or self-actualization (Dolgoff et al., 2012)? Alan Ritter (2013) raises the idea of a reciprocal awareness in anarchist community as an antidote to the state. "Just as the theme of self-development unifies the anarchists' various conceptions of individuality, so does the theme of reciprocal awareness unify their conceptions of community" (p. 115). The same way that the individual becomes more self-aware, the community can do so as well. This is where one can perhaps see further the distinction, at least according to this writer, between American notions of the libertarian and this particular form of anarchist thought. The development of the self and the reciprocal awareness of the awareness (individuality and community) are the true goals of anarchism, not freedom. "Freedom is prized by anarchists more as a means to individuality and community than as a final end" (p. 116). In effect, anarchism sees true aims only achievable in relation or dependence to each other. Thus true solidarity lies in the diversity of individuals, not homogeny. In fact, Ritter would say that solidarity requires the diversity of individuals. There is no polarity between individuality and community. They reinforce, rather than conflict with each other.

Discussion

A number of points deserve reflection. Social work has a history of advocacy that has made way for the project of professionalization (Reisch, 2019). Historical consciousness is waning for the profession. In other words, it would be of benefit to remind ourselves of our past. In fact, a history of political efforts at organizing exists during the "red scare" of the Cold War (Jennissen & Lundy, 2011) and the civil rights era (Burghardt, 2020).

Reisch (2019) further makes an important point regarding how we view history in the first place. The failure to engage in a form of historiography, where we acknowledge a limitation of our current context and perspective, makes for anachronistic understanding of historical ideas and peoples, as we are rooted in a form of presentism. So too it is important that we engage with ideas outside of our present time, inviting an opportunity to view our world from new perspectives in return.

Returning to the ideas of advocacy and social justice, Kim (2017) argues that a number of failures have impacted meaningful progress for social work. There has been a loss of social justice or advocacy related work in recent times in part due to the focus on race-based injustice. This has the danger of missing other factors that contribute to oppression and inequity in the first place. Kim further claims that social work has failed to define social justice in a meaningful way. The result is that social work is left having to rely on existing definitions. This means that social work therefore also doesn't have a particular political approach and must use the political vocabulary of others, which includes the ideology of others, and at its worst, accept austerity as a fixed reality in times of such measures by the state. We know that, at present, our system of welfare is becoming increasingly marketized and commodified under neoliberal influences (Reisch, 2019). It may be that anarchism can contribute to social work here. Acknowledging that justice is problematic in that it raises everyone to a generic standard rather than meeting each on their own terms can open the discourse to new approaches. Furthermore, if the state needs oppression to function, we can explore ways to understand racial inequity as a device of the state to maintain control. Put another way, racism is not the consequence of inequity but an essential feature of state control. Beyond a divide and conquer approach or even oppressive framework, racism legitimates the state's purpose. Building on a Hobbesian pessimism of the human condition, it reinforces the notion that society needs governance to protect it from itself.

Social work has a tendency to rise to the occasion during tumultuous times (Toft, 2020) to engage with social reform. At the present moment, with neoliberalism increasing economic insecurity and policies that increase the anxious middle class' concern for its own survival have resulted in anti-collectivist sentiments. It is difficult to imagine how such a climate can promote collective action or social reforms and call for social work to return to its role in this regard. However, some efforts are being made to increase political or policy making education in social work (Lane et al., 2018). Social work research has sought to raise awareness of social problems via innovative approaches, such as identifying youth suicide rates decreasing instates that have same-sex marriage laws (Cederbaum et al., 2018). However, it is also of concern that currently social work has been mostly passive or even neglectful in its role as social reformer (Lane et al., 2018).

Globalization and the associated exploitation of the Global South have raised notions of an international social work (Hick & Stokes, 2016). A common trend in this area is to consider sustainability which posits ideas where countries are empowered to become independent competitive entities in the global economy. Another way perhaps to reflect on the conditions that have been placed on the Global South is as the true face of capitalism. The profit motive is best served when populations are traumatized and dispossessed (Klein, 2007). The meager and substandard wages, housing, and exploitation of land that is the experience of the Global South reflects how far the economy is willing to go for their bottomless hunger for profit. The state in the west is adopting neoliberal policies a la the marketplace of ideas. The welfare state, via pro-business tax reform, increasingly needs to become more and more residual (see Hick, 2013). The privatization of welfare further reflects the neoliberal turn (Lightman & Lightman, 2017). Of concern then, is not only how international social work reproduces the same question where we are ameliorating conditions that are a result of the status quo, but also how the evidence of capitalism eroding the welfare mandate of governments in the Global South is a warning.

Conclusion

This chapter sought to examine the state from anarchist perspectives. The possibilities here can challenge how social work sees its relationship to welfare and the state. In thinking about the purpose and function of the state, we can consider the following concerns raised about capitalism and its extreme version of self-defense, fascism.

Our current moment appears to show disturbing indications of a turbulent time when voices are raised in concern of the overreach of the state apparatus. The revolutions of the past can still provide lessons for our future. We ignore them at our peril.

Charles Rappoport (2019) an anarchist Lithuanian Jew living in France, wrote about fascism prior to World War II. As we collectively cannot dismiss the reality of the second world war, his words may yet reach us. He argues that fascism is when capitalism defends itself and its position. "Along with reformist socialism, it is the last cartridge of a bourgeoisie backed against the wall" (p. 91). Why and how this relates to theories of the state is that this is "plan B"—when the state is under threat of revolution (Gelderoos, 2007). To extend the concern raised in structural social work (Mullaly, 2007), not only does reforming the state gloss over the harms of capitalism in the first place, it also serves to pacify citizens of the state. making them more vulnerable to a fascist takeover (Rappoport, 2019). It is important to know that wherever a socialist mentality increases, so does the idea of fascism—they rise together as capitalism defends itself.

> Telling proletarians that it is enough to wait for parliamentary majorities means opening the working class to fascist blows. Even if the proletariat has the majority in parliament the capitalist class will not surrender. (p. 93)

This was by no means an exhaustive review of social work nor of anarchist thought. It is perfectly reasonable for a reader to note that more can be added as to the rise of a critical social work that engages in a different analysis of the welfare state than perhaps more conservative or liberal approaches included here. This is a fair point and, in similar fashion, the same could be said about anarchist thought as well. The truth is that there is no claim being made here to a particular essential orientation to social work or anarchism. If the reader can follow how anarchist thought can contribute to developing a more complete critique of the state, then I have accomplished my goal. Quite simply, the assumption that social work promotes about needing to engage with the state is being challenged. Perhaps there is no reformation for a system that reproduces oppression in order to maintain authority. It is my hope that this analysis can expand the creative imagination of social work to engage with people who have been at greatest risk of harm by current authoritarian, neoliberal structures of power.

A valid question may be how anarchist thought avoids the paradox of critical and structural social work approaches. If the system needs to go, but we help those harmed by it, do we not ensure its ongoing validation? It is tempting to go further into this issue, but the length and purpose of this chapter does not make this possible. As an illustration, I am reminded of Uri Gordon (2013) writing about an anarchist dilemma regarding the Palestine's quest for statehood. After all, the paradox is inherent in anarchist thought—how do you support a Palestinian state as an anarchist? The point he makes is that if you support a solution, you cease to be an anarchist as you would be in support of a state. If you maintain your position of anti-state at all costs, you become useless or irrelevant to the plight of Palestinians. As with any form of activism, Gordon makes the point that we need to avoid the charge of paternalism in which anarchists claim to be better than Palestinians at identifying their "real interests" and disregard what Palestinians want—the oppressed losing voice rather than joining them in solidarity. Fortier (2017) notes how anarchists have struggled with ideas around Indigenous sovereignty that are similar to the ones Gordon is addressing. This echoes what Mullaly (2007) and other anti-oppressive and anti-racist social work approaches (see West & Mullaly, 2018) seek to address. As we strive to aspire to principles, like the abolition of the state, we must not be ignorant of the real issues that people experience in this world or dogmatically addled. It is fair to, "insist that in a liminal, imperfect situation, solidarity is still worthwhile even if it comes at the price of inconsistency" (Gordon, 2013, p. 136).

In effect, it is holding in tension the discrepancy as an anarchist regarding the state in order to "express a specific value judgment whereby one's anti-imperialist or humanitarian commitments are seen to 'trump' an otherwise fully uncompromising anti-statism" (p. 137). Furthermore, he makes the point that people that have historically been rendered stateless are the most vulnerable. Fighting to destroy the state while these people are at the mercy of this apparatus is reckless.

An intriguing point is made by Gordon (2013) in that anarchism engages with the struggle via direct action and mutual aid and will tend to view the state as something to ignore. By engaging in communities, to establish healthier alternatives to the state apparatus, the project is realized in fulfilling its irrelevance. Ultimately, it is about defending and preserving the humanity and dignity of all people. "The everyday acts of resistance that anarchists join and defend in Palestine and Israel are immediate steps to help preserve people's livelihoods and dignity, which are in no way necessarily connected to a statist project" (p. 138). These are principles that social work can get behind.

Finally, I am returning to the classroom. One frequent idea in policy making is to identify the values that matter in any given social issue (Jansson, 2003; Dobelstein, 2003). If society can see how their values are in conflict with the status quo, they can be moved to consider alternatives. While this remains located within systems that assume the state has a valid role, it also presumes that empathy building for the other is sufficient to bring change. I write the following knowing that this can be misunderstood. As a social worker, I am certainly a believer in that most people, if aware, will choose to be good. The challenge is that it is a vague concept. What if one must be cutthroat to others in order to take care of their family? This is the situation that a capitalist, neoliberal world is producing. It is difficult to define what is best, and for whom, if the decisions are restricted to a particular structural system. This is where anarchist thought can be of help. By identifying how we all are harmed by the current assumptions related to the necessity of the state, we can work together in solidarity toward a world that is more compassionate, equitable, and humane for all. These are the bars of our prison cells. Now that we can see them, we can plot our jailbreak together.

References

Barclay, H. (2013). Anarchy and state formation. In R. Graham (Ed.), *Anarchism: A documentary history of libertarian ideas: Vol 3: The new anarchism (1974–2012)* (pp. 99–113). Black Rose Books.

Bookchin, M. (2004a). Listen Marxist! In *Post-scarcity anarchism* (pp. 107–145). AK Press.

Bookchin, M. (2004b). Discussion on "Listen Marxist!" In *Post-scarcity anarchism* (pp. 147–163). AK Press.

Brown, C. (2016). The constraints of neo-liberal new managerialism in social work education. *Canadian Social Work Review, 33*(1), 115–123.

Burghardt, S. (2020). *The end of social work: A defense of the social worker in times of transformation.* Cognella Academic Publishing.

Carter, A. (2013). The logic of state power. In R. Graham (Ed.), *Anarchism: A documentary history of libertarian ideas. Vol 3: The new anarchism (1974–2012)* (pp. 119–129). Black Rose Books.

Cederbaum, J., Ross, A., Ruth, B., & Keefe, R. (2018). Public health social work as a unifying framework for social work's grand challenges. *Social Work, 64*(1), 9–18. doi: 10.1093/sw/swy045

Chappell, R. (2010). *Social welfare in Canadian society* (4th ed.). Toronto: Nelson.

Dobelstein, A. (2003). *Social welfare: Policy and analysis* (3rd ed.). Brooks/Cole.

Dolgoff, R., Harrington, D., & Lowenberg, F. (2012). *Ethical decisions for social work practice* (9th ed.). Brookes/Cole.

Ferrell, J. (1998). Against the Law: Anarchist criminology. Social Anarchism (25). http://library.nothingness.org/articles/SA/en/display/127

Fortier, C. (2017). *Unsettling the commons: Social movements within, against, and beyond settler colonialism.* Arbeiter Ring Press.

Gelderoos, P. (2007). *Fascists are the tools of the state.* https://theanarchistlibrary.org/library/peter-gelderloos-fascists-are-the-tools-of-the-state

Gordon, U. (2013). Israel, Palestine, and anarchist dilemmas. In R. Graham (Ed.), *Anarchism: A documentary history of libertarian ideas: Vol 3: The new anarchism (1974–2012)* (pp. 135–138). Black Rose Books.

Gouldner, A. W. (1970). *The coming crisis in western sociology.* Basic Books.

Graeber, D. (2018). *Bullshit jobs: A theory.* Simon & Shuster Press.

Graham, R. (Ed.). (2009). *Anarchism: A documentary history of libertarian ideas: Vol 2: The emergence of the new anarchism (1939–1977).* Black Rose Books.

Graham, R. (Ed.) (2013). *Anarchism: A documentary history of libertarian ideas: Vol 3: The new anarchism (1974–2012).* Black Rose Books.

Harrison, F. (1983). *The modern state.* Black Rose Books.

Hick, S. (2013). *Social welfare in Canada: Understanding income security* (3rd ed.). Thompson Educational Publishing.

Hick, S., & Stokes, J. (2016). *Social work in Canada: An introduction* (4th ed.). Thompson Educational Publishing.

Jansson, B. S. (2003). *Becoming an effective policy advocate: From policy practice to social justice* (4th ed.). Brooks/Cole.

Jennissen, T., & Lundy, C. (2011). *One hundred years of social work.* Wilfrid Laurier University Press.

Kim, H. C. (2017). A challenge to the social work profession? The rise of socially engaged art and a call to radical social work. *Social Work, 62*(4), 305–311. https://doi.org/10.1093/sw/swx045

Kinna, R. (2009). *Anarchism: A beginner's guide* (2nd ed.). One World Publications.

Klein, N. (2007). *The shock doctrine: The rise of disaster capitalism.* Alfred A. Knopf Canada.

Knuttila, M. (1992). *State theories: From liberalism to the challenge of feminism* (2nd ed.). Fernwood Publishing.

Lane, S., Ostrander, J., & Rhodes Smith, T. (2018). "Politics is social work with power": Training social workers for elected office. *Social Work Education, 37*(1), 1–16. doi:10.1080/02615479.2017.1366975

Lightman, E., & Lightman, N. (2017). *Social policy in Canada* (2nd ed.). Oxford University Press.

Macias, T. (2015). "On the footsteps of Foucault": Doing Foucaultian discourse analysis in social justice research. In S. Strega & L. Brown (Eds.), *Research as resistance: Revisiting critical, Indigenous, and anti-oppressive approaches* (2nd ed., pp. 221–242). Canadian Scholars' Press.

Marshall, P. (2010). *Demanding the impossible: A history of anarchism.* PM Press.

Martin, J. (2003). Historical development of critical social work practice. In J. Allan, B. Pease, & L. Briskman (Eds.), *Critical social work: An introduction to theories and practices* (pp. 17–31). Allen & Unwin.

Miller, D. P., Bazzi A. R., Allen, H. L., Martinson, M. L., Salas-Wright, C. P., Jantz, K., Crevi, K., & Rosenbloom, D. L. (2017). A social work approach to policy: Implications for population health. *American Journal of Public Health, 107*(3), 243–249. doi: 10.2105/AJPH.2017.304003. PMID: 29236535; PMCID: PMC5731070

Mullaly, B. (2007). *The new structural social work*. Oxford University Press.

Mullaly, B., & West, J. (2018). *Challenging oppression and confronting privilege: A critical approach to anti-oppressive and anti-privilege theory and practice*. Oxford University Press.

Rappoport, C. (2019). Fascism. In S. Faure (Ed.), *The anarchist encyclopedia* (pp. 91–94). AK Press.

Reisch, M. (2019) Lessons from social work's history for a tumultuous era. *Social Service Review, 93*(4), 581–607. doi:10.1086/706741

Ritter, A. (2013). Anarchy, law and freedom. In R. Graham (Ed.), *Anarchism: A documentary history of libertarian ideas: Vol 3: The new anarchism (1974–2012)* (pp. 113–119). Black Rose Books.

Tannenbaum, N., & Reisch, M. (2001). *From charitable volunteers to architects of social welfare: A brief history of social work*. https://ssw.umich.edu/about/history/brief-history-of-social-work

Toft, J. (2020). Words of common cause: Social work's historical democratic discourse. *Social Service Review, 94*(1). doi: 0037-7961/2020/9401-0003

Voline (2019). State. In S. Faure (Ed.), *The anarchist encyclopedia* (pp. 189–196). AK Press.

Chapter questions

1. This chapter makes the argument that welfare exists as a way for the state to defend its own right to exist. Do you agree with this? Why or why not?
2. If you could design an alternative to the welfare system, what would it look like?
3. The point is made that Hobbes is to blame for our negative view of human nature and the justification of the state. Can you think of an example that disproves, or proves this argument?

3
Supported employment
Wage slavery entrenched in recovery

The following paper is an examination of the ideas related to depictions of employment as recovery. The point is to challenge the problematic nature of how societal perceptions about work negatively impact our collective understandings around mental wellness, mental health, and recovery. The intention here is to engage with anarchist critiques of work to explore the hidden assumptions about what constitutes individual value and worth. By challenging efforts to define our collective utility to capitalist production, we can move toward a more humane and fulfilling perspective of the human condition. Ultimately, addressing harmful views of recovery will not only help those directly affected by these but society as well.

At the time of writing this, we are all practicing social distancing in an effort to slow the coronavirus pandemic. Those who can work remotely are doing so, while those considered "essential services" must remain in the field, risking their health and possibly their lives. Sweeping changes to our society included an examination of what can be considered "essential," which is in stark opposition to neoliberal notions of the economy and our collective role in its participation. As the global economy grinds to a halt in the face of unprecedented viral calamity, the question can be asked: "If most of our work is not essential, why do we need to engage in it?" Conversely, government leaders pushing for a resumption of business as usual are raising the question of what value citizens have as compared to the health of the economy under capitalism. Author and editor of *Autonomie Magazin*, Vidar Lindström (2020), while reflecting on the current pandemic, makes an important point that measures of quarantine to protect the elderly are hypocrisy as we have cast them out. They cannot contribute to society in productive ways, and hence we have already decided that their worth is not as great. Furthermore, the purpose of quarantine is flawed if people are allowed to spread the virus at work (see essential workers) but just not outside of labor time.

I had been thinking about writing this particular paper for a number of years, as I believe that tacit assumptions about work as an evaluation of our worth are deeply problematic. As a case manager and team leader for a Program for Assertive Community Treatment (PACT) team (Allness & Knoedler, 1998), I recall how we would focus on helping people see reasons beyond medication adherence to work with our program toward recovery. This would frequently result in people seeing employment as a primary goal, and we would measure our success as a program on how often we could, with and without supported employment services, make this dream come true. At the time, I found no cognitive dissonance in pursuing this course of action. Our program was hailed as being innovative, riding a new wave of person-centered approaches that would finally be responsive to individual hopes and dreams rather than an obsessive focus on clinical outcomes. While well-intentioned, I have become troubled by this simplistic view about something as complex as recovery. Furthermore, the tacit assumption of work as an indicator of recovery misses an important point related to hegemonic assumptions about work itself.

While completing my PhD at the University of Manitoba, I discovered in my research of patient records at a local mental health facility the way social work had been perceived in practice. It was particularly interesting how psychiatry would await the adjudication of social workers in determining the status for discharge of patients at Selkirk Mental Health Centre (SMHC). The main area of determination here was whether the patient had access to or was prepared and ready to be able to work.

What is recovery from mental illness? Numerous attempts have been made to find a suitable explanation (Burstow et al., 2014; Morrow, 2012; Stuart et al., 2012; Walsh, 2013). Frequently there are conceptions that tend to include the representation of citizens that can work and contribute to society in meaningful ways. The advent of supported employment is based on such assumptions. If the individual is unable to contribute to society in meaningful ways, then the simulation of paid employment remains a popular image that suggests "recovery."

David Graeber (2018) searchingly engages with the question of "bullshit jobs" and their popularity. What is it about the need for people to appear to be working that reduces the very idea of work to making people guard empty museum rooms and be vice presidents of nothing? Not only do these jobs appear counter to the logic of capitalism but there is also the concern of what this does to one's mental health when they knowingly "working" at these jobs. A salient example is one provided by Holley Cantine (2009) writing back in 1947 about how, toward the end of WWII, it was common practice to hire more workers than needed if the government contract was paid out according to the number of workers needed. These idle workers were still expected to show up on time and ready to remain at the factory until end of day. "The activity can be entirely meaningless, but it is work if it is paid for" (p. 115).

My perspective is based on the view that the tacit acceptance of employment as the standard for recovery influenced the development of supported employment programs and ultimately defined mental health from the perspective of the dominant ideology: capitalism. During a review of my original dissertation, I was struck by my own ignorance. I see the embrace by social work of vocational rehabilitation as uncritical and as a validation of a nonmedical focus in recovery. I am now struck by how the assumptions of labor activity have been embedded in my own thinking about recovery. Even when working with someone in defining their own recovery, I am struck by how often I still think about how empowering it would be for them to secure employment. I may not say this out loud, but I wonder how often this is coming across regardless.

When we examine vocational rehabilitation, it is the tacit assumption that work equals recovery from some kind of disability. Even when directly challenging ableist attitudes, there is the ongoing challenge of assuming the only legitimate being is one who is working, contributing to the economy in a meaningful way. For example, while the excellent volume "Mad Matters" (LeFrancois et al., 2013) chronicles the important emergence of the Mad movement, employment is usually introduced to illustrate issues related to access and exploitation.[1] Similar to "Paradigms Lost" (Stuart et al., 2012) or "Psychiatry Disrupted" (Burstow et al., 2019), the question of work itself is not directly investigated. That said, recovery is not represented by the former sources as homogenous and primarily defined as being able to work. Rather, the concern I am raising is about how our perspectives related to work are hegemonic. Even if someone describes their own idiosyncratic vision of recovery, it contrasts with this idea. Other literature on how oppression is

---

[1] A notable exception being Tam's (2012) contribution, which critiques an absence of reflection of the ways in which capitalism and racism intersect to create "different desirable or undesirable capitalist subjects" (p. 287), yet does not investigate assumptions of work itself as a value.

internalized and further validated (e.g. Mullaly & West, 2018) would suggest that how we have internalized the view of ourselves as only having merit in what we can do to be productive is of real concern.

The assumption of work as a natural condition of human living is mirrored in practice as well. I recall while working as a case manager at a community mental health center in the United States that, even in the absence of meaningful work, volunteer or "assisted workshop" activities were recommended to our "consumers" to give them "structure." This is never questioned. In fact, I recall when launching an intensive community mental health program) focusing on the employment rates of people in our program as evidence that our approach was "working" when it came to "recovery."

I find my own assumptions now challenged as I reflect on the ways in which we have all been conditioned to accept capitalism and production as the sole factors of purpose in our lives. The way social work has been complicit in communicating this message to those we intend to help, can now provide a window into how such messages are created and reproduced as facts of social life. In this way, I hope to contribute to a growing understanding about tacit assumptions about recovery that reproduce the misery of expecting people to adapt to modern life that values the commodification of labor power over the holistic, social beings that we have the potential to become.

Critical social work seeks to challenge assumptions about common approaches to social work. This includes a critique of approaches that view problems as rooted in the individual and leave context/society out of the analysis. In effect this echoes neoliberal explanations about poverty and unemployment. The goodness of fit is the focus, the individual simply needs retraining to adapt more effectively. Hence "critical social work" would challenge assumptions about society and focus on exposing how seeing people as somehow effective legitimates a world where capital accumulation and exploitation of labor are normalized (see Mullaly, 2007).

While Marxist-influenced social work approaches adeptly address structural questions on the nature of oppression in modern life, there is a tendency to return to a key weakness related to this theory. Marx posited that power is located with the working classes (Harrison, 1983; Knuttila, 1992). Antonio Negri (2017) evocatively summarizes Marx's view that it was the rebellion of an exploited working class that resulted in the state intervening, "using the force of law, to obligate the capitalists to shorten the length of the working day . . . to force them to understand that the life of the workers is not just brute raw material but vital activity" (p. 19). In other words, their attachment to the marketplace is key to achieving liberation. Essentially, this needs to be addressed, as those who are not able to participate in labor are excluded from realizing their own empowerment in this analysis. Furthermore, it tacitly accepts the notion that work is an essential factor of our lives. Labor and its relations are their own hegemony.

In order to investigate further the way social work makes these assumptions about recovery, the following will be an examination on how work itself is understood. Ultimately, the questions as to how we have arrived at a point where employment has become an essential category of the "human experience" and the damage this does to those unable or unwilling to participate will be explored. Finally, an antiauthoritarian theoretical approach will be introduced to challenge these assumptions and build resistance.

The role of work in society

Gouldner (1970) suggests that much of our present thinking about the utility of individuals in terms of their contributions to society lies in the emerging of a middle class during preindustrial economies. This is similar to how Knuttila (1992) refers to the mercantile class and its struggle with monarchies as leading to liberal theories of the state. Gouldner (1970) suggests that a middle class initially needed to find a way to identify itself. Given that the purpose of their existence lay in their function and their utility, this became their own defining characteristic. Ultimately, the advent of utilitarianism led to an evaluation of all other classes related to their usefulness to society. This was a dramatic paradigm shift, as prior to this, feudalism had been about stations assigned by birth (aristocracy, vasal, etc.) where who you were mattered. Now it mattered what you did. This new pragmatism supported an argument for a change in the hierarchies, or of societal rule, toward revolution. After all, the upper class are not useful to society by engaging in lives primarily occupied by leisure and luxury.

Gouldner (1970) illustrates his point by reminding that after the French Revolution, the middle class, or bourgeoisie enshrined the concept of "utility" in the Declaration of the Rights of Man, making it a moral value. While liberty may be compelling, establishing it as a key value of society has ramifications. The problem is that utilitarianism reduces the individual to what their usefulness is which, under capitalism, is hence commodified (i.e. market based).

> In large reaches of our society and particularly in the industrial sector, it is not the man that is wanted. It is, rather, the function he can perform . . . a man [sic] must submit to an education and to socialization that early validates and cultivates only selected parts of himself, those that are expected to have subsequent utility . . . there is a strong tendency to appraise and reward him in terms of his utility as compared to that of other men [sic]. (p. 73)

Modern life hence requires one to suppress or ignore large amounts of one's own personality in order to conform to this utilitarian view of the human being in civil society. This is captured in how we see unemployment as a failure, where refusal to work is seen as a moral outrage, and the character of the individual is viewed as somehow defective or morally questionable (Gouldner, 1970).

This has grave implications for society itself. If everything can be reduced to employability, all other spheres (i.e. not productive) lose importance and hence focus. "In a culture that measures value by gainful employment, of what value are painters and poets, priests and prophets" (Gouldner, 1970, p. 75). We pay the collective price of a society that has reduced individuals to their worth as workers. I am reminded of the concerns raised about how society increasingly lacks good sleep hygiene, rising levels of stress, and mental health-related illnesses due to the increasing demands of work. Black (1985) would argue that it is the unhealthy habits, such as substance abuse to cope with the stress of work, or even the fatal traffic accidents on the way to work that better self-care and meditation cannot address. Work kills. There is an irony when employees are identified as experiencing occupational stress directly related to the degree of autonomy they have at the work place (Kirby & Keon, 2006, p. 207; Sawang & Newton 2018). Work itself requires the abdication of autonomy as someone has paid for our labor for a specific time toward a specific end.

If society has been reduced to seeing its citizens as workers, strategies must be applied to those who do not conform to this collective identity. Gouldner (1970) refers to these as "useless men."

> There are various strategies for the disposal and control of useless men . . . they may be placed in special training or retraining camps, as are certain unskilled and unemployed American youth, frequently Black; or again, they may be placed in prisons or in insane asylums, following routine certification by juridical or medical authorities. (p. 76)

Another way this could be seen is that if we move from providing asylum to deinstitutionalization, we are following the same trajectory of increasing enfranchisement of the utilitarian individual. Recovery from mental illness as recast to be of economic value to society. Hence, the hallmark of a paradigm that only values utility means that if we are not reducible to our worth to the state, we need to undergo treatment to be able to do so. This follows what Goffman (1961) said about totalizing institutions. There is a transformation of the individual to a compliant rule-bound citizen that is implied in the treatment at institutions, notably in psychiatric facilities. Obeying the "tinkering trades" makes for someone who will participate in the standards set by the society they reside in.

I alluded to this premise about bullshit jobs (Graeber, 2018) before but believe this requires further consideration. If we accept that our neoliberal world fetishizes work as a primary anchor for defining individual existence in society, we have a challenge to consider. Those in society who are not able to participate in the occupational sphere. In my own prior work as a clinical social worker, I recall needing to evaluate and address the question in the context of helping people get financial support due to a disability. The language itself is plain—to not be able—not have utility.

Furthermore, by applying this metric it becomes the goal to help rehabilitate those who are seen as disabled, to engage in some form of employment even if only symbolic, where utility is simulated in positions either expressly created for the individual or in generic supported employment workshops. Frequently this is provided with well-intentioned appeals to help people feel that they have purpose and hence subjective improvement in well-being. If we accept the idea of bullshit jobs, this changes. Graeber (2018) documents the ways in which the existence and in fact growth of jobs that are essentially meaningless are not only paradoxical according to their utility for capitalism but can have a harrowing impact on the mental health of people that perform these. These parodies of gainful employment are deleterious because those employed are aware of the futility of their work. Given these concerns, it ought to give us pause when advocating for supported employment in the first place. What is it about work that we assume is natural? Why would we assume that rehabilitation or recovery equals success in terms of employment? The research on competitive employment has been inconclusive as to improving quality of life (Gold et al., 2016).

Work and mental health

Another illustration of the problematic assumptions around work and recovery as practiced by social work can be found in my own research. The following is an examination of patient records at SMHC beginning in the 1940s and ending in the 1970s that show the evolving conceptualization of employment as a standard for successful recovery in mental health. These data were recovered as part of a larger dissertation where themes of social work practice were examined. The time frame is based on the time before and leading up to deinstitutionalization in Manitoba, Canada.

My dissertation sought to trace the evolution of social work at a Canadian psychiatric institution leading up to the period of community mental health via deinstitutionalization. I find it interesting that the legitimizing of the profession can be seen in how medical professionals employed (pardon the pun) the services of social workers. The following entry from my dissertation is of value here. "It is apparent that employment served as a measure of recovery at SMHC. Throughout the period of study (1947–1979), there is reference to efforts in the patient record, to get the patient employed. This echoes current models of recovery that refer to meaningful activity as a measure of recovery (Becker et al., 2005; Bond & Campbell, 2008; Major et al., 2009)" (Sawatsky, 2015, p. 233).

In fact, while preparing my dissertation, other annual reports confirmed the tacit assumptions of the role of social work in psychiatric rehabilitation. "Our Social Service Worker is our main resource for rehabilitation services. She is in constant liaison with social agencies, and the Unemployment Insurance Commission, arranging work, assistance and training for discharged patients" (Department of Health and Public Welfare, 1960, p.135). While developing an emerging picture of how social work gained legitimacy as a member of the psychiatric helping professions, I came across further entries in the patient record that make the connection plainer. "The reliance on the social worker to effectively connect patients to employment is such that doctor's entries chronicle the expectation that patient discharge be contingent on the social work department' being able to find employment first. (Sawatsky, 2015, p. 184).

Not only is the social worker a member of the team, but their ability to secure employment acts as a gatekeeping function for people in the care of the institution. While at the time it was a way to identify how a social worker serves an important function in mental health, this ought to give pause. Totalizing institutions (Goffman, 1961) recast societal expectations of what is "normal." If we accept that the work of institutions is misleading, promising curative services a la a medical model, it makes sense that factors like employment and housing become incorporated into the medical treatment team's objectives. After all, if it isn't the mental illness but the material conditions upon discharge that are the real factors leading to increased distress (see Prilleltensky & Nelson, 2002) and likely readmission, it makes sense. This becomes even more problematic when social work sees its authority as transcending how individuals see their own recovery. One entry dated 1972 makes this plain when the social worker disregards an individual's request to take a professional course, instead planning to relocate them back in the city to work at a local vocational rehabilitation center (Sawatsky, 2015, pp. 203–204). In other words, the social worker assumes greater authority and claims to know what the individual would best benefit from, fully invalidating their own perceptions and desires claiming to do so in their best interest.Critical social work theory, as the term implies, is influenced by critical theories which have sought to find new ways of interpreting and expanding on classical Marxism including Foucault (Fook, 2003). However, fairly constant in Marxist theories is the assumption that a future state is needed and that it would reflect the material conditions extant then (see Knuttila, 1992).

The concern remains thus that the utility of the individual remains preserved as a condition regardless of form of government structure. This would mean that those found unable to meet some future standard would be subject to similar oppressions noted here. Perhaps it is good to put this more bluntly when referring to the present liberal welfare state: "... to transform the sick, the deviant, and the unskilled into 'useless citizens' and to return them to 'society' only after periods of hospitalization, treatment.... It is this emphasis upon the reshaping of persons that differentiates the Welfare State's disposal strategies from those that tended to cope with the useless primarily by custody ... insulation from society" (Gouldner, 1970, p. 77).

While Gouldner is referring to the development of contemporary welfare states, a Marxist oriented analysis would run the risk of continuing this perception. It may be more benign in intention and design, but no less oppressive and reductive to the human condition and those we claim to be helping in the first place. Critical social work theory has sought to challenge assumptions about treatment goals and interventions as already stated above. The ideas of classical Marxism hold to the notion of labor as the power—change only possible by the workers themselves usurping the system (e.g. Negri, 2017).

This would mean that nonworkers cannot appeal to Marx in the classic sense for a cogent analysis in the problem of work itself. Furthermore, classical Marxism seeks to hold power by the labor class and its assumption of the means of production (Knuttila, 1992). Hence this reifies the definition of the self as relating to work as primary. Given the prior concerns about this narrow and reductive definition of the human condition, another perspective is necessary.

Anarchist thoughts about the idea of work

Anarcho-primitivist John Zerzan (2018) argues that the advent of industrialization in the United States marked a watershed in how work itself was to represent modern life. Prior to the industrial revolution, artisan workers were able to interrupt work for play or fun activity. By referring to writings of the 1830s, he identifies reference to the imposition of work hours as effective social control with one writer even describing the 15 to 16 hours of daily toil to be more effective than law enforcement to control the behavior of the population (Zerzan, 2018, p. 226). The industrial revolution hence resulted in concentrating people around a mechanizing approach to work that reduced initiative, the joy of creative manufacture, and individuality. "Largely spontaneous games, fairs, festivals, and excursions gave way, along with working at one's own pace, to enslavement to the uniform, unremitting technological time of the factory whistle, centralized power, and unvarying routine" (p. 227).

The philosopher Bertrand Russell (1932) adds that the case for the desirability of work is a product of the preindustrial age. Those who benefitted from the surplus were the priests and warriors who most often benefitted from free time and leisure. Now that we are in post scarcity, leisure is no longer just for the idle rich. Hence, "The morality of work is the morality of slaves, and the modern world has no need of slavery" (p. 2). Essentially, he makes the case by commenting on how shocked the British would be at the idea that the monarchy does not deserve its wealth when in fact it is produced by society for this class to remain idle. The work ethic essentially replaces the need for force to compel workers to contribute to the elite.

As was mentioned at the outset of this chapter, current events beg the question: what constitutes essential work, the nature of our economic structure, and prior assumptions about work in general. Russell (1932) makes a similar point when reflecting on WWI in his own lifetime. In fact, during the war, the allied side enjoyed ongoing comforts despite the fact that a segment of the population that had previously been working and contributing to the economy was now unavailable, having been seconded to the war effort. If fewer people can do the same amount of work, why would their return from the front not result in a decrease of hours for all? "Why? Because work is a duty, and a man should not receive wages in proportion to what he has produced, but in proportion to his virtue as exemplified by his industry. This is the morality of the Slave State" (p. 3).

We have tacitly accepted that when overproduction results in losses, employers cut positions rather than cut production. As a result, the remaining workers continue to produce at the same rate. An odd double standard to be sure, where the poor have to be kept busy working and their leisure is suspect versus the idleness of the rich (Russell, 1932). As a result, most of us are unfamiliar with leisure and have forgotten how to experience this in a meaningful way. Our reaction hence is usually boredom or restlessness as we are not able to appreciate or benefit from leisure. Importantly, Russell connects the myth of the saintliness of women, which essentially valorizes their passive role in society, with the myth of the hard-working lower class and how the poor will inherit the earth and that feminists have discovered the lack of power this provides, claiming the right to both.

What we have is the concern about domestication via time and work hours (Zerzan, 2018) along with the illogical insistence of fixed work hours that don't even line up with any economic theory of supply and demand. In effect, the arbitrary insistence of a 40-hour work week in any profession does not equal the time it takes for work to equal need (of any given product) so excess is produced and things that are not needed are flooding the marketplace (Russell, 1932). It is fair to say that the commodification of our productive activity (i.e. work) is the problem. Profitable activity, by definition, is not about the work itself but what it achieves, always outside of the now. We are hence unable to appreciate leisure for the sake of leisure—there is no profit from it (Russell, 1932). Modern life has thus robbed us of the appreciation of leisure and the playfulness it brings. Speaking of modern life, Russell would point out that even when leisure is available, it is essentially passive such as watching a movie, a play, and so on.

The theme of valuing leisure is key here. According to Russell (1932) the progress of civilization needs leisure as this is the space where play, creativity, and fun produce questions and ideas that develop the sciences and arts.

Historically, leisure had been a luxury for a smaller group to enjoy. As this is essentially oppressive, a rationale had to be developed as to why this was acceptable: hence, the aforementioned monarchies and ruling classes with royal blood and other narratives that allowed for them to be supported by the work of others. By reducing work hours for all, this group is expanded, and society as a whole would benefit from the progress this would bring. In fact, rather than seeing work as the solution, it is the absence or reduction which is sorely needed. "Ordinary men and women, having the opportunity of a happy life, will become more kindly and less persecuting and less inclined to view others with suspicion. The taste for war will die out, partly for this reason, and partly because it will involve long and severe work for all" (p. 8).

Anarchist writer Bob Black questions the value of work at all and is in favor of laziness in his essay, "The Abolition of Work" (1985). One could argue that he does this by making strange the idea of work itself. He levels a charge that all ideologies, left or right, quibble about what kind of compensation ought to be appropriate for selling our life in timed increments but never why it should be at all. According to him, Marxists want bureaucracy to be the boss, while liberals the employer and feminists that it be a woman, regardless of whether bureaucrat or employer. Regardless of perspective, the current construct of leisure is based on the binary of work and time away from work and does not provide real leisure at all. "Leisure is the time spent recovering from work and in the frenzied but hopeless attempt to forget about work. Many people return from vacation so beat that they look forward to returning to work so they can rest up. The main difference between work and leisure is that work at least you get paid for your alienation and enervation" (p. 2).

Black (1985) makes the case that even preindustrial arrangements of paying parasitic landlords to use their fields is preferred to the surveillance of the office worker to ensure servility. In effect, we have accepted a degree of freedom being relinquished during working hours as a matter of course. What this means is that we have allowed someone else to dictate our actions during a set period of time. Taken to extremes, we are being told when we can use bathrooms and even what clothes we are allowed to wear during work hours. There is no freedom at the workplace, and hence this idea of democracy is flawed if 40 hours a week you are forced into labor with no real input or control.

Returning to the idea of essential services, Black (1985) claims only 5% of work is really needed to address basic necessities, such as food, shelter, and clothing. Even this work he would suggest we convert into playful activities we all participate in. We jettison the rest, as it isn't worth doing and only serves to validate the work week in its current iteration. By abolishing work and opening leisure, homemaking is removed. This is seen as an artificial division of labor brought about by capitalism, and hence the abolition of work is a feminist project as well. Ultimately, he is endorsing a socialism or communism that parts with any form that values work, leaving Marx out. "Any extant version of leftism, whose devotees look to be the last champions of work, for if there were no work there would be no workers, and without workers, who would the left have to organize?" (p. 10).

French political theorist Gilles Dauvé (2018) agrees that work as a construct is problematic and that labor time is seen as a neutral assumption. "In reading Marx, as long as there is no sale/purchase, labor time acts as a neutral given, which capitalism in its own way takes advantage of, and which communism would also use but in a totally different way" (p. 4). In effect, by continuing to use labor time as a construct, it reinforces the idea of work as a commodity and some variation of money (exchange value) will result.

Canadian feminist-anarcho-communist writer L. Susan Brown (2011) reminds in her essay, "Does work really work?" how we are essentially defined by the question "what do you do? " This results in a particular psychic dislocation, a kind of damage that we experience when losing a job—the question constrains us and is deeply problematic—that is an unemployed person is on the margins, cast out, and would rather answer this question as being between jobs than "nothing." She examines the construct from economics and political science as the "property in the person" which presupposes that you can sell parts of yourself, such as your skill, even appearance or sex appeal without selling yourself to your employer. The fallacy of this construct is that as you must be fully present to use your labor power, you are actually submitting to be being dominated for pay as a whole person. Hence the idea of wage slavery is a reality. After all, if we are selling our self-determination for a period of time to an employee, we are essentially slaves during work hours.

Brown (2011) argues that it is this tension of the worker believing the marketplace ideologies related to labor power, while directly experiencing the slavery part of it, that is central to our collective misery. This is not an impression but inscribed in the very expectation of employee–employer relations. "No matter what kind of job a worker does, whether manual or mental, well paid or poorly paid, the nature of the employment contract is that the worker must, in the end, obey the employer" (p. 3). This unhappiness is not something that needs Prozac or therapy but is a very normal response to domination. Echoing prior voices on work, she envisions a new work based on what we already do after hours, baking, writing poetry, refereeing soccer matches, and so on. What is important is the distinction she makes between play and effort. Play does not mean easy, as play can be difficult and challenging, but the rewards are more intrinsic not in exchange for currency and all the trappings of a capitalist exchange that reduces self-determination and promotes a form of slavery. What is important is that we challenge the constructions of ourselves that are based on the false assumptions about work. We need to reflect on who we want to be since, "If one's identity is based on work, and work is based on the employment contract, and the employment contract is a falsehood, then our very identities have at their foundation a lie" (p. 6).

Anarchist historian Peter Marshall (2010) sums it up nicely when, while agreeing with Russell, he argues that work has historically been about moving things around and telling other people what to do. If we abolish the latter, we can develop a society that sees work in context. Essentially, he would argue that a collective self-interest along with a noncoercive view of work would result in a healthier society. Anarchists would be interested in separating essential work from useless labor. Again, noting Russell's view of laziness as being the result of the right person at the wrong place or location is a clue as to how an anarchist society would look at work. In other words, the work that needs to be completed, be it playful and enjoyable or unsavory but important, would be completed but with a different approach. The decommodification of labor opens up the possibility for all to explore their interests and passions, making work itself no longer a burden to be carried. Even the most unpleasant of labors would be completed collectively as it is to everyone's benefit to share such work. "When people are able to choose the nature of their work and control its process they do not wish to avoid it like the plague" (p. 656).

While this has already been alluded to, the notion of play needs attention. If we can make work play, what is play? War resister and writer, Holley Cantine (2009) wrote back in 1947 about how capitalism and its fetish for production, utility, have harmed an essential part of the human condition. His argument centers around the idea that what we do in childhood through play is later exchanged for a stale maturity defined by what one cannot do. In effect, the adult, "... is free to take a job—in fact compelled to—but the possibility of exercising his [sic] faculties in his work is infinitesimal in comparison with the creative outlets that even a slum-child possesses..." (p. 114).

The point here is to consider not only the artificiality of defining the human condition based on notions of labor but also how society has been encouraged to discourage the free creative spirit present in childhood. Any person that holds on to their creative and free spirit had best get a career in the arts which is the commodified version of the same (Cantine, 2009). Those who do not are ridiculed for being childish, immature, or, if attempting but failing to commercialize their work, a failed artist. "An artist who cannot sell his art is not considered a full adult" (p. 115).

An interesting position is advanced here. We are not meant to be working in conditions that segment our days into artificial divisions where we follow orders so we can appreciate a standard of living in society. The last vestiges of our drive toward creativity and play have been co-opted in leisure activities that simulate capitalist production (Cantine, 2009). We engage in passive activities that we must pay for, such as going to plays and movies, or even watching paid athletes play games. Furthermore, our desire to afford luxuries beyond bare necessity (and which keep us firmly entrenched in the wage slavery system) are likely further attempts at compensating for the innate play desire that is frustrated in the modern age. So too in art, there is the latent expression of activity not toward a specific end as in regular work activity. We are enchanted by it for what it represents—a way of being and seeing the world free of pragmatism and function. Unfortunately, we perceive this desire in capitalist terms and resolve to purchase, to own art made by others.

Social work and work as rehabilitation/recovery

The following quote from a paper on work illustrates the hegemony of labor as an essential part of recovery. "Gainful employment is integral to the mental health recovery process as it promotes reintegration into the community, social participation, and the fulfillment of important work roles for working age adults" (Gregitis et al., 2010, as cited in Fitzgerald et al., 2018, p. 28). This is a common claim in the literature (e.g. Hall et al., 2018; Mueser et al., 2003; Yu et al., 2016), the therapeutic benefits of work. Furthermore, work has been viewed as essential in preventing relapse, as now one has a reason to abstain. "Meaningful progress toward employment can reduce the potential for relapse" (Young, 2000, p. 47). If work as defined in our current world of labor relations is so therapeutic, why are social work students reporting the deleterious effects of work as they study, raising the specter of early burnout (Benner & Curl, 2018)?

The issues around recovery illustrate problematic assumptions we make about work itself. The following quote illustrates some of the challenges. "Current analyses demonstrated that, among people with psychiatric disabilities, participating as equal citizens in regular employment environments is positively associated with personal empowerment, above and beyond their demographic and clinical characteristics" (Sá-Fernandes et al., 2018, p. 261). Being considered as someone who is participating as "an equal citizen" is embodied in employment. As already stated, it is not about getting work done but that we expect to be identified by our labor. While some acknowledgment exists about the harms of employment on those in supported employment programs (e.g. Besse et al., 2018), the response is to develop supports to ensure greater success at the work place. In effect, by admitting that the same stressors of work affect people in these programs, the solution is not to investigate work itself but to develop more resources to ensure successful placement. Ultimately there is a tacit assumption that work stress management is needed, and over time, work mastery or accomplishment will ensure success.

There is of course a challenge when employing ideas like false consciousness (Mullaly, 2007). Who am I to disagree with someone who defines their recovery as including employment? For example, Mood Disorders Society of Canada (2009) found that 80% of people with serious mental illness want to work while 70–90% are unemployed. Dismissing their reality by claiming they are misinformed and hold a false awareness of the world is condescending and wrong. The fact is that in our current world, employment is needed to succeed beyond bare subsistence. There is an arrogance in questioning this right, while enjoying it myself, that I want to avoid. However, internalized oppression is real (Mullaly & West, 2018). So too is the problematic of how we have been convinced to accept our reality as if a better world were impossible.

Conclusion

This chapter sought to challenge preconceived notions about work itself. By seeing recovery as located within the capacity to successfully be employed, we are imbuing work with some form of sacred essence. Work is somehow the best therapy. This is often couched in terms like meaningful or productive activity. Even if we move to more liberal notions of recovery, where people are encouraged to find their own definition of recovery, it is still true that much of modern life is structured around work and the labeling of people by their occupations. Hence the message remains—only useful people are valid and whole.

The literature on supported employment, as noted above, validates this construct by uncritically extolling the virtues of social contact and skill development by virtue of paid employment. In fact, it is tempting to continue to embrace efforts to get people into competitive employment. The truth is that the welfare state does not provide enough meaningful support for sustainable living. People who are identified as disabled would benefit from a greater income. It is tempting to continue to focus on employment goals as they echo social work values—the environment as locus for change and recovery versus a reductionistic medical model. However, we are contributing to another form of reductionism. We valorize work as the solution without consideration. Work has been found to be a culprit in health and mental health issues. Furthermore, this chapter has reviewed concerns of how we have become conditioned to accept work as a fact of life, rather than a construct that disempowers us all under capitalism. The question we need to ask ourselves is not only whether our efforts at getting people employed is another way for us to engage in hiding or obscuring the contradictions of capitalism (Mullaly, 2007) but also how we are doing harm by reinforcing oppressive ideologies. In other words, are we helping people be miserable like the rest of society in the eternal hamster wheel of work? Any version of work that involves wages supports a ruling or owning class one is beholden to (Buick & Crump, 2013). We are thus validating a system that, by default, will result in the oppression and exploitation by one group over others for gain.

Another important issue regarding social work in mental health practice is that we make strange the expectations involved in the clinical encounter. It is fair game to wonder how a social worker's concern with the idea of work itself may be reproducing oppression by shaping the goals of people identified as in need of mental health services. Social workers have participated in a system that anti-psychiatry and Mad activists would say reifies an oppressive system. It goes to the large point above about how social work has sought to control the course of treatment for people identified as recipients of the system (of psychiatry/mental health). Again, I appreciate those Mad scholars and activists (Burstow et al., 2019; LeFrancois et al., 2013) from whom

I continue to learn. I want to aspire, for example, to be a "negative worker," an accomplice to the powerless who helps identify needs in opposition to the aims and agendas of bourgeois institutions (LeFrancois et al., 2013, p. 15). The assumptions around work are hegemonic—our own expectations around the good life and utility are harmful to ourselves and to people historically impacted by our profession.

Ultimately, it is my hope that this chapter has stimulated questions, provided some new ways of examining these concerns, and helped the reader to challenge tacit assumptions about the good life. We need to make strange the idea of work as a healthy part of living. By challenging these ideas in our own lives, we can explore alternatives. For example, when I used to be a case manager, I was cautious of engaging with people whom I was assigned to work with in weekly coffee times. This was unproductive and did not facilitate any treatment plan goals. After all, if the time was only spent chatting and drinking coffee, how is this person becoming more social, getting a more developed informal support system together, gaining experience in social skills, or applying themselves to more productive activity? These are all thoughts based on my own productivity and how I am anxious to measure my impact and utility as a social worker. While I may be seeking to empower and reduce dependence on the professional support network, I am not truly thinking about what this person wants. I am thus lost in the mindset of utility, which brings me back to work and its importance. By engaging in my time with people I must be present with them. Instead, I am anxious about my performance. If social work is about helping others, it needs to start with challenging ideas that do harm in how we see our collective reality. It is time to challenge what we think about work. The people we want to be helpful to deserve this from us.

References

Allness, D., & Knoedler, W. (1998). *The PACT model of community-based treatment for persons with severe and persistent mental illnesses: A manual for PACT start-up*. National Alliance for the Mentally Ill (NAMI).

Benner, K., & Curl, A. L. (2018). Exhausted, stressed, and disengaged: Does employment create burnout for social work students? *Journal of Social Work Education, 54*(2), 300–309. https://doi.org/10.1080/10437797.2017.1341858

Besse, C., Poremski, D., Laliberté, V., & Latimer, E. (2018). The meaning and experience of stress among supported employment clients with mental health problems. *Health & Social Care in the Community, 26*(3), 383–392. https://doi.org/10.1111/hsc.12527

Black, B. (1985). *The abolition of work*. The Anarchist Library. https://theanarchistlibrary.org/library/bob-black-the-abolition-of-work

Brown, L. S. (2011). *Does work really work?* The Anarchist Library. https://theanarchistlibrary.org/library/l-susan-brown-does-work-really-work

Buick, A., & Crump, J. (2013). The alternative to capitalism. In R. Graham (Ed.), *Anarchism: A documentary history of libertarian ideas. Vol 3: The new anarchism (1974–2012)* (pp. 297–307). Black Rose Books.

Burstow, B., LeFrancois, B. A., & Diamond, S. (eds.). (2019). *Psychiatry disrupted: Theorizing resistance and crafting the (r)evolution*. McGill-Queen's University Press.

Cantine, H. (2009). Art: Play and its perversions. In R. Graham (Ed.), *Anarchism: A documentary history of libertarian ideas. Vol 2: The emergence of the new anarchism (1939–1977)* (pp. 112–120). Black Rose Books.

Dauvé, G. (2018). *Getting rid of work*. https://ediciones-ineditos.com/2018/03/08/getting-rid-of-work/

Department of Health and Public Welfare. (1960). *Province of Manitoba. Highlights from the Annual Report*. Queen's Printer of Manitoba (1961).

Fitzgerald, S., Kimmel, K., Locust, A., & Miller, S. (2018). Uncovering the early vocational recovery phases for persons with psychiatric disabilities participating in a supported employment program. *Journal of Vocational Rehabilitation*, 48(1), 27–36. doi:10.3233/JVR-170913 IOS

Fook, J. (2003). Critical social work: The current issues. *Qualitative Social Work*, 2(2), 123–130. doi: 473-3250[200306]2:2;123-130;033273

Goffman, E. (1961). *Asylums: Essays on the social situation of mental patients and other inmates*. Anchor Books.

Gold, P. B., Macias, C., & Rodican, C. F. (2016). Does competitive work improve quality of life for adults with severe mental illness? Evidence from a randomized trial of supported employment. *Journal of Behavioral Health Services & Research*, 43(2), 155–171. https://doi.org/10.1007/s11414-014-9392-0

Gouldner, A. W. (1970). *The coming crisis in western sociology*. Basic Books.

Graeber, D. (2018). *Bullshit jobs: A theory*. Simon & Shuster Press.

Hall, A. C., Butterworth, J., Winsor, J., Kramer, J., Nye-Lengerman, K., & Timmons, J. (2018). Building an evidence-based, holistic approach to advancing integrated employment. *Research and Practice for Persons with Severe Disabilities*, 43(3), 207–218. https://doi.org/10.1177/1540796918787503

Harrison, F. (1983). *The modern state*. Black Rose Books.

Kirby, M., & Keon, W. (2006, May). *Out of the Shadows at Last: Transforming Mental Health, Mental Illness and Addictions Services in Canada*. The Standing Senate Committee on Social Affairs, Science and Technology.

Knuttila, M. (1992). *State theories: From liberalism to the challenge of feminism* (2nd ed.). Fernwood Publishing.

LeFrancois, B. A., Menzies, R., & Reaume, G. (2013). *Mad matters: A critical reader in Canadian mad studies*. Canadian Scholars' Press.

Lindström, V. (2020). Land of the living dead. In *To reach out and touch one another: Collected reflections on quarantine*. Salish Sea Black Autonomists. https://theanarchistlibrary.org/library/salish-sea-black-autonomists-to-reach-out-and-touch-one-another

Marshall, P. (2010). *Demanding the impossible: A history of anarchism*. PM Press.

Mood Disorders Society of Canada. (2009). Quick facts: Mental illness & addiction in Canada. https://mdsc.ca/documents/Media%20Room/Quick%20Facts%203rd%20Edition%20Eng%20Nov%2012%2009.pdf

Morrow, M. (2012). Recovery: A progressive paradigm or neoliberal smokescreen? In B. A. LeFrancois, R. Menzies, & G. Reaume (Eds.), *Mad matters: A critical reader in Canadian mad studies* (pp. 323–333). Canadian Scholars' Press.

Mueser, K. T., Noordsy, D. L., Drake, R. E, & Lindy, F. (2003). *Integrated treatment for dual disorders: A guide to effective practice*. Guilford Press.

Mullaly, B. (2007). *The new structural social work*. Oxford University Press.

Mullaly, B., & West, J. (2018). *Challenging oppression and confronting privilege: A critical approach to anti-oppressive and anti-privilege theory and practice*. Oxford University Press.

Negri, A. (2017). *Marx and Foucault*. Polity Press.

Prilleltensky, I., & Nelson, G. (2002). *Doing psychology critically: Making a difference in diverse settings*. Palgrave MacMillan.

Russell, B. (1932). *In praise of idleness*. http://www.anarchistlibrary.org

Sá-Fernandes, L., Jorge-Monteiro, M., & Ornelas, J. (2018). Empowerment promotion through competitive employment for people with psychiatric disabilities. *Journal of Vocational Rehabilitation*, 49(2), 259–263. 10.3233/JVR-180971.

Sawang, S., & Newton, C. J. (2018). Defining work stress in young people. *Journal of Employment Counseling*, 55(2), 72–83. https://doi.org/10.1002/joec.12076

Sawatsky, A. (2015). *The evolution of social work mental health practice: Patient records research at Selkirk Mental Health Centre (SMHC), 1947–1980* [Unpublished doctoral dissertation]. University of Manitoba.

Stuart, H., Arboleda-Florez, J., & Sartorius, N. (2012). *Paradigms lost: Fighting stigma and the lessons learned*. Oxford University Press.

Tam, L. (2012). Wither indigenizing the mad movement? Theorizing the social relations of race and madness through conviviality. In B. A. LeFrancois, R. Menzies, & G. Reaume (Eds.), *Mad matters: A critical reader in Canadian mad studies* (pp. 281–297). Canadian Scholars' Press.

Walsh, J. (2013). *The recovery philosophy and direct social work practice*. Lyceum Books.

Young, N. (Ed.). (2000). *TIP 38: Integrating substance abuse treatment and vocational services*. Substance Abuse and Mental Health Services Administration (US).

Yu, L. B., Tsui, M. C. M., Zhang, G. F., Lu, A. J. B., Li, D., & Tsang, H. W. H. (2016). Impact of integrated supported employment program on people with schizophrenia: Perspectives of participants and caregivers. *Journal of Rehabilitation*, 82(3), 11–17.

Zerzan, J. (2018). *A people's history of civilization*. Feralhouse.

Chapter questions

1. The argument is made that social work has been complicit in supporting the idea that recovery from mental illness includes employment. What would you think is the main reason for this? Does social work stand to lose if this was no longer a valid definition of recovery? Why or why not?

2. If the definition of our worth to society is based on our utility, our productivity, do you see any concerns for social work as a way of identifying ourselves?

3. Do social work professional codes of ethics validate a reductive view of human nature? Are we contributing to oppression by supporting it?

4

Green anarcho-social work

Social ecology, the social world, and nature

A pandemic has struck the world. As we remain ensconced in our socially distanced homes, it becomes important to consider not only how we have arrived at this point but also where to direct our attention for change. Social workers are seen as "change agents" (Lucas-Darby, 2011) when it comes to social problems. Advocacy is a field of practice born from history. Some may say that this only makes sense given our frontline work—we see evidence of how vulnerable, oppressed, and disenfranchised fellow human beings are impacted by a society that has either forgotten them or has convinced itself that there is no alternative.

While this chapter is about environmental justice and social work, the question may be asked as to why the current pandemic is the lead sentence? As governments urge for us to stay home, it may help flatten the infection rate, but it may not be as healthy for each of us. Depending on income and social standing, home, if not a homeless shelter, could still be an environment harmful to one's health. There are living conditions, directly impacted by the physical environment caused by a pattern of neglect and exploitation by industry and capital, that have not only impacted the natural environment but also left it on the doorstep of the most vulnerable and exploited to weather.

Another related rationale for locating this chapter within the pandemic has to do with how this worldwide scourge has impacted our environment. There are numerous reports around the world that the pollution rates are declining as we have drastically changed our lifestyles. What decades of alarm bells regarding our dying world have not been able to impact is now being affected by a global health emergency. As we look to the future and return to a new normal, it is important to focus on the concerns raised about the environment. The new normal needs to involve ways to address prior patterns of exploitation of the natural world. From this horror, what good could be found as a learning opportunity to make another world possible? The following will be a review of ideas related to social work and environmental justice. This will be followed by anarchist environmental thoughts with the goal of considering new approaches to "green social work."

Social work and the environment

Social work has had a history of viewing the environment as an important factor in human development. Jarvis (2019) describes how Mary Richmond herself was advocating for clean water and living conditions for the poor. Early agencies dedicated to the prevention of the cruelty of animals were the origins of child welfare (Bretzlaff-Holstein, 2018; Hick & Stokes, 2016). The ecological model was an attempt to examine transactions between individuals and their environment in order to understand the location of problems (Pease, 2003; Zastrow & Kirst-Ashman, 2016). The 1960s was a period where civil rights reforms and Marxist and Feminist critiques of society promoted a perspective where the social environment increased in importance as a location of analysis (Hick & Stokes, 2016). A Person in Environment (PIE) perspective is in effect such an analysis (Bretzlaff-Holstein, 2018; Lucas-Darby, 2011; Teixeira & Krings, 2015). Despite this history, little has been done by social work to develop a critical consciousness regarding the climate crisis (Jarvis, 2019; Norton, 2012; Weber, 2012). Notions around environmental justice are emerging, however, and the case has been made that it is social work's hallmark of interdisciplinary collaboration, as well as work toward social justice in community development, that make this discipline ideal for addressing climate change (Jarvis, 2019). Ethically, if our position is to be on the side of the most vulnerable, it is important to note how the physical places that such people reside within are the most affected by pollution and related hazards of climate change (Dominelli, 2012; Jarvis, 2019; Teixeira & Krings, 2015). It is the wealthy that disproportionally use resources, and the poor that carry the environmental burden (Norton, 2012; Weber, 2012). Addressing the climate crisis is about ensuring the marginalized have the greatest self-determination given that current conditions in the environment are limiting (Teixeira & Krings, 2015). Unfortunately, the legacy of environmental models has been more for social workers to think of the same in terms of the social, not the natural, world (Dominelli, 2012; Jarvis, 2019; Zapf, 2009). One perspective has been that this is due to social work seeking professional status by embracing the medical model which has shaped the evolution of this discipline. The result being that social work has not been able to see it's connection to the natural world (Teixeira & Krings, 2015).

Issues around climate change have international implications, as 95% of the people impacted by pollution-related health concerns reside in "developing nations" (Teixeira & Krings, 2015). In Europe, one example are the Roma people who, after a history of discrimination and oppression, are currently part of the population most impacted by pollution. However, those developing nations most impacted by climate change are where we can look for emerging ideas around a green social work practice. Social workers in developing nations are engaging with ideas about sustainable development and environmental concerns and are hence leading the way as these problems are at their doorstep (Weber, 2012).

When looking at the literature, ideas such as environmental justice and sustainability emerge. Following even the reference to a "humane capitalism" (e.g. Norton, 2012) another concern for social work is plain. One charge leveled against the discipline has been that it has served the interests of the ruling class. Social work as agents of social control have demonstrated an alarming capacity to normalize problematic assumptions of the welfare state that reproduce damaging stereotypes of the poor as lazy, scheming, and morally dubious. Even well-intentioned attempts to help the marginalized survive this harsh climate can be seen in what Mullaly (2007) would consider the softening of the contradictions of capitalism and hence reinforcing of the status quo. Humane capitalism seems to be such a construct, whereby community development for environmental sustainability has an implicit bias for seeking solutions that empower local communities in the economic bounty that can be a result of market-driven alternatives, such as jobs and keeping money in the local economy (Weber, 2012). What such approaches do is legitimize economic incentives in solving climate concerns which are the result of the economy in the first place. Put another way, commodifying solutions disappears any strategy to save the planet that doesn't have financial incentive. If all problems must be profitable, solutions will be risk averse. Furthermore, as will be explored more at length when examining green anarchism, notions of environmental justice are problematic as—already stated—there is no equality in the production of environmental damage. Nevertheless, the distinction has been made in social work between environmental justice, which is human centric, and the right of people to have a healthy environment and ecological justice, which is nature centric—where human activity is harmful to the world, and we exist inside the physical world as a part of all activity. Concerns here extend beyond humanity to the non-human natural world (Bretzlaff-Holstein, 2018).

Several textbooks on social work and the environment have attempted to find ways for the profession to engage with climate change. Zapf (2009) argues for the need to consider a place-based social work practice. Erickson (2018) argues that environmental social work can be found as early as with Jane Addams who began community work by focusing on improving sanitation and garbage pickup for the most impoverished communities (p. 6). Zapf (2009) laments how our view of the social environment serves to de-emphasize the origin of this approach. The concern with a toxic environment heralding a future without birdsong is reduced to our social interactions. By having done this, we are missing an opportunity to develop a framework for practice that includes the natural world.

Zapf (2009) also notes that there has been a failure to consider rural social work. He laments the disappearance of rural social work from the academic literature and attributes this to several factors. This includes the preference for analytic practice as well as the focus on urban locations for practice. This can in part be understood as to where the schools of social work are located and what the focus of social problems has been. Zapf argues that the "generalist practitioner" approach has frequently been viewed as the only realistic approach for rural practice. Historically, rural social work has operated from a deficit model which further adds to the problem of seeing this area of practice as having a legitimate perspective. In effect, rural social work is defined in the context of what it is missing compared to urban environments. Zapf encourages us to reflect and consider a strength-based approach to rural practice instead. This would require seeing place or environment as shaping practice in new and exciting ways. In fact, such an assets-based focus can lead to new ideas around community capacity building that incorporates the physical world. Furthermore, Zapf see potential for a less controlling approach that allows for the inclusion of the environment—even incorporating a sense of stewardship to the environment—that can be spiritual in nature, if we choose to transcend the rationality we tend to employ as professionals.

While Erickson (2018) locates the time of Rachel Carson's book *Silent Spring* within "second state environmentalism" (p. 6), Van Wormer and Besthorn (2011) see her work as having been foundational in raising the consciousness of the world (p. 271–272). They credit her with helping make the link between the environment and human flourishing. Biodiversity as a concept then, is how variation in nature among and between species helps keep every being across species healthy. This is what can be understood by Indigenous activist and scholar, Winona LaDuke (1999), when she says, "There is a direct relationship between the loss of cultural diversity and the loss of biodiversity. Wherever Indigenous peoples still remain, there is also a corresponding enclave of biodiversity" (p. 1).

Dominelli (2012) argues for a green social work that attends to the impact of climate change on people most vulnerable and at the margins. For example, when a natural disaster strikes, to ensure that children who have been separated from parents are reunited, social workers are uniquely qualified to help. Gray, Coates, and Hetherington (2013), on the other hand, talk about the need to ensure that social workers are educated about international human rights legislation and law in order to ensure environmental justice for the marginalized. This does not necessarily mean that legal mechanisms can bring about needed change. Tester (2013) points to examples, such as when the Inuit claimed a violation of their human rights due to the environmental degradation that was being caused elsewhere. The government response was that there was not enough evidence to support the claim. However, if we take the position that that legal challenge wasn't about whether it would succeed but about whether it would raise awareness, then it may have been effective because it did draw attention to the fact this conversation is really about human rights in relation to climate change.

A good illustration of the harms that emerge for people outside of the Global North comes from Lena Dominelli (2012), who points to how climate change has impacted groups such as nomads moving to the slums of Nairobi due to the loss of grazing lands. This is related to drought and desertification due to climate change. Also related to this is how the environment and climate change issues are made worse by colonial legacies. For example, tribal people living around Kenya, Somalia, and Ethiopia are not able to move across borders because of delineations of national lines drawn by European colonizers in Africa. The result is that even though social workers (as relief workers) have set up refugee camps for any population that is being displaced, government regulations clearly state that if you're Kenyan you cannot use these refugee camps. In fact, they have gone as far as saying that if you enter the Dadaab camp (located in Kenya) you will lose your citizenship rights.

Dominelli also cautions the touting of green technology as a panacea. Environmental impact assessments, for example, tend to focus on economic cost–benefit analyses, which provide a quantitative figure regarding the costs of materials and labor that goes into building a dam. However, building hydroelectric dams impacts local communities and biospheres, which developers rarely factor into the costs—in fact it's neglected by them. Dominelli illustrates this issue by noting how in Turkey there's been protest against damage and loss of cultural heritage sites like Hasankeyf. Even though the government was providing assurance no harm would come of a proposed construction of a dam to produce hydroelectricity, the Ilisu Dam will raise water levels up to 200 feet, destroying ancient cultural artifacts of great value. Even when an environmental impact assessment does factor in the cost to people and local communities, it tends to be a simplistic formula that assumes that increased technological innovation, replacing natural resources with artificial or manufactured ones, and the more efficient approach to the use of those resources will just solve all the problems due to the project the first place.

What is frequently missing, according to Dominelli, is a fair path to acknowledge emotional attachments people have to their homes and to their places. These impact assessments don't look at ways to address poverty or help marginalized populations who are trying to safeguard these resources for their own future generations. It is a rare thing for corporations to consider long-term damages or any unintended consequences caused to the physical environment by development. For example, in the case of dams, the drought caused downstream from where the dam is located is a real danger to local communities. Dominelli recommends social workers engage with these stakeholders (government, corporations, and so on) to facilitate consciousness raising of these powerful groups. Encouraging more holistic impact assessments that factor in these harms is another strategy where social workers could leverage their social capital to speak truth to power. On a local level, social workers are encouraged to promote a return to seasonal foods, foster opportunities for developing nations to engage in food cooperatives, and establish solutions based on local or Indigenous knowledges versus those imposed by neoliberal globalization.

Some authors in social work are challenging educators to engage students with examples of dispossession as it relates to water and land access or use (Teixeira & Krings, 2015). Such illustrations can be employed to use traditional skills of analysis provided via a social work education but serve to raise consciousness pedagogically by leveraging students' growing skills in critical thinking. Little changes in curriculum would be required to engage in various forms of environmental consciousness raising for social work educators (Bretzlaff-Holstein, 2018). The connections have been made that our patterns of consumption reflect societal beliefs about the environment and how harmful this is to our world (Lucas-Darby, 2011). Solutions frequently are bound within ideas of the role that the state has via regulations. Education, while raising the consciousness of students, remains entrenched in ideas related to personal behavioral change (Lucas-Darby, 2011). To borrow from business language, it is a focus on downstream solutions.

The good news is that social work is focusing on the role the physical environment has on people and society. As an illustration, concerns were raised by social workers about "urban heat islands" (UHI) and how human made geography and pollution increase the temperature in impoverished neighborhoods (Hamilton & Erickson, 2012). Dominelli (2012) sees social workers as being assets in helping to anticipate and predict as well as develop plans to mitigate the damage caused by disasters. This includes working with older people and children, for example, during heat waves as well as before. She recommends that social workers help educate and raise awareness around hydration and managing and watching for symptoms that might signal the onset of heat exhaustion, to avoid heart attacks or death. As an example, she refers to the country of Spain where there's a national warning system that social workers helped create that has prevented deaths due to heat. Further to the Spanish example, there is a special registry where those most at risk can sign up for special services during a disaster. It was social workers that were directly involved in ensuring that these resources were available when needed.

Solutions for how social workers can get involved betray the ongoing challenge for the profession, however. Educating those most at risk and setting up cool zones and working with local public service workers to monitor for safety are ways to address the present concerns (Hamilton & Erickson, 2012). However, the conditions that allow for UHI to exist in the first place receive far less attention.

Concerns have been raised about the rights of migrants to be able to use international laws to claim status as environmental refugees (Powers et al., 2018). Social work is asked to address how such migrants are received in their new locations to build on their capacities and empower them to have voice as new communities with wisdom and resilience to share. This can be expanded and built upon by employing Indigenous approaches which see knowledge as less compartmentalized, compared to Western approaches, and thus more essential in looking at complex interrelated issues such as environment and migration. Social workers are called on to help mitigate harm to those affected by climate change with policies to protect vulnerable populations.

Green anarchisms

Many variations to anarchism exist, but a common feature tends to be a conviction that society ought to exist without the artifice of a state controlling its function. The following is a summary of some of the ideas related to anarchism and the environment. It is not intended to be comprehensive but to generate interest and discussion of possibilities, of ways to see ideas from this school of thought and how they can help social work imagine ecological practice.

Anarchism has a history of challenging the destructive nature of industrialization upon ecology (Marshall, 2010; McKay et al., 2008). Early anarchist writers like Proudhon and Reclus noted the value of nature and expressed these concerns while the Russian anarchist Kropotkin insisted that a Darwinian view of evolution was a misread of nature where cooperation and diversity are true survival strategies (McKay et al., 2008). Murray Bookchin's work on social ecology is largely seen as a significant contribution to the environmental movement. He challenged the ideas related to nature as proof of hierarchy. Accordingly, he claimed that "There are no 'kings of the beasts' and no 'lowly ants.' These notions are the projections of our own social attitudes and relationships to the natural world" (Bookchin, 2013, p. 161). Bookchin saw humanity's drive to conquer and dominate the natural world as a product of our patterns of domination. This is seen in the domination by men over women and each other. Our world is based on a perception and way of thinking that is a product of our collective rearing within a paradigm of hierarchical relations. Hence the state is not only an institution but also a manifestation of our state of mind, shaping the very way we perceive and order the universe (Marshall, 2010). This has resulted in society and the state meshing in our minds and daily relations to the point that we cannot distinguish them as separate.

Our current world is no longer based on the kind of scarcity Marx had imagined would trigger revolution. Rather than engage in a form of neo-Marxism, Bookchin examines anarchist alternatives (Marshall, 2010). "Where Marx posed the choice between socialism or barbarism, Bookchin suggests that we are confronted with the more drastic alternatives of 'anarchism or annihilation'" (p. 610). In fact, he critiques Marxism as being a "form of bourgeois sociology" (p. 615) because it tacitly accepts capitalist production without exploring or investigating the culture that maintains/normalizes it.

Bookchin (2013) looks to preindustrial societies for a glimpse at alternatives. He describes a shift in thinking that coincided with preliterate organic communities getting divided into classes first based on gender division of labor and kinship connections, then hierarchical organization (of classes), and ultimately more sophisticated structures forming society and creating a separation between the members of the former organic community. In part this is created by narratives that validate this division.

> The reduction of humans to objects, whether as slaves, woman, or children, finds its precise parallel in Noah's power to name the beasts and dominate them, to place the world of life in the servitude of men ... the Promethean powers of the male are collected into an ideology of repressive rationality and hierarchical morality. (p. 164)

Women, then, are the embodiment of life, of nature and must be dominated in turn, which reflects how men view the ecology of life and nature as well. Laws are the manifestation of how domination is validated. Notions of justice, which underpin laws, are problematic as they flatten experience—not validate it. "The notion of justice, as distinguished from the ideal of freedom, collects all of these values into a rule of equivalence that denies the entire content of archaic equality" (p. 165).

Accordingly, the march of progress under capitalism is the real danger to all life on earth. Here Bookchin (2013) appeals to the Marxist idea of production for the sake of production and expands this to raise concerns about how such a society is essentially anti-ecological, with the result being a once diverse and complex organic world that "has been degraded by technology into the inorganic stuff that flows from the end of the assembly line" (p. 167). In effect, the destruction of our world is due to hierarchical notions—the food chain—and if we want to survive, we need to change our relationship to the world itself. According to Bookchin, this means changing the relations within society itself, so we relate differently to each other. Building on an idea from German Romanticism, he envisions a humanity with the potential to view itself as nature rendered self-conscious if realizing a new ecological society (Biehl, 1999, p. 39).

The recommendation hence goes beyond changing to green technologies. Bookchin describes a green society as decentralized, leaving the mega cities and their pollution (e.g. waste management) but more of a consolidation of town and country into new eco-communities. "[T]his sweeping reversal means that we must begin to decentralize our cities and establish entirely new eco-communities that are artistically modeled to the ecosystems in which they are located" (Bookchin, 2013, p. 168).

It is Bookchin's optimism about the environment that is significant. His idea of biodiversity is key for survival—the industrial capitalist approach of simplifying, mass producing, and reducing nature to parts for commodification are harmful to the world (Marshall, 2010). If we take our relationship with each other as the template for how we treat the natural world, the inverse can be applied as well. Bookchin would say that society is strongest when it is diverse and nonhierarchical as an ecological society.

The concept of social ecology is perhaps his most well-known contribution to the environmental movement. What is important to note is how he saw a distinction between a green anarchism and environmentalism. In essence, any act to conserve or protect the environment sets up a dualism where we are separate from the natural world, and the existing structures that dominate and perceive a hierarchical order remain unchallenged (Marshall, 2010). Such an instrumental approach simply allows for the existing relations of capital and state to continue and make any real climate concerns impossible to resolve (McKay et al., 2008). The notion is that environmentalism is merely a kind of reforming of the system and "without dealing radically with the need for an expanded concept of revolution, it will merely serve as a safety valve for the existing system of natural and human exploitation" (Bookchin, 1980, p. 43, as cited in McKay et al., 2008, p. 386). In effect, the abolition of private property and commodity relations would be greener than incremental, regulatory efforts within the state. The hallmark of an organic and ecological society would be one that is characterized by diversity, interdependence, and mutual aid (Marshall, 2010).

To expect capitalism to reform itself is illogical given its essential mandate that requires exploitation to exist in the first place. Capitalism, "turns the plunder of nature into society's law of life. To quibble with this kind of system about its values, to try to frighten it with visions about the consequence of growth is to quarrel with its very metabolism" (Bookchin, 1980, p. 66 as cited in McKay et al., 2008, p. 387). Taken further, any attempts by capitalism to address such things as pollution are reduced to market-based solutions, where some form of commodification and hence surplus value are produced. The passing on of costs (externalities) or investing in new means of production are key to increasing productivity. Pollution is then passed on as an externality to a third party, such as the marginalized in society who reside closest to the site of industrial production. The endless growth cycle of capitalism is the key for industry to survive is to grow or die. "To speak of 'limits to growth' under a capitalistic market economy is as meaningless as to speak of limits of warfare under a warrior society" (Bookchin, 1989, p. 93–94, as cited in McKay et al., 2008, p. 387). Essentially a neoliberal solution via regulations, like cap and trade, is employed; or else capitalism will seek to engage in denial strategies, refusing to admit the severity of the climate crisis or asserting that science will solve the problem in time.

Anarchist positions on environmentalism have become more insistent in that a failure to reconcile the paradox of capitalism reforming itself is that groups that are deeply anti-ecological in their orientation/ideas have joined the green movement. "Thus we find fascists expounding on their environmental vision or defenders of capitalism proposing 'ecological' solutions based on expanding private property rights" (McKay et al., 2008, p. 435). This idea of privatization presupposes that if you own the property, you will want to maintain its ecological value given that it's your own property. The problem with this is the false assumption that a system that relies on possession does not seek to maximize its utility to accumulate capital. What if it's worth more as a deforested dump than a pristine forest? Furthermore, in this age of "Tiger King" (Goode & Chaiklin, 2020), if you have a preserve for endangered species, what if it is more profitable to sell them off?

Science is not a neutral epistemology. Under capitalism, the most common form of science is objective since it reifies the existing world as it is (McKay et al., 2008). Malthus' "law of population" is an example of science that, while flawed and questionable in following science's own standards, is accepted by ruling elites, as it supports their worldview. It is important to take the time to examine this idea, as it has been used to justify responses to our growing ecological crisis. In fact, it has, unfortunately, even been used by some green activist groups (McKay et al., 2008). Malthus' argument is essentially that poverty and any associated misery is a result of overpopulation, in effect, blaming the poor for behaviors (such as having too many children) that exacerbate their own suffering. This is a popular myth that serves the interests of those in power to maintain the capitalist status quo. Ironically, Malthus was initially intending to use this work to challenge, in part, the writings of an early anarchist named William Godwin (McKay et al., 2008). The point was to prove that social stratification and hence status quo is a law of nature. Interestingly, he prefigured Darwin, who saw his own work on the theory of natural selection as an extension of Malthus' doctrine. While Malthus' ideas have been challenged, a return of his ideas via the neo Malthusians has brought back notions where the poor and hungry are basically at fault. In effect, they live too long and breed too much.

McKay et al. (2008) make the case that when you dispossess people of material conditions, their culture, or any other form of self-expression/emancipatory living, population rates will increase. Hence population increases are related to the damage caused by capitalism itself and not the other way around. In fact, when Malthusian arguments are made, one can point to how nations struggling with poverty and famine are able to export with profits for the ruling elites. Hence, it cannot be about material conditions but rather relations of authority and power.

> When people are ground into the dirt by poverty, education falls, women's rights decrease, and contraception is less available. Having children then becomes virtually the only survival means, with people resting their hopes for a better future in their offspring. Therefore, social conditions have a major impact on population growth. (p. 472)

The other argument that population explosion explains high consumption never asks how many luxury yachts the average person has as this is based on the mistaken assumption of average consumption equaling real per person use.

Eco anarchism would see environmental degradation as directly related to the degradation of ourselves. From this perspective, class divisions are important to consider in ecological terms. If we focus on healing the earth from the assumption of everyone doing their part, it misses an important difference. Young people, old people, non-White, women along with exploiters would all have the same responsibility to affect change which is a gross denial of social reality. "Be they starving Ethiopian children or corporate barons, all people are held to be equally culpable" (Bookchin, 1980, p. 33, as cited in McKay et al., 2008, p. 437). This de-contextualization from the social is neither accurate nor helpful.

While anti-oppressive approaches to the environment may support economic critiques, anarchism goes further to challenge the state directly. In effect, the state is essentially anti-nature as a construct. No form of representation can accurately capture each individual's perspectives, desires, or needs. Hence, by default, a state will need to manage via abstraction. This results in "Standardised citizens ... uniform in their needs and even interchangeable ... for purposes of the planning exercise, no gender; no tastes; no history; no values; no opinions or original ideas, no traditions, and no distinctive personalities to contribute to the enterprise (Scott, 1999, p. 22–23, as cited in McKay et al., 2008, p. 438). Hence if this is how the state treats us, the natural world will be viewed in the same fashion, which would go against the diverse ecosystems that actually exist in nature. The state will resist any changes that threaten it—hence any changes will be hard fought battles for reform and, in the same instance, will be followed by constant efforts/attempts by industry to violate, ignore, or undo said reforms in the name of profit. Hence eco-anarchists reject the parliamentary domain as a locus of change, as it legitimates the reality of the state and forces the environmental justice movement to restrict itself to government reforms—playing in a field where one has no say or control over the rules, and industries prevail.

While many currents of anarchism find purchase in these critiques, it is important to note, in particular, the ideas related to anarcho-primitivism. This approach takes the extreme position that all technology is essentially bad and calls for a return to an earlier time without technology. McKay et al. (2008) engage in thorough examination of this current of thought and raise significant concerns as well as flaws in its logic. It is their position that primitivism holds an extreme view that at best does not capture anarchist ideas of choice and freedom and at worst would welcome genocide as their approach and would accept mass starvation as an acceptable consequence of returning to some earlier, mythical state of being. It is important to draw the contrast between social ecology and primitivism. The former, per Bookchin, would see the use of technology as acceptable to produce needs—not wants, which exist in a consumer-oriented society (Kinna, 2009). Hence production is less wasteful, and what is in excess is repurposed or recycled by the community. The latter as already stated, would dogmatically oppose and even impose the authority to deny all technology (McKay et al., 2008). In fact, the argument has been made that primitivism is not really a form of anarchism, as it advocates a vanguardism or transitional period more in common with Marx. Furthermore, if tactics are to reflect the ideas that spawned them, there is a significant element of authoritarianism that would disqualify primitivists. McKay et al. (2008) raise an important distinction where the examination of past societies can help us critique our present world. What is less useful is when we seek a mythical past as something to return to. The latter will invariably disappoint, as it creates a static utopia that reduces the power of such ideas to motivate and rather venerate a stagnant dogmatic future (Kinna, 2009). It is perhaps part of the reason why primitivist arguments seem to be based on a rose-colored view of a past that glosses over any anthropological data that do not reinforce their view of civilization and history (McKay et al., 2008). In conclusion, this chapter aligns more closely with anarchism that seeks to transform society for the good of our environment, not the kind that calls for the destruction of civilization.

Returning to the problem of the state, then, it is important to examine the ways in which our own social relations reflect hierarchical and essentially capitalist ways of viewing the world. By reworking these relations (e.g. gender, race, age, and so on) to address issues of domination and oppression, we avoid reproducing these dynamics in nature. In this, McKay et al. (2008) are echoing how Bookchin has framed our relationship with nature in a strategic way. The state cannot help in this process, as at a fundamental level "there is no real difference between private and state capitalism. That this is the case can be seen from the willingness of capitalist firms to invest in, say, China in order to take advantage of their weaker environmental laws and regulations plus the lack of opposition" (pp. 439–440). The state thus will only reproduce relations that reproduce capitalism in varying structural forms which will continue to impact the environment in damaging ways. While as a social worker I am always motivated to see education and consciousness raising as the best way to promote change, it is important to ask whether this is always the right assumption. If capitalism and its enabler, the state, will always seek profit over any other factors, expecting knowledge to change behavior may be naïve. Naomi Klein's work, "The Shock Doctrine" (2007) is a sobering exposition on how disaster capitalism manages to adapt and exploit opportunities brought about by climate change. Our collective ecological calamity is not about lack of information. It may be a lack of morality, unless we accept that capitalism has its own set of morals. "This can only be ended by ending capitalism, not by appeals to consumers to buy eco-friendly products or to capitalists to provide them" (McKay et al., 2008, p. 441–442).

What is the alternative?

A number of ideas are useful to consider in how anarchism can be applied to address concerns about the environment. Bookchin refers to usufruct, complementarity, and the irreducible minimum (Marshall, 2010). "Usufruct" is the idea that you take what you need, not because you own it or have the right or possession over it. Complementarity is an alternative to contracts, where people engage in a process of giving and receiving without preconditions. All of this is based on the idea of the irreducible minimum, which posits that all people have basic needs met regardless of their contribution or utility to society. What Bookchin is saying, in essence, is that if people had what they needed, coveting more would cease to exist.

If a large part of our world's ecological woes is based on unquenchable desire and limitless growth, meeting the needs of society and its members seems a reasonable step. Bookchin's "affinity groups" (Marshall, 2010) embody the idea that change needs to emerge from associations of people with shared connections and concerns about the world. Furthermore, considering decentralization, if cooperatives are any indication, the decentralized and worker-run production of needs would invariably decrease pollution, as those who control said production are local residents and most directly impacted by the work (McKay et al., 2008). Bookchin (2004) expresses optimism that an eco-technology is possible in an organic society. If technology was designed as most opportune for all, it would be done, not based on an imaginary profit/loss calculation. At this time, only the wealthy can afford a Tesla, while the rest must remain complicit in creating further environmental damage as we have been economically excluded from this green strategy.

In what McKay et al. (2008) refer to as "eco-anarchism," they see alliances with feminist and peace movements as essential with a common cause. War is seen as significant ecological calamity, so the ends are the same as the peace movement, while male domination and the domination of "mother earth" are directly related (given assumptions of psychology of hierarchy and domination) and hence common cause to abolish androcentrism and patriarchy.

Further strategies include challenging narratives of liberal hegemony that assure us we can work inside a system, which is rigged against us, in the name of the profit motive. For instance, the idea that using the law to challenge owners of private property or capitalism in general (the use of lawsuits) ignores that a basic plurality does not in fact exist. The wealthy can afford the best teams of lawyers to fight indefinitely in courts while the rest of us must go bankrupt (McKay et al., 2008). In fact, "it soon becomes clear that people may put up with externalities imposed upon them simply because of economic necessity and the pressure big business can inflict" (p. 453).

If we don't challenge the illusion of freedom and choice in current neoliberal landscapes, we risk being unable to create viable alternatives to our current climate crisis. Environmental pollution is systematic. The ruling class will attack labor unions, which historically have tried to keep the masses informed and active in the process and the same infernal short-term logic is applied to them in order to achieve ends. "After all, tolerating pollution in return for some money is more tempting when you are struggling to make ends meet" (p. 454). Furthermore, when businesses require workers to sign waivers, it is not about freedom. "Choosing" to not hold the business responsible for the hazards incurred by working there does not mean there was a real choice. If you must feed yourself and your family and this is the only option for you, refusal to sign is no choice at all.

We need to problematize the way modern life has created harmful practices in the name of consumer culture. "The fast food chain's vast purchasing power and their demand for a uniform product have encouraged fundamental changes in how cattle are raised, slaughtered, and processed into ground beef." (Schlosser, *Fast Food Nation*, pp. 8–9, as cited in McKay et al., 2008, p. 455). Furthermore, we need to challenge market-based solutions that increase the consumption of "green" products. Ethical consuming is about individual solutions to a collective, systemic problem. "Real change comes from collective struggle, not individual decisions within the marketplace which cannot combat the cancerous growth principle" (p. 471). In effect, we need to question values rooted in utility and consumption and encourage a transformation to valorizing the importance of living interconnected to the world we are inextricably bound within. We need to challenge harmful narratives that push the blame of capitalism itself onto overpopulation myths.

Heller (2013) makes a valuable point regarding green movements as opposed to green anarchism. Like primitivists, there can be a tendency to idealize nature, which becomes fetish. This can be harmful, as it separates us from nature, dogmatically insisting on its conservation and ignoring society itself in the process. "Nature cannot be a 'country home' of our desires ... By placing the idea of nature within society itself, we may transform society into a ground on which we may build, collectively, a new practice of both nature and community" (p. 177). In fact, Marshall (2013) reminds that being protective of the environment ignores a reality of nature: it can heal and grow without intervention. "We should no longer act as business managers of the cosmic process but as fellow voyagers in the grand and mysterious odyssey of evolution" (p. 180). We need to step away from models that encourage seeing nature as a valuable resource, as this simply reifies the value of commodification. Nature has intrinsic value beyond what it can do or provide.

Other possibilities for social work

Another promising direction for social work may be in degrowth. In fact, I would argue, there are interesting intersections that seem to infer an anarchist perspective to the environment and social work practice. Macias (2022) offers an intriguing premise: what if we inverted the concept that the earth belongs to us? In fact, we belong to the earth. "What would happen if instead of a list of learning outcomes, environmental issues, and professional competencies ... we were given a chance to build from there?" (Macias, 2022, p. 549). Degrowth is about challenging the idea of capitalism's need for infinite growth. In fact, like anarchism, it questions the attempts by capitalism to recuperate the current climate crisis, brought on by capitalism in the first place. Recently the degrowth movement has expanded beyond economics to broader social and systemic forces—where degrowth is not the objective but the product of the objective to fundamentally alter democratic institutions and governments toward greater autonomy for us all. This fits well with autonomous movements—including anti-capitalist, anti-neoliberal, and decolonizing approaches.

Macias (2022) makes the point that we need to *challenge how our minds have been conditioned* to separate ourselves from the world and that this binary thinking is replicated in solutions for the environment. In some ways, I see the idea of degrowth as helping us rediscover our humanity, our identity beyond and removed from economic entanglement. This includes the challenge of how we see ourselves as professional helpers, as social workers.

> Social work remains steeped in modernist notions of disciplinarity and professionalization; it is part of the colonial matrix of power within which it emerges, and on which its epistemic and classificatory fictions find meaning ... Within this colonial matrix of power, it becomes difficult for us in social work to read any other script or map than that of social work. (p. 555)

Degrowth includes intentional communities, a prefiguring of living outside of neoliberal systems—rather than glorifying an imaginary past (which would be a modernist view), it is about bringing the past forward into a better future—a path not investigated or taken leading us in a better direction then the one we took for the sake of the accumulation of wealth and colonial projects. By doing so, Macias (2022) sees degrowth as offering a way to deconstruct assumptions and to engage in a praxis of unlearning the capitalist/ colonial mindsets and engaging in an ethics of care that is fundamentally different. It is modernity that needs to be confronted as it tends to conflate and reduce difference in anodyne pluralism at best. What remains privileged are Western ontologies of scientific rationality which reinforce a capitalist present. For example, modernity has historically presented the knowledge of the Indigenous as myth or folklore. In contrast, western ideas are framed as enlightened knowledge. In doing so, the colonized subject is cast as being incapable of thinking or creating valid theory or philosophy that would challenge these privileged, western ideas.

Ecofascism

This chapter cannot conclude before talking about a worrisome trend: the rise of eco-fascism. While the scope of this chapter cannot encompass more than a passing reference, it is important to acknowledge that even the right wing has a response for climate change. The following then is an attempt to summarize some of the broad ideas connected to the fascist ideas about the environment. I do this hoping that further work (see the final chapter) on this topic will be the topic of future endeavors, as the threat from the right is not only in the political landscape but also in the environment.

Moore and Roberts (2022), when unpacking the origins of ecological fascism, return to Malthus and the need to clarify terminology. First, they would avoid terms such as anthropocene as this implies that we are in the era of human action causing climate change. Rather, it is more appropriate to refer to our current era as the "capitalocene." It is not humanity that is causing our current climate crisis but the specific economic system of capitalism. It is also important to note that the colonial project has been concerned about the environment for some time. Even Christopher Columbus warned against deforestation because of colonial expansion. While his understanding may have been limited (he feared lack of forested areas would reduce rainfall) and primarily concerned with interfering with colonialism (not to cease expansion after all), it is an acknowledgment of what the colonizer is doing to the environment. It wasn't about preserving nature for its own sake but conservation and protection of the environment to get as much bang for the buck as possible. Furthermore, colonial states seeking to preserve nature were not appealing to a pure, untouched view. The land was already reorganized through the introduction of norms and species brought in from European landscapes and profoundly organized by the genocide of the Land's prior inhabitants.

A Malthusian understanding of the world does not only blame those who are poor and vulnerable. Policies that use this logic can be devastating and deadly (Moore & Roberts, 2022). When the Irish were begging for relief during the great famine from 1845 to 1852 an Oxford economist opposed government famine relief using the argument that the main cause of famine was overpopulation greater than the land could support.

The Nazis have a long tradition of veneration for nature but also used this as subterfuge to build tanks when there was a ban on this post Treaty of Versailles (WW I). One of the architects of ensuring an expansion of the Aryan landscapes, the preservation of a purity in nature, was Alvin Seifert (Moore & Roberts, 2022). He felt that the entire landscape of newly captured territories needed to be "Germanized." Seifert's "advocates for the landscape" were hired at Auschwitz, where they experimented with composting and constructing a tree nursery. This resulted in the construction of a 180-acre biodynamic plantation at Dachau which grew medicinal herbs and other products for the Schutzstaffel (SS). Many prisoners died building these greenhouses.

Suffice it to say, eco-fascism today tends to be protectionist, if a fascist admits to climate change at all. When it is acknowledged, it is about protecting one's country. The solution then is to just plant more trees to provide ways to ensure one's land is able to defeat CO_2 emissions and prevent the 'other' from polluting the homeland with their presence(Malm & The Zetkin Collective, 2021). Nature is still seen as an object separate from us and is venerated via the same mythic past as the elite race they claim to be. It is also important to note that there are mass shooters, such as the Christchurch killer in New Zealand, referring to themselves as eco-terrorists. The dangerous rhetoric of ecofascism has deadly real life consequences for those most often harmed by white supremacy. Hence this topic is an important one to engage with as we think about the environment, social work, and beyond.

Conclusion

The environmental issues raised in this chapter aren't new. Nor are the social issues related to climate change. In fact, 21% of all civil unrest since the 1950s are related to the weather phenomenon known as El Niño (Besthorn, 2013). It is also true that climate change is not monolithic and will be experienced differently by each nation, but international collective action is needed to make mitigation of climate change possible. Climate change is a social, political, and cultural issue. It is expected that up to 216 million people could be displaced due to climate change by 2050 (Worldbank.org, 2013). It is anticipated that due to rising seas, famine and disease people made vulnerable to poverty, especially those in developing countries will be and already are the most impacted by climate change (Besthorn, 2013). It is these groups, the ones social work is supposed to help the most, that lack not only the means to cope with climate change, but have lower socioeconomic capital. They lack education, private savings, let alone private transportation to leave areas that are becoming uninhabitable. Furthermore, economically disadvantaged people are more likely to choose less savory places to live as they cannot afford better which results in them being disproportionately impacted by climate change as they bear the brunt of being in the path of hurricanes, flooding, and so on.

Within these groups, there are intersectional concerns that need to be acknowledged as well. For example, women are more vulnerable as in some communities the androcentric breadwinner model means that women are not as attached to land so are expected to make food for the husband and be the last to eat (Besthorn, 2013). Indigenous people are more likely to be located near fragile ecosystems and will experience the effects of climate change sooner and more severely. The case for their inclusion in the climate change conversation, given their unique position, is essential. As they are frequently at these epicenters of fragile ecosystems, their insights—due to their experience with climate prediction based on survival—along with culture (caretakers of the earth), allows them a perspective that may hold keys to addressing climate change. Finally, we need to acknowledge that older people are throughout the world at greater risk of harm due to the extreme temperatures brought on by climate change. This risk includes extreme heat and cold as well as poor air quality brought on by bush and forest fires, causing respiratory issues.

This chapter seeks to challenge the reader to examine alternatives to common responses to our current climate crisis. While social work has become involved in seeking a green alternative to practice, it is reasonable to expect these to be embedded in current worldviews and systems. While by no means complete nor comprehensive, ideas from anarchism were introduced that address a different way of approaching our environmental issues. It is important that I avoid the temptation to provide a prescription or solution based on the literature presented here. For some, anarchism may be a new source of inspiration while others may be more familiar with these ideas than I have been to date.

The purpose of this chapter is to encourage further discussion and exploration for a better world that I believe social work can help advance. We must be willing to engage with our paradoxical relationship to the current neoliberal welfare state that provides for our work to never be complete as poverty increases and our world burns. Anarchism is a way to think about the challenges of hierarchical relations, how we repeat these not only with each other but with the natural world. Unpacking the way capitalism reinforces exploitation and questioning approaches that seek to factor market-based ideas such as sustainability are key. We need to consider how saving our planet may require a radical transformation of our own values and of those in the society we live in. I want to conclude this paper with the optimism found in anarchism. One popular phrase I keep returning to is that a better world is possible. I look forward to further engagement with my fellow social workers as we seek to find this better world together.

References

Besthorn, F. (2013). Radical equalitarian ecological justice: A social work call to action. In M. Gray, J. Coates, & T. Hetherington (Eds.), *Environmental social work* (pp. 29–45). Oxford University Press.
Biehl, J. (Ed.). (1999). *The Murray Bookchin reader*. Black Rose Books.
Bookchin, M. (2004). *Post-scarcity anarchism*. AK Press.
Bookchin, M. (2013). Toward an ecological society. In R. Graham (Ed.), *Anarchism: A documentary history of libertarian ideas volume 3: The new anarchism (1974–2012)* (pp 161–169). Black Rose Books.
Bretzlaff-Holstein, C. (2018). The case for humane education in social work education. *Social Work Education, 37*(7), 924–935. doi: 10.1080/02615479.2018.1468428
Dominelli, L. (2012). *Green social work: From environmental crisis to environmental justice*. Polity.
Erickson, C. L. (2018). *Environmental justice as social work practice*. Oxford University Press.
Goode, E., & Chaiklin, R. (Producers). (2020). *Tiger king: Murder, mayhem, and madness* [video]. Netflix. http://www.netflix.com

Gray, M., Coates, J., & Hetherington, T. (2013). *Environmental social work*. Oxford University Press.

Hamilton, B., & Erickson, C. L. (2012). Urban heat islands and social work: Opportunities for intervention. *Advances in Social Work, 13*(2), 420-430.

Heller, C. (2013). Ecology and desire. In R. Graham (Ed.), *Anarchism: A documentary history of libertarian ideas: Vol 3: The new anarchism (1974-2012)* (pp. 176-179). Black Rose Books.

Hick, S., & Stokes, J. (2016). *Social work in Canada: An introduction* (4th ed.). Thompson Educational Publishing.

Jarvis, D. (2019). Environmental justice and social work. *Columbia Social Work Review, 11*(1), 36-45.

Kinna, R. (2009). *Anarchism: A beginner's guide*. One World Publications.

Klein, N. (2007). *The shock doctrine: The rise of disaster capitalism*. Alfred A. Knopf Canada.

LaDuke, W. (1999). *All our relations: Native struggles for land and life*. Haymarket Books.

Lucas-Darby, E. T. (2011). The new color is green: Social work practice and service-learning. *Advances in Social Work, 12*(1), 113-125.

Macias, T. (2022). Degrowth, decoloniality and the unsettling of the knowing subject: A utopian praxis for social work education. In S. S. Shaikh, B. A. LeFrancois, & T. Macias (Eds.), *Critical social work praxis* (pp. 547-564). Fernwood Press.

Malm, A.; The Zetkin Collective. (2021). *White skin, black fuel: On the danger of fossil fascism*. Verso.

Marshall, P (2010). *Demanding the impossible: A history of anarchism*. PM Press.

Marshall, P. (2013). Liberation ecology. In R. Graham (Ed.), *Anarchism: A documentary history of libertarian ideas. Vol 3: The new anarchism (1974-2012)* (pp. 180-185). Black Rose Books.

McKay, I., Elkin, G., Neal, D., & Boraas, E. (Eds.). (2008). *An anarchist FAQ : AFAQ volume 1*. AK Press.

Moore, S., & Roberts, A. (2022). *The rise of ecofascism: Climate change and the far right*. Polity.

Mullaly, B. (2007). *The new structural social work*. Oxford University Press.

Norton, C. (2012). Social work and the environment: An ecosocial approach. *International Journal of Social Welfare, 21*(3), 299-308. doi: 10.1111/j.1468-2397.2011.00853.x

Pease, B. (2003). Rethinking the relationship between the self and society. In J. Allan, B. Pease, & L. Briskman (Eds.), *Critical social work: An introduction to theories and practices* (pp. 187-201). Allen & Unwin.

Powers, M. C. F., Schmitz, C. L., Nsnowu, C. Z., & Mathew, M. T. (2018). Environmental migration: Social work at the nexus of climate change and global migration. *Advances in Social Work, 18*(3), 1023-1040. doi: 10.18060/21678

Teixeira, S., & Krings, A. (2015). Sustainable social work: An environmental justice framework for social work education. *Social Work Education, 34*(5), 513-527. doi: 10.1080/02615479.2015.1063601

Tester, F. (2013). Climate change as a human rights issue. In M. Gray, J. Coates, & T. Hetherington (Eds.), *Environmental social work* (pp 101-117). Oxford University Press.

Van Wormer, K., & Besthorn, F. (2011). *Human behavior and the social environment, macro level: Groups, communities, and organizations* (2nd ed.). Oxford University Press.

Weber, B. A. (2012). Social work and the green economy. *Advances in Social Work, 13*(2), 391-407.

Worldbank.Org. (2013, September 9). *Climate change could force 216 million people to migrate within their cwn Countries by 2050.* https://www.worldbank.org/en/news/press-release/2021/09/13/climate-change-could-force-216-million-people-to-migrate-within-their-own-countries-by-2050#:~:text=13%2C%202021%E2%80%94The%20World%20Bank's,within%20their%20countries%20by%202050

Zapf, M. K. (2009). *Social work and the environment: Understanding people and place.* Canadian Scholars' Press.

Zastrow, C. H., & Kirst-Ashman, K. K. (2016). *Understanding human behavior and the social environment* (10th ed.). Cengage Learning.

Chapter questions

1. Have you found courses in social work that discuss the physical environment? What are the themes that emerge there?
2. The person in the environment perspective is being criticized for conflating the physical world to mere allegory for the social world. Do you think this is a valid argument? Why or why not? Defend your answer.
3. If you were to practice a green social work practice, would you incorporate anarchist ideas? What would this look like?

5
Crime, social work, and anarchism
Seeking to abolish the carceral state

There are some things that are more obviously different between Canadian and American social work practice than others. When I arrived in Canada, I was surprised to learn that many social workers are employed as probation or parole officers. This was quite different than the imposing and intimidating ex-police officers I had met through my work at a community mental health center in the American Midwest.

At the time of writing this chapter, the streets of United States cities are alive with protests and confrontations with police. What Black Lives Matter (BLM) has done is raise the question of whether policing as an institution should exist. Related to this, the question of whether the carceral system itself ought to be abolished is becoming a topic of debate in the mainstream. Given the coronavirus pandemic and the horror of rampant exposure in prisons, it seems even more timely to explore ending the entire prison industrial complex. Finally, calls are being made to replace the police with social work. It seems therefore even more relevant to the profession that the relationship between crime and social work be considered.

Recently, the National Association of Social Workers (NASW) has been involved in a skirmish between the organization and its members over the topic of police abolition. At issue is the seemingly unilateral decision by the board of NASW to issue a statement in support of police reform (See Wilson & Wilson, 2020) that sees social workers as working alongside police to help in reform efforts. Some members have articulated the same arguments of social work's own past in legitimating oppression and do not support reformation, but abolition, of the police and are calling for NASW to adopt this strategy instead (Sato, 2020). It should be noted, that in Canada, the Canadian Association of Social Workers (CASW) adopted a stance, in a call to action to Justin Trudeau, that describes a plan for a review of the police and Royal Canadian Mounted Police (RCMP) with the intention to redirect funds to community supports as well as the mandatory adoption of body cameras (Wood, 2020).

I am in no way claiming to be the authority on the experiences of others. As a White, middle-class, cis-male academic, I am aware of my privilege. Even in my early years as the child of missionaries, I was privileged in my experience of poverty. What I mean to say is that most people in lower socioeconomic classes experience associated anxiety. I can't speak for my parents, but it is true that all essential needs were met via the denomination that supported the project. It is true that I have not experienced the fear and terror that police officers can produce nor the totalizing experience of the prison system.

I recall a time when I was still working on an inpatient unit at a psychiatric hospital in the United States. It was a night shift, and a friend of mine, originally from Sri Lanka, arrived late for work. He was pale, and his eyes were wide, and he was shaking. The story emerged that he had been pulled over twice on the way to this very shift that night by police. He was terrified by the experience. I cannot relate to this because I have never been pulled over without any apparent reason. I may drive "cleaner" when I spot a police cruiser in my rearview mirror, but that is about it. My friend was welcomed to the United States by a very different experience, due to driving while brown-skinned.

Now, as a social worker, it is important that I am aware of the reality that marginalized and oppressed people live in. It is not one where the police are seen as protecting and serving the community. Their lives, the spaces they occupy, have been criminalized. In Canada, the abolition of residential schools and the increase in apprehensions and incarcerations of Indigenous youth and adults suggest an uncomfortable correlation. Canadian prisons, according to poet and activist/academic El Jones (2016, as cited in Maynard, 2017, p. 109) are both the afterlife of slavery and the new residential schools. Hence, social workers need to be versed in both theories on crime and their role in perpetuating racially biased oppression in the field of corrections. This chapter is an exploration of theories about crime and punishment as they have evolved into our current system of law enforcement and corrections. Voices from carceral abolitionists and anarchists will follow. By engaging with these ideas, I want to challenge myself and the reader to consider alternatives to policing and incarceration and social work's role in these. It is my hope we can reflect on anarchist and abolitionist voices so we can help bring about change in policing and law enforcement for the good of all.

Police and crime

Kristian Williams (2015) traces the origins of current law enforcement to slave patrols in the United States. Robyn Maynard (2017) draws a link between Canada's own 200 years of practicing slavery where the runaway slave was portrayed as "thieves and criminals" and that, "After slavery's abolition, the associations between Blackness and crime served important political, social, economic, and cultural functions in maintaining the racial order . . . the corresponding wildly disproportionate arrests . . . associations with Blackness . . . remain markedly unchanged" (p. 85).

Academic and activist, Angela Davis (2003), asks the question "Are prisons obsolete?" She makes the case that in the United States, Black, Indigenous, and People of Color (BIPOC) people are more likely to be incarcerated than to get a "decent" education. She describes the scourge of incarceration as exposing a growing group of people to authoritarian regimes, physical brutality, and the psychological violence of seclusion via penal strategies at asserting control. Aside from the deleterious consequences to prisoners, the communities from which they have been taken suffer alongside as well. Further concerns include the troubling rise of the prison industrial complex, which is intimately tied to capital investment/corporate production and the rise of the war on drugs under Reagan. Maynard (2017) ties the war on drugs to the misery of police encounters and associated rising rates of incarceration in Canada.

Davis (2003) adds that we have engaged in a form of abstraction where we cannot imagine a system that is flawed but rather conflating those who commit crime with skin color. Rather than looking at the communities where conditions create such behavior, we control perception by removing individuals from our sight. Taking this further, she argues that the causes of community damage are due to large migrating corporations searching for cheaper labor pools abroad during globalization, leaving devastated communities in their wake with the perfect candidates for the prison industry to warehouse for profit. In effect, the contradictions of capitalism managed by capitalism itself and sanitizing itself in the process—these are just evildoers after all. This is where she identifies the role of the media. Prison movies, even those with themes of escape, are serving to normalize the institution and to condition the popular imagination to accept this as a natural reality.

As the United States is reeling from unrest related to incidents of police brutality, the conversation around defunding and even abolishing the police are becoming increasingly common. The reactions to these ideas are mixed. Some express concern about how society would be protected and by whom. This is at times framed as reasons to dismiss arguments for a world without policing as naïve and dangerous. Davis (2003) argues that the long struggle to abolish slavery can act as an object lesson to how we think about prisons today. Those calling for the end of the practice of slavery were seen as extremists as the popular imagination couldn't conceive of a world without this system in the United States. Taking this further, she challenges assumptions around incarceration in the first place. She argues that historically the prison was where you were detained until your sentence was carried out. The emergence of the penitentiary—where you were punished and rehabilitated emerged in the United States around the time of the American Revolution. She unpacks the 13th Amendment and how it was a reincarnation of slavery: the conditions in penal systems were virtually identical to slavery, and the South's crafting of laws that exclusively applied to black people (vagrancy laws and so on) resulted in hard time with labor requirements for minimal recompense. In effect, prison life become virtually identical to slavery.

Davis (2003) finds that racial profiling has roots in the racialization of crime. It is not unusual for a perpetrator to claim having seen an unknown black man leave the scene of the crime to avoid their own consequences. Maynard (2017) adds that if a population is targeted by police for their skin color, sheer repetition of engagement with this group will result in criminal detection. If this is not done with other groups, such a slanted sample will further support the view of the dangerous other. Further, she makes the point that many crimes perpetrated by white Canadians receive less attention and severity of response.

The US criminal justice system is based on white supremacy (Hackett & Turk, 2018). Similar to how Maynard (2017) describes the evolution of how the runaway slave was presented as a figure to fear, Hackett & Turk (2018) refer to a similar project by white supremacy. By engaging in historical misrepresentation of the murderous savage or the diseased drug addict, white supremacy remains safely entrenched in a system of control for the public good. White supremacy is based on the belief that in a hierarchical formation, whiteness is at the top—all others are substandard—nonwhites are inferior "thereby rendering resources, land and socioeconomic capital to white settlers or those who align themselves with whiteness" (p. 25). In this light, it is better to understand the roots of modern policing in the slave patrol. This was an "organized form of extralegal terror against slaves to catch plantation escapees and to prevent revolts" (p. 25).

With the abolition of slavery, new Black codes emerged such as "vagrancy laws." The practice of enforcing these laws enabled for newly freed black people to be streamed into the carceral system (Hackett & Turk, 2018). The important point here is that white supremacy was not defeated post slavery but just became more devious and developed throughout the current judicial system of policing and incarceration. White supremacy has not only found expression via the prison system but has impacted all aspects of experience. Anti-immigration policies, voter ID laws, and standardized testing are all examples of how White supremacy has infiltrated the societal psyche and become institutionalized. Thus Hackett and Turk (2018) "wish to add to a growing abolitionist analytic that critiques the institutional embedment of white supremacy not only in the criminal legal system but also in the broader society that necessitates prisons in the first place" (p. 28). In other words, they argue that research needs to be done outside of prisons as the overall framework of modern life legitimizes the carceral system. Given current debates around community policing, it is salient to note that under Bill Clinton in the United States, the Community Oriented Policing Services (COPS) program increased police by 100,000 officers (Hackett & Turk, 2018). Since then, the prison population has only grown. Another area of concern is how reforming the carceral system uses language reminiscent of the Elizabethan Poor Law. The main thrust of this old law was how some people are deserving, and others not, of poor relief (Long, 2004). Current debates about nonviolent drug offenders being decarcerated and decriminalized create categories of deserving and undeserving.

> When we invoke these ideas about who deserves our empathy and compassion based on whether a crime was violent or not, we are disregarding the racial reality of the justice system. For example, according to Hackett & Turk (2018), the fact that African American people are convicted of violent offences at disproportionately higher rates than White offenders, means that, "Those prisoners convicted of nonviolent charges that receive—and therefore deserve—state mercy are those who appeal to liberal White sympathies and who do not threaten status quo White racial interests." (p. 31)

In effect, prison is seen as the way that the white supremacist system keeps the dispossessed from challenging the status quo—from disrupting the generational wealth and civic privilege of the status quo. "Moreover, the obsession with the violence of a 'dangerous few' and their street-level crimes masks structural violence" (p. 31). Reforming this system is problematic as eliminating bias (via reform) in one part does not diminish white supremacy which is embedded throughout the penal system.

Drug policies are an example of the inherent racism that the system of law enforcement and justice perpetrate. If the war on drugs, as initially launched by Reagan in the United States and Mulroney in Canada, is about ending illegal drug trafficking, it seems ill-advised to go after poor women of color as drug mules. According to Maynard (2017), the consequences to the drug trade are minimal, given that the supply being confiscated is a fraction of what arrives in the country. The conditions, like poverty, that might move someone to participate in the smuggling of small amounts of drugs into the country are largely ignored, as penalties are leveled against these women. The larger infrastructure of the drug trade remains essentially untouched.

Davis (2003) adds that the trend in the United States to turn over the prison system to for-profit companies only increases the problem. This is nothing new. In the 19th century, coal companies, that used the incarcerated as workers, would urge the justice system to discourage short sentences to keep the prisoner as long as possible to turn a profit in the mines. Given this past, we should be concerned, as currently money is to be made off the backs of prisoners. It isn't just the for-profit prison system that is the problem; prison labor is being used in many ways by the free market to produce at low labor costs. As the prison population continues to rise, we should not only be asking if outdated crime and punishment models work but who benefits from a growing group of people that can be exploited for profit. If a for-profit industry benefits from a prisoner remaining in the carceral system, why would efforts to rehabilitate even be a goal? There is a legacy of using prisoners as surplus medical subjects for experiments for corporations like Johnson & Johnson. This continues, as corporations like Nestle, AT&T, and Dial Soap benefit from lucrative contracts with prisons in the United States (Davis, 2003). There is a way to manage the contradictions of capitalism and turn a profit. The appetite of capitalism serves to keep prisoners longer, while the racialization of crime serves to deflect the public by appealing to their fears. In effect, "we—the police and associated prisons—will keep you safe by locking away the Black and brown bodies you have been taught to fear."

Schmid (2018) raises further the disturbing concerns about how prisons were used to study and control the bodies of women. "The violence, sexual abuse, medical experimentation, sterilization, and death of a few hundred captive women in the nineteenth century laid the foundation for the field of gynecology" (p. 84). Given the era of hyper-incarceration resulting in thousands of BIPOC women being incarcerated during the prime of their lives, the carceral system has become a eugenics project, perpetuating white supremacy with a form of genocide.

> A woman in her late teens or early twenties sentenced to twenty or more years in prison will lose her years to reproduce right along with her freedom. What does this say of a country that incarcerates women of color at a rate 3.8 times higher than white women? (p. 85)

A sobering thought given reports as late as 2013 in California where tubal ligations were being performed post birth on women prisoners without their permission (p. 85–86).

This brings us to the idea of reform or rehabilitation. Current voices are growing to look at police reform. While prison reform ought to be a significant correlating topic of concern, much of the recent focus has been on what occurs at the point of contact between stewards of the system (i.e. police) and marginalized communities. Regardless, words such as reform and rehabilitation are integral to the concept of law and order which serve to legitimate their function (Davis 2003) and deserve further attention here.

French philosopher Michel Foucault (2008) offers a compelling argument for the existence of the carceral system and its prevalence today. Early models of crime and punishment had to do with the authority of the king. Crime threatens the king (i.e. the state) and, as such, punishment is a ritual that not only serves to keep the king in power but also has to show the inverse of a coronation (election), where power is identified and located at the top—the inverse hence means that whatever is done to the prisoner has to not only be a punishment for infraction but a demonstration of the prisoner's powerlessness—that is, a stripping of power has to occur.

Kenney (2010) refers to the legal fiction perpetrated by the courts today as illustrative of this concept. He argues that the current judicial system is based on a 12th-century move toward the King's Law needing protection and the victim's rights being relegated to civil court options to seek redress. The legal fiction has to do with the myth that this whole thing involves the state and the accused only: there is no other relationship that matters (hence shutting even victims out and leaving them without rights to redress).

The public spectacle of execution, then, is this demonstration for the masses. This is what happens if you defy the king. "[E]very crime constituted... a rebellion against the law and that the criminal was an enemy of the prince" (Foucault, 2008, p. 65). The public display of punishment is still extant today—the sentencing phase is open to the public or available via media reports. Current legal decisions by a judge are not only about determining the truth of a crime but also about enshrining further a reality we all must understand and accept.

> [T]he sentence that condemns or acquits is not simply a judgement of guilt, a legal decision that lays down punishment; it bears within it an assessment of normality and a technical prescription for a possible normalization. Today the judge... certainly does more than 'judge.' (p. 27)

This technical prescription can be understood as the idea of rehabilitation for the crime committed. Davis (2003) makes the point that if prison and reform are forever linked, using terminology related to reforming the system simply reinforces the validity of ideas of crime and punishment. It is, to pardon the pun, inescapable. Foucault (2008) sees the shift from corporal punishment and execution to incarceration as a greater demonstration of power—to destroy or break the soul rather than the body. Davis (2003) offers another perspective: that incarceration as rehabilitation is touted as a product of the Enlightenment. Society perceives itself as being more moral and sophisticated than its past efforts at addressing crime. She argues that incarceration was never conceived of as a final solution to crime. According to Davis (2003), it is the emergence of capitalism and a bourgeoisie entrenching something that should be thought of as a particular response to a particular set of historical settings.

The influence of capitalism can be felt in how the law inscribes what is in our minds, in that sentencing correlates with the commodified perception of work hours—the cost of time to the individual in sentencing correlating with this (Davis, 2003). Given the Enlightenment's legacy of couching the state as the expression of objective rationality, sentencing thus has the veneer of a quantifiable way of practicing "justice."

Dubler and Lloyd (2018) offer another perspective of the origins of incarceration that predate the Enlightenment and the rational discourse. They point to the religious connotations behind the idea of the penitentiary. The root of the term is about seeking penitence, essentially a time of reflection and reform and an opportunity to seek redemption. Here we have the question: What role does religion have in the ongoing support of mass incarceration? While prison culture is rooted in deep-seated problems beyond the individual and includes notions of "original sin and sacrifice" (p. 118), the absence of faith or religion in the current period of hyper-carceration has contributed to the problem.

> To focus on ideals, and not on policies, has become the purview of children and cranks. In such an impoverished landscape, justice as an abstract ideal ceded its existence to the criminal justice *system* (italics in original). This system is now everything. Justice has come to mean little more than the proper functioning of the law. (p. 120)

In this legal landscape, devoid of a phenomenological center, the cult of law enforcement emerges as a form of heresy, of the worship of false gods.

In the pulp sci-fi novel *Agent of Chaos* (Spinrad, 1972), the all-seeing eye of the state can detect crimes and instantly vaporize offenders. It is revealed that, in fact, the state will randomly kill a civilian regardless of whether a crime is being committed or not. Given the sheer size of the population, it is the belief that crime will be instantly discovered and punished, and that hegemony is preserved, that matters. Davis (2003) credits the utilitarian philosopher Jeremy Bentham and his idea of the panopticon as central to the way prisons work. The very construction of the prison is intended to produce the idea that you never know if the warden is watching you, so you act as if they are. This is integral to the process of rehabilitation. To act as if one is always under surveillance, so obedience to the system is maximized.

Well-intentioned acts of reformation of the carceral system only reproduce oppression. Davis (2003) recasts John Howard and Elizabeth Fry's attempts at prison reform as ways that just make the system more effective in producing its myth of rehabilitation. The dehumanizing impact of prison life begins at the processing stage. Davis (2003) makes the compelling point that outside of prison, the strip search would be deemed a sexual assault. The context reduces this to a dehumanizing process that sets the stage for how the prisoner has less standing and fewer human rights.

Before continuing further, it is essential that a discussion around law enforcement include the ways in which Indigenous and First Nations people of North America have been impacted by this issue as well. I echo Robyn Maynard's (2017) point that it is not possible to talk about the racism of the system toward one racialized group without acknowledging this. It is again, with great awareness of my own social location and privilege as a White academic, that I take care to make my positionality known. I am only able to write about what I have learned; I am not the expert of this story, nor do I want to communicate this. However, it would be a mistake to omit the reality that the laws of colonial occupying society have wreaked enormous damage upon Indigenous and First Nations from the moment of first contact onward. From land treaties that were designed to privilege the occupying forces to apprehending children to continue genocide via the 60s Scoop and residential schools, the law—with the aid of social work—has been used to validate these horrors.

Recent efforts by land defenders to place themselves in the path of corporate and state power illustrate the resistance that still lives in these communities. However, the state continues to use laws as a way to characterize this resistance as criminal. Crosby and Monaghan (2018) chronicle the ongoing efforts by corporations, supported by the state, to define such resistance as threats to the energy sector and actors as potential ecological terrorists. Further, government has been the servant of capitalism by undermining legitimate Indigenous governance through a divide and conquer strategy by simply appointing leadership that would support the co-opting of treaty land claims in favor of resource extracting corporations.

In *Indians Wear Red* the devastating impact of the criminalization of Indigenous youth can be palpably felt when one participant shares that he knows what will happen to his resume when he leaves the store. It will end up in the garbage, as the assumptions based on his appearance have already defined the odds of successful employment for him (Cormack et al., 2013).

Pamela Palmater (2020) refers to the overincarceration of Indigenous peoples as further genocide. Tracing the history of Indigenous encounters with the police that lead to false convictions, death, and disproportionate sentencing and convictions, she painfully demonstrates the findings of the 2004 Saskatchewan Commission on First Nations and Metis Peoples and Justice Reform. There exists a major issue regarding racism in how police relate to Indigenous Peoples. It is difficult to ignore when statistics tell the story. In Manitoba, 80% of inmates are Indigenous. This is also the province where half of the missing and murdered women are Indigenous, and 90% of all kids in (foster) care are Indigenous. Considering that "more than two-thirds of

Indigenous prisoners have been impacted by the foster care system" (p. 66), it is no surprise to see the connection between these systems and the devastation they have wrought to Indigenous Peoples in Canada. Further, she argues for decarceration versus reforming the prison system. Cultural sensitivity or increasing Indigenous input in prison reform does not address that people are "languishing in prisons for little more than navigating poverty" (p. 67).

Palmater (2020) argues that if the laws are constructed to perpetuate oppression and genocidal structural violence, there is no value in being obedient to them. By pointing out the discriminatory laws around the tobacco and cannabis trade, she illustrates how the Canadian rule of law ignores cultural heritage and defends a status quo built on advancing the interest of a colonizing force. The discourse around these issues tends to portray Indigenous Peoples as engaging in criminal enterprise, further damaging the collective perception of Indigenous Peoples as criminal and dangerous. Noting how Maynard (2017) argues that this is a way to dehumanize and legitimate state violence toward another group, it should be concerning. Furthermore, Palmater (2020) stresses that bills intended to promote greater security are leading to the characterization of any resistance by groups such as Idle No More as "threats of concern" in the vein of domestic terrorism. When Crosby and Monaghan (2018) were able to access the RCMP's secretive Project SITKA this is precisely the worrisome trend they saw emerging: a security apparatus that was able to justify surveillance of Indigenous activism under the auspices of national security concerns. Effectively constructing the image of the domestic terrorist to describe the behaviors related to defense of land, culture, and identity while supporting the agenda of extractive capitalism.

The Indigenous experience with police brutality is not uniquely Canadian, and it is not my intention to say so. According to Heatherton (2016, p. 109), New Mexico has been referred to as having the highest rate of police killings as of 2014 (Heatherton, 2016, p. 109), with Indigenous Peoples being statistically the most likely victims. Nick Estes, in his role as a council member of the Red Nation, comprised of Indigenous and Non-Indigenous activists, draws from Antonio Gramsci, the Italian Marxist theorist who described "common sense" as an ideology not necessarily actively theorized but more like a knee-jerk response (p. 110). Indigenous people are not intentionally being considered as not having the right to exist, it is simply a part of mainstream society's worldview. In effect, the existence of Indigenous people in North America is an anachronism. Thomas King (2012) echoes a similar point in his book, *The Inconvenient Indian*, where the "dead Indian" can be celebrated in movies and in art or literature, but the living one is not. Estes (as cited in Heatherton, 2016, p. 112–113) refers to the "unnatural deaths" that are the result of property having more value than Indigenous life, where vagrancy laws keep people without homes on the move, unable to access needed resources. Hence, death due to exposure, for example, is a violence perpetrated on Indigenous lives by a system of law and its enforcement by colonial society. Ultimately the point is that there exists a connection between law enforcement and colonization. In the words of Nick Estes and Melanie Yazzie, "Colonization is a failed project, because they didn't kill us all. That's why they have to constantly police us" (as cited in Heatherton, 2016, p. 119).

While by no means exhaustive, the prior points serve to illustrate that one cannot talk about police and prison without Indigenous Peoples' experience of oppression and colonization. As anarchist and abolitionist ideas will show in the following pages, Indigenous and non-White voices are represented here as well. It is my hope that the reader will take these introductions and explore further by reading the work by these important contributors to the ongoing issue of law enforcement and even the laws of state authority itself.

Harsha Walia (Walia & Dilts, 2018), for example, would challenge the very notion of nations and the fiction of the legal citizen as problematic. The practice of managing and defending borders becomes internalized as a state of mind. "The internalization of borders is happening in so-called public institutions—schools, hospitals, transit—that are operating as checkpoints and either denying migrants access and often as border guards to detain and report people to immigration authorities" (p. 13). The premise behind the idea that no one is illegal is straightforward. No one should be criminalized for simply existing or being. It is the state that is illegal, a construct foisted upon the minds and bodies of people. The lines are arbitrary and not real. It has to do with settler-colonial existence being fundamentally predicated on a series of illegal acts. Hence the boundaries of nations are illegal, not the person crossing them (Walia & Dilts, 2018). Therefore, to be opposed to criminalizing immigrants, by this logic, means to be in support of Indigenous rights and the people's claim to nationhood.

In this current period of opportunity and change, it is perhaps timely to look to anti-capitalist ideas related to crime. Perhaps there is space to consider how such ideas could help equip current social workers with tools to support a better world without policing and incarceration. Given our role in child welfare and our stance of being on the side of the vulnerable, we ought to be concerned about the ways that offenders are pathologized while frequently being victimized.

Anarchist notions of crime

As one can likely already guess, anarchists generally are opposed to incarceration and the carceral system. Russian anarchist, Peter Kropotkin saw crime as mainly the product of idleness, law, and authority (Marshall, 2010). According to him, most crime is related to property. Hence, this would disappear when property (which is the dominion of the elite few) becomes that of the community. If some few remain antisocial and aggressive or violent, punishment is not an option "since the severity of punishment does not diminish the amount of crime" (Marshall, 2010, p. 31). It was his view that prisons cannot be reformed. "The more prisons are reformed, the more detestable they become: modern penitentiaries are far worse than the dungeons of the Middle Ages" (Marshall, 2010, p. 31).

A number of early anarchists made plain their disdain for crime and punishment. French anarchist Proudhon's famous paradoxical slogan that 'property is theft'(Marshall, 2010, p. 239) and his ideas related to mutualism portray this idea (Graham, 2013, p. 484–485). If ownership of things ceased to exist, social problems such as vice, crime, hunger, and so on would be eliminated. Russian anarchist Bakunin exposes the false assumptions around crime by noting that when all of these criminal acts are done for the sake of country in a patriotic frenzy, they are absolved (Graham, 2013). The veneer of a form of humanitarianism obscures the barbarity of the invading force. One need only reflect on modern attempts at bringing democracy to countries around the world for current examples. "When anarchists resort to violence, they are held criminally responsible, and their beliefs denounced as the cause. When government forces engage in the wholesale destruction of war, no one (at least among the victors) is held responsible" (p. 547).

Gelderloos and Lincoln (2005) raise concerns about how prisons are portrayed—as a consequence of crime—and that there is an intentional obscuration of prisons, located in remote places, with small windows and razor wire. And thereby the sensation of the crime resolving in the disappearance of the offender behind prison walls. Anarchists themselves have written from a similar perspective as prison abolitionists, having personal experience within the carceral system as Gelderloos and Lincoln (2005) make plain.

Protest can be the motivation of acts that the legal system will revise to be about unlawful trespass rather than an act of political expression. In their case, it enables them to speak from experience about the reality of prison. The popular message that prisons are populated with hardened killers fails to ring true when you discover that most prisoners are people of color, poor people, and nonviolent offenders. Most people of color in fact make up only one-quarter of the total US population but 65% of the prison population. This is, in fact, in contrast with how the majority of federal prison staffs—around 65%—are white. This makes sense if you consider that the lower one's income, the less likely one can afford good lawyers, so poor people have a higher chance of being convicted. Gelderloos & Lincoln (2005) hence point to the numbers that find that 80% of people who go to prison could not afford a lawyer and were using a public defender at the time of trial. Furthermore, in 1996, 64% of jail inmates had incomes under $1000 in the month before they were arrested, and 36% were unemployed. Seventy percent of those sentenced to state prisons in 1998 were convicted of nonviolent offences. In some US states, in fact, the majority of prisoners are in prison because of parole violations. At the federal level, more people are locked up for immigration violations than any other offence (Gelderloos & Lincoln, 2005). These numbers essentially point to how deeply racist the carceral system is. While we point to apartheid-era South Africa as the definition of systemic racism—hence, we are not so bad—US incarceration rates tell a different story. In the United States, the incarceration rate of black males is eight times higher than the South African government perpetrated during apartheid (Gelderloos & Lincoln, 2005, p. 7). Maynard (2017) reminds that in Canada, a similar phenomenon has taken place where criticism of law enforcement is deflected by pointing to the United States as an ever more egregious example of the problem.

Another concern raised is the deleterious health impacts of incarceration. In effect, if 20 years in prison decreases life expectancy by 16 years, a 20-year sentence can de facto become a death sentence (Gelderloos & Lincoln, 2005). Poor diet and a lack of sunlight contribute to this. They argue that sometimes access to health care is used as a bargaining chip to coerce prisoners into participating in medical experiments.

Further worrying signs of the meshing between prison and natural life outside are occurring (Gelderloos & Lincoln, 2005). The interior architecture of prisons can be reminiscent of elementary schools. In the United States, drug searches and zero tolerance policies including adding guards, security cameras, and metal detectors as well as other control methods echo the prison experience. This follows what Maynard (2017) describes as the school-to-prison pipeline with its inherently racist prosecution of student behaviors. If a six-year-old is subdued by school police in handcuffs, it is not difficult to imagine.

In effect, policing and, by extension, the prison system are the results of capitalist accumulation and the resulting injustices. In the United States policing really did not exist when it was first founded (Gelderloos & Lincoln, 2005). This institution evolved in combination with the slave patrols in the South and the city watch, which was designed to control immigrant populations and support political parties in the North. What else would explain the reason for the institution of policing to grow during a time when crime is decreasing, and there was no actual need for them? Gelderloos & Lincoln (2005) argue that the development of criminal codes was a way to, during a shortage of crime, help the government expand police authority and definitions of criminality. This now included behaviors that had not been considered crimes before. Not surprisingly, criminal codes tended to focus on lower classes by defining their behavior as criminal. Examples such as vagrancy, homelessness, gambling. drinking in public, loitering, prostitution, and disorderly conduct illustrate this well. Essentially, police exist therefore as a way to defend the wealthy from any kind of significant crisis of democracy, for the lower classes would find voice and rebel.

Gelderloos & Lincoln (2005) make an anarchist case in exploring the lie of legal analogies. Whenever there is a concern about the limits of free speech in the United States, it tends to go hand in hand with the idea of yelling fire in a crowded theater. What may not be known is that this analogy was first used by Supreme Court Justice Oliver Wendell Holmes to justify the government locking up several people for passing out pamphlets against the draft during World War I. Given this precedent, we must ask ourselves: If our government recasts political prisoners as criminals, then what is the difference between our actions and those of other repressive countries that we tend to point to and say, "those people don't have any rights?" Given current unrest and conflict with people protesting police brutality, labeling protest as riots and protestors as terrorists takes on a more sinister tone.

It is almost like the symbolic impact of nuclear weapons, talismans we can look to in order to assuage our fear of annihilation by the "red scare" during the Cold War. We have been convinced that life is increasingly more unsafe due to rising crime. Now our new symbols of security are prisons (Gelderloos

& Lincoln, 2005). Looking at them, we can see that the bad guys—that reality shows and news channels have convinced us are always on the prowl—are being kept away. Such a constant anxiety in the public mind makes it difficult to conceive of alternatives.

Anarchist collective CrimethInc (2020) raise the point that if police reform was effective, one should be seeing a decrease in police shootings post Ferguson. This is not the case. According to CrimethInc, there were more police killings in 2019 than 2014, when the Ferguson uprising occurred. The point being made here is that widespread attention to the issue of police violence does not bring about meaningful change, as reforms do not have any real impact. CrimethInc (2020) argues that if political activism was meaningful, it is difficult to explain how, at the time of Georg Floyd's killing, a local, predominantly democratic administration was unable to improve the scourge of police-perpetrated violence. So, if voting was a strategy to reform police brutality, it should have worked here; but the killing continues despite these progressive political parties in charge. Another question that begs explanation is how a Black president can stand by while Freddie Gray, Philando Castile, and others were being murdered by the police. CrimethInc (2020) would suggest that the answer is political power. Political leaders know that when the public can no longer be relied on, power must be preserved by force. During volatile times, such as the present moment, the people in charge will not alienate or antagonize their armed defenders of the status quo.

Gelderloos and Lincoln (2005) ask the question why police and, by extension, any authority system needs to be involved in deciding about crime? If we were to see crime as a social harm, friends, neighbors, and community would be drawn into the conversation. People directly involved in the crime have the voice and the freedom to decide how it ought to be dealt with. Furthermore, if there is no victim, there cannot be a crime. They argue that there are real crimes out there and, generally, they are happening in their own homes. Here we are talking about domestic violence, physical and sexual abuse of children and spouses. However, our society creates the narrative that men own their partners and that parents own their children. The solution to crime brings its own problems. For example, if the offender is incarcerated, their family may now further spiral into poverty. In fact, this reality results in the difficult decision by some to remain in violent and abusive relationships. Hence, the criminal code results in prolonging the problem, not resolving it.

It can be difficult to imagine a world without police, as we have been conditioned to believe that without them, we would be overwhelmed and at the mercy of vicious criminals. Gelderloos and Lincoln (2005) point out that there are alternatives. Indigenous communities still exist today that do not have police or any other authority from the outside. Deviance of any kind is viewed as a problem that the whole community must confront so it can continue to live in harmony. Colonizers who have occupied these territories invariably recast crime as any action against the state, therefore allowing them to have surveillance and authority to apprehend any voice of resistance. Kropotkin echoes a similar idea when referring to prelaw societies where instead of coercion and control, disputes were resolved via custom and usage (Marshall, 2010). In effect, the law is the implementation of fixed decrees made by conquerors that served their interests, and the invocation of superstition applied a veneer of justice to these.

Gelderloos & Lincoln (2005) note the danger of participating in reformist approaches. They argue that engaging in policy reform is simply validating the current system of law. By creating new laws to redress inequities, the government gains strength. The power of government then is expressed via enforcement of these laws. They are the tools of the state, and only the state has the authority to employ them.

Perhaps the reform or revolution debate is a false dichotomy. It is possible to address the deleterious effects of current carceral approaches with the aim to improve the plight of those impacted in the present, while working toward abolition in the long run. Gelderloos & Lincoln (2005) see this as addressing prison conditions in the short term while in the long-term aiming for complete abolition of prison systems and the capitalist conditions that create them in the first place.

Ultimately, we must ask ourselves, what kind of society needs police to maintain its status quo? According to Gelderloos (2014), the answer is one where a parasitic class is benefiting from inequity and the dispossession and oppression of others. Policing is a fairly recent invention coinciding with significant social changes, such as industrialization and the accumulation of wealth. This should give us pause. It certainly is not a new idea. While not describing himself as anarchist, William Godwin has been described as an influential philosopher on ideas of anarchism (Marshall, 2010). He claimed that most crime is in response to the accumulation of wealth/property and would wither without this incentive (Marshall, 2010). In other words, it is a society that upholds inequity that is the genus of crime.

> Since the main cause of crime—the breaking of law—is the unjust distribution of property, there would be fewer incidents in a freer, more equal and sustainable society. Any disputes and misdemeanours could be dealt with by popular juries which aim at restoring social harmony rather than imposing punishments. (Marshall, 2013, p. 182)

Godwin further saw the administration of punishment by the state as admission of its own failure. Punishment then is worse than the crime itself, as the state knowingly uses force instead of rational and intelligent discourse. Furthermore, he argued that if the environment is the genus of crime, it should be held accountable, not the criminal.

The problem of course is that force alone is not effective nor needed. The populace has accepted capitalism which serves to perpetuate its oppressive requirements (Martin, 2013). Legal systems are built on violence, the core of capitalism is based on private property. The legal system is never investigated and largely accepted by society.

> Petty theft, big-time swindles and organized crime are not major challenges to the property system, since they accept the legitimacy of property and are simply attempts to change ownership in an illegal manner... Principled challenges to property, such as squatting and workers' control, are far more threatening. (p. 257)

In other words, there is no antagonism between capitalism and the state—they are hand in glove. With the increasing use of private security, detectives, or policing by stores, business and so on, the link becomes ever clearer. Martin (2013) points out that there are more private police in the United States than standard, government-paid police forces.

As previously noted, anarchist views aren't monolithic but tend to support abolition of the powers of the state which are personified in the legal system, from police to prison. Christian anarchist Leo Tolstoy wrote passionately about crime and punishment when a mass execution of 20 peasants took place in retaliation to an attack on a landowner's property (Marshall, 2010). His response, titled "I cannot be silent" unpacks how he feels complicit in the act of execution. This is argued as something he is responsible for, as the Russian government claimed to be enforcing their law in the best interests of its citizenry. He rather would be in prison or at the gallows with the punished than to be associated with the state. Further, his conviction as to the evil that is personified in the state and it's agents of control is captured well in a letter he wrote to Mohandas Gandhi where he argues that, "all our taxes collected by force, our judicial and police institutions and, above all, our armies must be abolished" (Tolstoy to Mohandas Gandhi, 7 September 1910, *Letters*, op. cit., II, 706, as cited in Marshall, 2010, p. 381). So in summary, Tolstoy's take on crime and punishment is that when we do not act against the status quo, we share in the sin of authoritarian solutions, including executions. The use of force is always wrong, regardless of who is doing it. There is no moral high ground to its use.

In terms of solutions, Tolstoy believed that the influence of public opinion and censure as strategies to address criminal behavior would be effective. Another interesting question is whether rehabilitation is a useful construct. Individualist/Egoist anarchist Stirner saw psychiatric correction as another form of violence (Marshall, 2010). Rather than rehabilitate the individual to society via correction, the individual is corrected toward themselves—another form of coercion and control. It is important that we do not conflate this idea as a hallmark of all anarchists since many do prefer rehabilitation to punishment and see community as the place for this (Marshall, 2010).

Perhaps the following quote best captures anarchist concerns about the tendency to want to punish those who have wronged us. The following is in response to the invocation of the image of the guillotine in revolutionary efforts to change current systems of oppression via the state.

> By and large, we tend to be more aware of the wrongs committed against us than we are of the wrongs we commit against others. We are most dangerous when we feel most wronged, because we feel most entitled to pass judgment, to be cruel. The more justified we feel, the more careful we ought to be not to replicate the patterns of the justice industry, the assumptions of the carceral state, the logic of the guillotine. Again, this does not justify inaction; it is simply to say that we must proceed most critically precisely when we feel most righteous, lest we assume the role of our oppressors. (CrimethInc, 2019, p. 8)

In effect, the seeking to identify with a form of power to get redress for grievances is the path of authoritarianism, counter-revolution, and misery. CrimethInc makes the case that it is okay to want revenge as this is based on outrage, on compassion, and empathy for those harmed (maybe ourselves even) but that this needs to be separated from politics rather than retrofitting a political ideology to justify acting on revenge. One could say the same for a carceral system.

In describing an anarchist criminology, Jeff Ferrell (1998) offers another intriguing possibility in challenging the current system of law. The Industrial Workers of the World (Woblies) took an unusual approach to resistance. At times they would turn the law against itself by sometimes following the rules and regulations of the workplace to such a degree, and so exactly, that it would grind all work to a halt. When resisting directly, they would violate the law with such volume that courts and jails would be so overloaded, that the system would be forced to dismiss their cases.

Interestingly, in the 70s the American Society for Political and Legal Philosophy actually voted overwhelmingly for anarchism as a topic which resulted in a series of articles by criminologist Harold Pinsky (Ferrell, 1998). Peacemaking criminology, originally called a form of communist anarchist criminology, was the result. The concerns raised by Ferrell (1998) include the way the interests of community remain as talking points while in actuality, the state continues to legislate what this means. He compellingly refers to the stale dichotomy of legality and illegality (p. 6), where human communities no longer have a center, as the abstraction of the state continues to divide in its attempt to consolidate and centralize control systems. The point is that if all aspects of social (and hence cultural) life are subject to binary definitions of legal/illegal we all are at risk of being under the thumb of state power. Perhaps this allows us to understand the police's response to the public demonstrations after the murder of George Floyd. These actions by the public are threatening to police, as they are the reclaiming of public spaces with impunity, not subject to the law-based restrictions. This is a threat to the traditional rule of law, as citizens are expected to engage in vapid and toothless activism at the voting booth.

Finally, Ferrell (1998) makes the case that an "anarchist criminology" punches up, not down. An anarchist criminology then goes beyond the binary definitions of deviance set up by the state, where criminal conduct is viewed as mindless misbehavior or even a failure of character (the moral deviant). Part of its role ought to be the blurring of the line between crime and political acts of resistance. While some acts may be based and predicated on essential need, others bear the mark of defiance or resistance to the system. Basically, if laws are created in a political context and hence related to this, any criminal act carries political implications. Examples, he suggests, include graffiti, art, or music that's been deemed illicit or dangerous or obscene, curfew violations, shoplifting, as well as illegal labor.

Adopting an important position on the nature of law itself, Newman (2013) takes a kind of criminogenic position. He refers to Jaques Derrida's denunciation of the authority of the Law as helpful to understand how this formal institution itself is built on a foundation that required an act of violence. This may now be disavowed, but that does not change the origins of the law itself (p. 430). In effect, the law must be based on a prior act, which means it is based on something illegal. The elaborate construction of law is to obscure this fact—hence law is also not natural but antagonistic or political in origin and practice. We only need to recall colonization itself to see evidence of this process. This reminds me of the popular slogan, "No one is illegal on stolen land."

Activist and intellectual, Harsha Walia, makes this particular case when arguing that borders and their creation are part of the problem (Walia & Dilts, 2018). The practice of bordering is creating illegal persons which is entirely a process from inside of nations. Schools, hospitals, and so on serve to facilitate the internalization borders, where they act as "checkpoints and either denying migrants access and often acting as border guards" (p, 13). The high rates of sexual violence against domestic workers in Canada is due to the Temporary Worker Program that increases the vulnerability of these people while acting as a form of control that is bordering and incarcerating in nature.

The use of concepts such as "public safety" or, in the case of migrants, "for their own safety," enables the state to surveil and detain them (Walia & Dilts, 2018). Hence, "surveillance is less about safety and more about invasion of privacy and increased social control" (p. 16). The principle that no one is illegal is in direct opposition to the evolution of corporations as persons. If states and corporations can be persons, they can be trespassed on. This of course is a theoretical construct and ridiculous in reality, hence the tenet that no one is illegal. "We cannot criminalize a person simply for existing" (p. 18). It is the violence of non-status or undocumented labels inflicted on people by a state that is not legitimate in the first place.

An Indigenous anarchist perspective ties the entire carceral project to fascism and colonization (Kesīqnaeh, 2017). Essentially, here we have a compelling case about fascism as the imperialist aspirations to control other worlds. This process of dominating and denigrating others has always been experienced by colonized peoples. The efforts in North America of civilizing the Indigenous to make the land available for exploitation is understood to be fascism recast. Carceral systems can thus be understood as imperialism coming home to roost, applied to its own people.

> In the settler colonial context this violence is one that was perfected within the exceptional state of the expansion of the frontier the clearing and civilizing of Indigenous people to make the land ripe for settlement and the carceral continuum that has marked Black existence on this land from chattel slavery to the modern hyper ghetto. (p. 7)

In effect, a version of fascism here is understood as a North American project that is founded on two axes of violence—toward Indigenous and Black people.

Abolition

If the current system reproduces oppression, and the agents of this system contribute to brutalizing individuals. If contemporary models of crime and punishment continue to obscure the uncomfortable reality of those who are harmed by our neoliberal present under capitalism. If law enforcement measures don't actually reduce crime let alone prevent it, then it is perfectly legitimate to ask—What are the alternatives then? The following will explore this very question, from both anarchist and prison abolitionist perspectives.

Angela Y. Davis (2003) makes the case that even if no alternatives to current carceral systems existed, the absence of the current one would already decrease crime. This is predicated on the assertion that the current system in fact serves to increase crime. Factors that contribute to crime, such as economic inequity and the accumulation of wealth by the few at the expense of the many, need to be the focus. Essentially, Davis (2003) argues for a better society that doesn't promote these contradictions inherently in capitalism. She raises an important point in that current trends at dealing with crime fail because they universalize problems. Given the complexities surrounding crime in the first place, a simple universal solution may not be the most effective focus. This is yet another reason why current efforts at confronting crime are failing to be effective.

Some initial reforms, according to Davis (2003) ought to include efforts to demilitarize schools and shifting systems of justice toward rehabilitation and reconciliation. Echoing what others identified as the watershed of current carceral woes (e.g. Maynard, 2017), decriminalizing drugs would go a long way toward reducing rather than growing the penal system.

Housing is another important issue from abolitionist perspectives. The effort to preserve white supremacist interests can be found in housing and neighborhood formations, supported by public policies and governmental behaviors. Housing and social housing per se are important to abolitionism as housing determines proximity to resources (school, work, etc.) and thus will predetermine the life journey of one's likelihood to be incarcerated and so on.

Abolitionism is a movement that seeks to engage with changing the status quo from the ground up rather than relying on the system to rehabilitate itself because true emancipation cannot be granted by a state that creates structural violence in the first place; it is the collective struggle by communities and individuals toward this new world that matters the most. Hackett and Turk (2018) capture this sentiment well when reflecting on the concept of rehabilitation from a carceral perspective.

> Rehabilitation officially defined, focuses on successfully teaching "offenders" how to lawfully abide by norms of society and to learn new ways of being in the world to prevent future criminality . . . places blame on the deficiencies of criminalized people for *social* (italics in original) failings . . . instead of understanding street crime as a survival tool or a rational response to the bounded realities of disadvantage. (p. 41)

CrimethInc (2020) raise an interesting observation from an anarchist perspective. During the protests in Minneapolis over George Floyd's murder, local gangs were organizing to help. They would work to protect protesters from far-right groups as tensions were escalating. Perhaps this illustrates a way forward for alternatives to police and the carceral system? After all, if the police continue with impunity to murder, we need alternatives. They argue that abolishing the police is the only reasonable response as all other measures so far have failed. In other words, there are no bad apples—the entire batch is rotten. Ultimately, communities that watch out for each other, that regulate traffic, that mediate conflict at work, engage in community outreach with those who have mental health issues, offer a brighter view of a world without police.

Reddy (2018) addresses solutions via deschooling, to decarcerate the minds of students before they enter the larger world having been convinced of the status quo. Reddy argues that, "the educational system in a capitalist society is geared toward class stratification and the maintenance of class privilege through capitalist exploitation" (p. 125).

Reddy refers to concerns raised by the work of Roman Catholic priest and social critic, Ivan Illich, about the way in which current educational systems create passified students who fail to critically interrogate the ideas and institutions that support coercion and control by the state. (Ivan Illich, Deschooling society (2002), as cited in Reddy, 2018, pp. 125–126).

The way in which the academic can contribute to a world without police hence is to engage in subversion—of poaching from the system while appearing to represent it in order to engage in guerrilla tactics to redistribute what has been privatised—education and knowledge and thus contributing to abolition by helping underserved communities in the process (Reddy, 2018). To students who struggle to carry ever increasing student debt and balance these with employment rather than personal development goals for education, Reddy (2018) offers this advice: "I usually stress that each student work to fulfill their true talents, whatever they may be, and keep themselves connected to struggles for social justice" (p. 129). If this must occur outside of the classroom, then so be it.

Harsha Walia offers further food for thought when it comes to allyship when challenging the carceral system (Walia & Dilts, 2018). Being an ally in the struggle can become an identity rather than a verb which needs to be avoided. It is actually impossible to be an ally in the sense of holding such an identity given our intersectional identities "because we all carry multitudes of experiences and oppressions and privileges. Most people are simultaneously oppressed and privileged, and even those are always specific and contextual" (p. 17). In fact, intersectionality can become a barrier to real allyship, as it can collapse into a fixed way of creating categories that lead to dichotomies where one is either ally or oppressed.

> Anti-oppression analysis becomes rigid in its categorizations when the question becomes who is more oppressed, rather than engaging in a dialogue of *how* (italics in original) oppression, which is relational and contextual, is specifically manifesting. Oppression develops a strange quantifiable logic, a commodity that can be stocked up on. (p. 17–18)

Restorative justice has a history within the legal system seeking a more humane alternative to the state's punishment and rehabilitation model. The anarchist going by the pseudonym of Peter Kletsan (2018) argues that we need to lean into the community aspect of restorative justice. By seeing the community as the interested and most affected stakeholder in addressing the harm, it counteracts the state's erasure of this voice as they claim to represent and act on behalf of. Anarchist communities are interested in addressing conflict internally from a restorative perspective rather than involving police in the first place. This does not mean that there is any revolutionary potential in restorative justice, but if communities engage in this practice, it is a way to create healthier communities, not become a de facto alternative to state punishment.

It should be noted, this is one perspective. Another sees restorative justice as the epitome of an anarchist criminology, that by divesting from state alternatives to crime, we starve this beast into no longer having utility or relevance (Kletsan, 2018). Kletsan is concerned that restorative justice may become co-opted by a state in a reformation of the current legal model. Rather, it is a good model to employ in the direst circumstances of criminal behavior that is not related to property—the interpersonal realm. It is here that there is transformative potential that is worth pursuing. From an anarchist perspective, the social conditions that most commonly make up crime (such as those related to possession) are a condition of this current capitalist environment, and it would be inappropriate to consider employing any rehabilitation as this would serve to validate current economic and political relations.

What possibilities for social work?

The role of social work as it relates to and engages with the legal system deserves further attention. The following will be a brief foray into social work literature to illustrate such attempts.

Perhaps it would be best to lead with a recent conversation I had with another social worker who is working to develop a course in social work and criminology. In looking for a suitable textbook, he stated that this was difficult for a Canadian context, as little exists despite social work being a crucial and important component in the field of corrections (personal correspondence, A. Goodchild 02/01/21). The book, *Essential Law for Social Work Practice in Canada* (Regehr & Kanani, 2010) is a good illustration of this issue. The focus of this textbook is on how to help the social worker navigate the world of law "in order to be able to assist and empower clients, to comply with the law in the manner and method through which they deliver such assistance, and to participate in the Canadian legal system themselves" (p. 7). In other words, the primary focus being the framing of social work as alongside current and existing legal frameworks rather than challenging them. Advocacy is presented as helping victims to make impact statements or to even pursue legal channels in the first place. What is interesting is that the social worker as probation officer is not explored.

Giwa (2018), in writing about community policing in Canada, argues for a role for police social work that echoes current debates when looking at abolishing or defunding law enforcement. The author notes that a growing awareness of a two-tiered system for Whites and BIPOC exists. It is not in dispute that a differential response from police is predicated on race. The metric here is the disproportionate number of BIPOC being charged with drug-related offenses, suggesting racial bias in profiling. Giwa (2018) notes that in the 1970s there was an uptick in the trend of alternatives, including team policing and foot patrols, but more experimental, cohering into a semblance of more familiar community policing approaches in the 1980s in the United States. What distinguishes Canadian law enforcement is that virtually all police services in Canada (RCMP, etc.) incorporate community policing as their "model of intent" (Giwa, 2018). However, an attempt at community policing in Toronto named the Toronto Anti-Violence Intervention Strategy (TAVIS) was eventually disbanded due to ongoing heavy-handed treatment of minorities by TAVIS officers. This model had been implemented as a response to increasing gun violence in Toronto in 2005.

What is important to note is that "community policing" is a vague term that has never been defined universally (Giwa, 2018). Generally agreed upon features usually include a focus on crime prevention by collaborating with an interested and invested public. Prevention means installing a neighborhood watch where the community is encouraged to call police if suspicious activity is witnessed. Another principle of community policing is some form of partnership with power sharing as well as problem solving with the community to address conditions that encourage crime including, "illegitimate opportunity and related social determinants" (p. 6). Power sharing is seen as an essential factor for this approach to be effective rather than descend into purely symbolic tokenism.

Giwa (2018) asks why community policing has such appeal when little empirical evidence is available about its effectiveness. One could describe the model as a set of aspirations dressed up in community packaging. The results remain unclear as to how much influence a community actually has on policing. Critiques include the concern that police can just use this idea of community policing as a way to improve their image when it has been tarnished.

Further concerns have to do with the White gaze and policing missing key problems in implementation of community policing responses. For example, neighborhood watches are more successful in White communities because racialized communities are more collectivist, will have had strained relations with law enforcement, and hence will resist working with the police in the first place (Giwa, 2018). Essentially community policing overlooks the structural relations and subordinate relationships inherent in racialized communities and the police. Giwa (2018), employing a critical race perspective, identifies how police's insistence that they treat everyone the same way is discriminatory and oppressive as not everyone is the same nor has the same opportunities or privilege.

Giwa (2018) sees the problems with community policing as being the precedent for social work to be involved. After all, social workers are already collaborating with police in child welfare matters. Police Social Workers would be trained in understanding, compassion, and locating people in the context of their environment, which the author argues police cannot do as their focus is more on public safety. The idea is that a social worker on the police force would be without uniform, and their presence on the force would help increase confidence by the public that meaningful change is taking place. These social workers would be accountable to the CASW code of ethics, which ensures another level of protection of the public. Giwa (2018) believes that this will send the right message and ensure greater success of meaningful community policing alternatives as social workers are trained to engage groups and communities effectively. As the reader can see, much of this chapter has raised concerns about these arguments and we will return to these in the conclusion below.

There are several other areas where social work is seen as important in the field of justice. As far back as in 1976, Kaslow and Werner argued that social workers need to attend to offenders post sentencing more. They referred to what they saw as the profession's education in the areas of humanistic psychology that allows for important interventions where criminal thinking can be addressed and a therapeutic community versus the punitive correctional environment can be championed. They adopt a position where incarcerated persons have mental health issues rather than being bad actors. The social worker is seen as a member of a mental health team where interdisciplinary work can be accomplished, a therapeutic milieu cultivated and even clinical social workers providing marital counseling for prisoners within six months of release to ease transition back into community. It is the social worker that is able to think beyond the binary of offender and sentence. "As team leader, the social worker helps convey the importance of matching the treatment modality and goals to the needs and objectives of the offender, not to the crime" (p. 661). Hence the argument that since rehabilitation in community is generally performed by probation and parole officers, social workers are ideally suited for this work. Of note is that the social worker here is seen as best in promoting a better fit as they can model how they use their authority constructively to help the offender adapt and behave in better ways to prevent reoffending. In fact, the social worker is seen as ideal to even become a director of corrections given their training to understand systems from a person in environment perspective. Umbreit (1993) sees social work's skills set in community organizing and program development as reasons why this profession is best suited to be involved in victim–offender mediation.

Rogowski (2014) finds that in the UK, crime management has taken a neoliberal turn where context is ignored and youth are seen as fully autonomous and responsible for their behavior. Hence punishment is seen as the appropriate answer to youth crime. Further evidence of the influence of neoliberalism is seeing the managerial approach creeping into dealing with youth crime. Risk management models currently reign versus etiological or structural approaches as they fit better with the demonization of youth offenders in the public sphere. Rogowski (2014) provides a glimpse of the importance of social work in the field of youth offenders when he raises the alarm that the emergence of a youth offender services worker has led to the disappearance of social work as the youth offender is now being treated apart from the larger child welfare and family framework. His solution is to engage in subversive or gentle resistance to challenge this worrisome trend. Examples include being selective with information presented to lead to a certain decision, being intentionally slow or delaying paperwork, or even intentionally ignoring or bending rules to advantage those the social worker is helping. Further, consciousness raising for youth offenders can be a form of resistance to the status quo. While communal strategies are not possible given the fractiousness of current neoliberal approaches, working with individual youth offenders to raise consciousness of the socioeconomic dimensions of crime can still be done by social workers who are practicing from an anti-oppressive practice (AOP) and or engaging in critical social work practice.

Sliva and Samimi (2018) take a more direct approach at raising concerns about the prison industrial complex. Big business is incentivized to exploit the prison population as their use is more efficient and economical than migrant labor. The findings on the merits of prison labor are questionable given the methodological weakness of many studies; yet this has not stopped the ongoing use of this practice. According to Sliva and Samimi (2018), social work schools provide less education for students in prison and crime-related areas of practice. They lament the lack of opportunity for social workers to learn how to integrate the values of social work despite field placements in these areas. Their solution calls for ways to increase literacy for social work students about prisons and related issues around vocational programming. Suggested prison reform alternatives include higher reimbursement of prisoners engaging in prison work. In this way prisoners are better able to pay victims and support their own families and communities impacted by the crime as well as having the work directly benefit communities versus large conglomerates.

Prinsloo (2014) takes another look at how students are exposed to youth offenders in prison in South Africa as a way to challenge preconceived notions. By taking students into youth prisons, they are challenged to practice Umbutu (humanity). This form of exposure resulted in experiences where students were able to see people rather than offenders. This was seen as especially important given the likelihood, due to rising crime rates in South Africa, of students having personal experiences as victims of crime themselves. It remains problematic that the framing of criminal behavior in this study remains at the individual making bad choices; structural factors do not get investigated here. However, social work education is framed as the personal experience to remove stigma of offenders and improve student's capacity to work with them and share in their humanity.

Noakes (2014) describes the efforts of social workers in the field of law to influence and shape the disposition of law students in legal practice toward offenders. She describes how, within a holistic law office, the insight is developed that the original offence is only a fraction of what offenders are dealing with. Social workers would work to provide new perspectives about the client's information that both transformed their behavior and enabled the law students working at this office to view them in a new light. She provides examples such as social workers starting programs for anger management, counseling, and addictions, which would translate into reduced sentences. In effect, the judge would be impressed that a social worker was involved and hence translate into a better outcome for the client of the legal office. Essentially, Noakes (2014) illustrates the role of social work similarly to how it is envisioned by Regehr and Kanani, (2010). Social workers work with those who are experiencing encounters with the law to act as change agents for those who are being charged. The system remains unchanged. Berlin and Kravetz (1981) see the role of social work to advocate on behalf of victims of crime. In effect, it is the role of the social worker, regardless of whether directly involved in the judicial system or in the social service system, to reduce further trauma or damage to the victim.

Perhaps it is easy to question the value of social work in the field of crime—be it management of offenders or advocacy for those harmed in the legal encounter. What bears consideration are that aspects of community have been parceled out, given to the experts to solve. However, "even if it is true historically that professionals have 'stolen' the community's conflicts . . . there is little current evidence that the community is making vigorous efforts to get them back" (Olson & Dzur, 2004, p. 147). The problem with professionals being in charge is that they tend to "shrink the space of democratic authority when they claim expertise and authority over tasks involved in achieving public purposes" (p. 148). Hence, one solution is for these professionals to give back these responsibilities to "activate civic action" (Olsen & Dzur, 2004, p. 149).

Conclusion

This chapter sought to explore how police and law can be understood from several perspectives. Ultimately, the question remains how social work can reflect anarchist and abolitionist perspectives while critically reflecting on its own relationship to the legal system. I am reminded of how in an ethics class, we discussed how social workers are held to a higher standard of ethical principles. What this means in practice is that we may at times have to choose between following the law and behaving ethically. In other words, our conversation held the possibility that the law can be unethical. Following laws without critically reflecting on our ethics leaves us vulnerable to engaging in harmful behavior. The support by social work of the 60s Scoop is certainly such an example. There is more to this argument, however.

Current debates within NASW and the role of social work in police enforcement illustrate this problem. Are professional codes of ethics enough? Should we follow a code of ethics that has been applied to and seen as congruent with conservative social work approaches? Jennissen and Lundy (2011) tell the story of the progressive or radical social worker leaving or being ejected from social work (as faculty in the 70s and in practice in the 40s in s Canada) for their political orientation. The Canadian Association of Social Workers is largely silent about this at the national level.

If we consider the concerns raised both by anarchist and abolitionist voices, we need to reconsider our involvement in the field of law enforcement. Social workers already have a relationship with policing as our work in child welfare involves surveillance. If families do not comply, apprehension is the threat to leverage submission. We have colluded in making it acceptable for lower income people and BIPOC to be more likely to have their private lives surveilled and invaded due to a Eurocentric, White supremacist-grounded notion of normality in child-rearing that disappears any structural factors. Law enforcement follows the same logic. In effect, policing involves the prosecution of justice that is "blind" and in fact reproduces oppression with this position in the first place. Treating everyone the same is ignorant of difference and is dangerous.

Profiling based on demographics implies a fatalism about the human condition and supports discrimination and racism. Social workers know that if their child welfare appointments disproportionately occur in "the poor part of town" it is likely in part due to poverty as a factor. Perceptions are managed by experience. If most of our surveillance occurs with a specific demographic, we will have larger representation of this group. This tracks with how police engage with BIPOC (Maynard, 2017). If you pull over cars because someone is driving while Black, you are sampling disproportionally from the larger population. You will either find more crime or define the actions as more criminal. From that, you extrapolate the racist logic of BIPOC being more criminal and needing to be under more surveillance for society's protection (Maynard, 2017). Ultimately if we reproduce the narrative of BIPOC and poor people being more represented in child welfare with the same logic, we are a part of the problem, not the solution. Our work becomes surveillance and oppression while upholding a white supremacist, capitalist status quo.

The conversation of social work being the more holistic and beneficent alternative to policing remains active in the public imagination. Certainly, by pointing to how social work has been present in prisons and probation makes for a compelling argument. However, the history of supporting government-sanctioned oppression in child welfare should give us pause. Social worker, activist, organizer, and lecturer, Shira Hassan (2021), responds to the siren song of police social work by noting that in child welfare, the mandate to report removes the worker's agency and simply upholds an oppressive system. This is a clear and present danger in the here and now that illustrates how fallacious it is to assume that social work's presence will reform a system. Looking to the past and telling ourselves we will never make these mistakes again ignores reality. In some ways it echoes the efforts by Canadian police to point to the United States as a worse example so they can avoid looking at their own problematic behaviors (Maynard, 2017). The school-to-prison pipeline is real, and social work's role ought not be to contribute to this evil.

Abolition requires the transformation of society, not just the removal of police and prisons (Rasmussen & James, 2020). The reasons for why this is necessary can be found in headlines, the BLM movement, and the civic unrest during this time. We may very well be at a critical moment where the conversation about what kind of a community and world we want to live in is possible. This is where I can see the potential for social work. Whenever I teach, I try to refer to what I used to tell the case managers I supervised in a former life—"Your job is to make yourself obsolete." In order for us to become redundant, we need to return to the idea that social work is the result of community offloading it's collective role to experts (Olsen & Dzur, 2004). A transformed society would need to have their collective potential returned to them. This can be a frightening prospect for several reasons. We have been told that we should assume that in the absence of an authority, our baser selves will run amok, barbarism will ensue. Our work needs to include conscientization as liberation pedagogue Paulo Freire (2004; Torres, 2014) would say. The stories we tell ourselves need to be critically examined. Anarchist critiques of the state ought to help us consider who benefits from such cynical views of the human condition that the only way we can live is in the safety of the cage of the law enforcement apparatus. As said many times throughout this book, a better world is possible. If we work to challenge collective thinking errors that reproduce colonized and oppressed minds, social work, by striving to erase the need for itself, will counter the atomized, neoliberal existence we are all beholden to. A world without police is possible.

References

Berlin, S., & Kravetz, D. (1981). Women as victims: A feminist social work perspective. *Social Work*, 26(6), 447–449.

Cormack, E., Deane, L., Morrissette, L., & Silver, J. (2013). *Indians wear red: Colonialism, resistance, and Aboriginal street gangs*. Fernwood Press.

CrimethInc. (2020, May 31). *What will it take to stop the police from killing?* https://crimethinc.com/2020/05/31/what-will-it-take-to-stop-the-police-from-killing Retrieved from http://www.theanarchistlibrary.org

Crosby, A., & Monaghan, J. (2018). *Policing Indigenous movements: Dissent and the security state*. Fernwood Press.

Davis, A. Y. (2003). *Are prisons obsolete?* Seven Stories Press.

Dubler, J., & Lloyd, V. (2018). Mass incarceration is religious (and so is abolition): A provocation. In Abolition Collective (Eds.), *Abolishing Carceral Society* (pp. 116–122). Common Notions.

Ferrell, J. (1998). Against the law: Anarchist criminology. *Social Anarchism* (25). http://library.nothingness.org/articles/SA/en/display/127

Foucault, M. (2008). *The spectacle of the scaffold*. Penguin Books.

Freire, P. (2004). Pedagogy of the oppressed. In L. Heldke & P. O'Connor, (Eds.), *Oppression, privilege and resistance: Theoretical perspectives on racism, sexism, and heterosexism* (pp. 5–23). McGraw-Hill.

Gelderloos, P. (ed.), & Lincoln, P. (2005). *World behind bars: The expansion of the American prison sell*. Signalfire Press. https://theanarchistlibrary.org/library/peter-gelderloos-and-patrick-lincoln-world-behind-bars-the-expansion-of-the-american-prison-sel

Gelderloos, P. (2014). *Learning from Ferguson*. Anarchist Library. https://theanarchistlibrary.org/library/peter-gelderloos-learning-from-ferguson

Giwa, S. (2018). Community policing in racialized communities: A potential role for police social work. *Journal of Human Behavior in the Social Environment*. doi:10.1080/10911359.2018.1456998

Graham, R. (2013). Afterword: The anarchist current: Continuity and change in anarchist thought. In R. Graham (Ed.), *Anarchism: A documentary history of libertarian ideas. Vol 3: The new anarchism (1974–2012)* (pp. 587). Black Rose Books.

Hackett, C., & Turk, B. (2018). Shifting carceral landscapes: Decarceration and the reconfiguration of white supremacy. In Abolition Collective (Eds.), *Abolishing carceral society* (pp. 23–54). Common Notions.

Hassan, S. (2021, March 31). *Harm reduction, abolition, and social work* (workshop). Haymarket Books. https://www.youtube.com/watch?v=_iFwX_Jzunk&t=969s

Heatherton, C. (2016). Policing the crisis of Indigenous lives: An interview with the Red Nation. In J. T. Camp & C. Heatherton (Eds.), *Policing the planet: Why the policing crisis led to Black Lives Matter* (pp. 109–119). Verso Books.

Jennissen, T., & Lundy, C. (2011). *One hundred years of social work: A history of the profession in English So called Canada 1900–2000*. Wilfried Laurier Press.

Kaslow, F., & Werner, S. (1976). Educating social workers for evolving roles in corrections. *The Journal of Sociology & Social Welfare* 3(6), 656–671.

Kenney, J. (2010). *Canadian victims of crime: Critical insights*. Canadian Scholars' Press.

Kesīqnaeh, E. W. (2017, February 11). *Fascism & anti-fascism: A decolonial perspective*. https://theanarchistlibrary.org/library/ena-emaehkiw-wakecanapaew-kes-qnaeh-fascism-anti-fascism-a-decolonial-perspective

King, T. (2012). *The inconvenient Indian: A curious account of Native People in North America*. Anchor Canada.

Kletsan, P. (2018). Revolution and restorative justice: An anarchist perspective. In Abolition Collective (Eds.), *Abolishing carceral society* (pp. 195–206). Common Notions.

Long, D. (2004). Introduction to social welfare. In A. L. Sallee (Ed.), *Social work and social welfare: An introduction* (pp. 2–22). Eddie Bowers Publishing.

Marshall, P. (2010). *Demanding the impossible: A history of anarchism*. PM Press.

Marshall, P (2013) Liberation ecology. In R. Graham, (Ed.), *Anarchism: A documentary history of libertarian ideas. Vol 3: The new anarchism (1974–2012)* (pp. 180–185). Black Rose Books.

Martin, B. (2013). Capitalism and violence. In R. Graham (Ed.), *Anarchism: A documentary history of libertarian ideas. Vol 3: The new anarchism (1974–2012)* (pp. 253–260). Black Rose Books.

Maynard, R. (2017). *Policing black lives: State violence in so called Canada from slavery to the present*. Fernwood Publishing.

Newman, S. (2013) The politics of post-anarchism. In R. Graham, (Ed.), *Anarchism: A documentary history of libertarian ideas. Vol 3: The new anarchism (1974–2012)* (pp. 423–434). Black Rose Books.

Noakes, Susan. (2014). Transformative social work in the criminal justice field. *Journal of Law and Social Policy, 23*, 175–187. https://digitalcommons.osgoode.yorku.ca/jlsp/vol23/iss1/11

Olson, S. M., & Dzur, A. W. (2004). Revisiting informal justice: Restorative justice and democratic professionalism. *Law & Society Review, 38*(1), 139–176.

Palmater, P. (2020). *Warrior life: Indigenous resistance and resurgence*. Fernwood Press.

Prinsloo, R. C. E. (2014). Social work values and principles: Students' experiences in intervention with children and youths in detention. *Journal of Social Work Practice, 28*(4), 445–460. https://doi-org.ezproxy.boothuc.ca/10.1080/02650533.2014.913236

Rasmussen, C., & James, K. (2020) *Trading cops for social workers isn't the solution to police violence* (op-ed). Truthout. July 17, 2020. https://truthout.org/articles/trading-cops-for-social-workers-isnt-the-solution-to-police-violence/

Reddy, S. K. (2018). We don't need no education: Deschooling as an abolitionist practice. In Abolition Collective (eds.), *Abolishing carceral society* (pp. 124–133). Common Notions.

Regehr, C., & Kanani, K. (2010). *Essential law for social work practice in Canada*. Oxford University Press.

Rogowski, S. (2014). Radical/critical social work with young offenders: Challenges and possibilities. *Journal of Social Work Practice, 28*(1), 7–21. https://doi-org.ezproxy.boothuc.ca/10.1080/02650533.2013.828280

Sato, M. (2020, August 20). *Social workers are rejecting calls for them to replace the police*. TheAppeal.org. https://theappeal.org/social-workers-are-rejecting-calls-for-them-to-replace-police/

Schmid, A. (2018). Crafting the perfect woman: How gynecology, obstetrics, and American prisons operate to construct and control women. In Abolition Collective (Eds.), *Abolishing Carceral Society* (pp. 71–88). Common Notions.

Sliva, S. M., & Samimi, C. (2018). Social work and prison labor: A restorative model. *Social Work, 63*(2), 153–160. https://doi-org.ezproxy.boothuc.ca/10.1093/sw/swy009

Spinrad, N. (1972). *Agent of chaos*. Belmont Books.

Torres, C. A. (2014). *First Freire: Early writings in social justice education*. Teachers College Press.
Umbreit, M. S. (1993). Crime victims and offenders in mediation: An emerging area of social work practice. *Social Work, 38*(1), 69–73.
Walia, H., & Dits, A. (2018). Dismantle and transform: On abolition, decolonization, and insurgent politics: A conversation between Harsha Walia and Andrew Dilts. In Abolition Collective (Eds.), *Abolishing Carceral Society* (pp. 12–21). Common Notions.
Williams, K. (2015). *Our enemies in blue: Police and power in America*. AK Press.
Wilson, A., & Wilson, M. (2020). *Reimagining policing: Strategies for community reinvestment: Pre-arrest diversion and innovative approaches to 911 emergency responses*. NASW. https://www.socialworkers.org/LinkClick.aspx?fileticket=GjXJr6rDzss%3d&portalid=0
Wood, J. C. (2020, June 15). *CASW letter to the right honourable Justin Trudeau: Call to action*. CASW. https://www.casw-acts.ca/en/casw-letter-right-honourable-justin-trudeau-call-action

Chapter questions

1. If in your work there was a safety concern, do you call the police? What concerns do you have about this? Would you want to have an alternative? What would you want it to look like?
2. The abolition of police has included the systems of incarceration in this chapter. What are your greatest concerns about a world without police and prisons? Do you think social work could be a part of alternative models for addressing crime?
3. This chapter suggests that borders and national identities have been further examples of the problems of securitization and ultimately how we use policing. Do you agree? Can you think of examples where the opposite is true? Why or why not?

6
Education, social work, and anti-capitalism

A theoretical exposition of teaching social work differently

Michel Foucault made the point that schools and prisons are locations where people have the least control (Blanchot & Foucault, 1987). Paulo Freire (2004) believed that education is a pathway to true democracy, as illiteracy keeps the dispossessed at the bottom of an oppressive system.

Social work emerged as a practice to address social problems brought on by industrialization (Tannenbaum & Reisch, 2001; Jennissen & Lundy, 2011). Some have claimed that due to educational reformer, Abraham Flexner, in a speech he gave in 1915, that social work is not a profession, education in social work evolved to address the need for a unique knowledge base that could give the growing discipline the status of a profession (McGrath Morris, 2008). This evolving knowledge base has emerged with what some could view as a problematic construct of the discipline itself. Parton and O'Byrne (2000) lament what they see as the overt bureaucratization of the profession that has left social workers demoralized, their professional skills undermined or disregarded. A core theoretical base, they argue, is needed for the discipline to counter this trend in practice. It is interesting how such a crisis of representation has been addressed. Some may want to become defensive, pointing out the diverse influences in the fields of psychology and sociology, for example, as a way to justify what may appear to be a field of knowledge with no center. I believe that the shifting ingredients of social work are rather a reflection of its greatest strength—its ability to respond to the context of the social world which by definition is forever in flux.

Given the above concerns about the purpose and function of education, this can be further confounding to the social work educator. How do we teach social work that not only mirrors the approach in field but addresses the concerns about power in the classroom? Traditional pedagogy replicates ways that education is understood—as a method of coercion and control. Good citizens raise their hands and follow orders, after all.

Critical pedagogy is useful in seeing new ways to teach and treat knowledge itself. Along with examining these approaches, anarchist writings on education will be explored to give further credence to the idea that social work, if it is part of the liberatory project, can be taught in a nonhierarchical fashion that emphasizes a new paradigm of how we conceive of knowledge and how we pass it on in social work education.

Social work education

There is a long standing concern regarding a growing gap between the academic focus on theory and lack of application by the social worker in practice (Fook, 2002; Ives et al., 2020) or as Mullaly and West (2018) describe how some social workers in the field claim that, "Theory has little direct relevance and actually may obscure the practical nature of social work.... New graduates... are often described by some experienced practitioners as naïve... in need of 'seasoning'" (p. 68). From its early traditions, it has been perceived as a profession (Payne, 2005) leading to qualified social workers in the field (Haight & Taylor, 2007). But what does this mean?

> The discipline of social work is the result of drawing from a broad field of social and biological science. Key is how this interdisciplinary body of knowledge has been re-interpreted from the point of view of social work ethics and values. This breadth of knowledge has been seen as a strength but could also be a challenge as social work seeks to define itself, social problems and their solutions. (Haight & Taylor, 2007)

It will not be possible to sufficiently address the myriad of issues surrounding social work education in this chapter. However, it is important to examine the field of social work education in context of the theories of education. How we teach reflects how we think about the discipline and its potential at the intersection of theory and practice, or praxis.

Critical theories and education

Some have appealed to the notions of the social world as the locus of care, highlighting structural oppression and institutional discrimination as the real culprits of the ills confronting the individual's as well as society's wellbeing (Payne, 2005). Critical theory has taken aim at the "lifeworld" and it's increasing occupation by hegemonic forces of global capitalization and the information industry (Agger, 2006). Adopting what Marx said about how the ideology of any time is a reflection of the ideas of a ruling class (Agger, 2006; Prilleltensky, 1994), we ought at least to pause and consider what it is we are doing in the classroom.

The 20th century has been a rich period for the development of critical thought. Many new schools of thought emerged to challenge the rosy picture of progress espoused by the period of enlightenment (Leonard, 2001). Critical theory advanced the idea that enlightenment predicates an industrialized laissez-faire worldview. Here we have a future with more and more of the world's population experiencing oppression as ever wealthier, global, industrial elites dominate the world's landscape (Leonard, 2001). This bleak picture of our collective future need not be. The notion that knowledge is accrued in ever increasing fashion and that such an advancement is morally superior is the same arrogance that aided the west in pushing its ethnocentrism on the world in the first place (Leonard, 2001). We don't have to accept the idea that there is a grand narrative that is steadily progressing toward a higher evolution of a good society. Our classrooms can reflect this difference in perspective to include alternative perspectives.

Foucault's ideas about power are essential here. He wrote about the use of expert language to co-opt local knowledge and subjugate its position in discourse (Jupp, 2005). Taking this idea further to the realm of clinical practice, we have Goffman(1961) talk about totalizing institutions. Social control is possible when we label socially unsavory behavior as "abnormal." By silencing perspectives that make us uncomfortable, we need not look at ourselves as despotic, but benevolent. The individual, under the thumb of public perceptions of normative standards, will internalize these notions of their own abnormality (Pease, 2003). If the individual is strong enough to resist this, they are further pathologized by the "totalizing institution" (Goffman, 1961).

What threatens us, as well as what serves us, is less reason than the various forms of rationality, an accelerated accumulation of rational apparatuses, a logical vertigo of rationalizations which are at work and in use as much in the penal system as in the medical system *or even the school system.* (Italics added, Blanchot & Foucault, 1987, p. 80–81)

If we adopt notions of critical pedagogy, it becomes important to understand how intellectuals like Paulo Freire and Michel Foucault have contributed to education.

Critical pedagogy

Paulo Freire, drawing from his Christian faith and Marxist philosophy, developed a framework where the goal of education is to recognize that we are all subjects of our lives (Kamberelis & Dimitriadis, 2005). He argued that a denial of the political nature of education and a narrow focus on objective training of skills disappears this reality (Jackson, 2007). Education thus becomes a liberating agent, as the consciousness of society is raised (Kincheloe & McLaren, 2005). Critical pedagogy therefore takes the form of a co-constructed enterprise, where both student and instructor collaborate in the process of learning. Curriculum development is co-constructed in order to maximize the ownership gained by both the student and the teacher (Taylor, 2008). Certainly, this kind of approach to social work education will serve to counter the challenges of this discipline's past. It is difficult to be a coercive agent in perpetuating the benevolent oppression of the disenfranchised when the student has learnt how to subjectify, versus objectify, what is known about the social world. No longer does the social worker know what is best for others based on a normative standard. What is best for any individual or group is best understood by listening to those we serve as they discover what this is for them.

Some concerns have been raised about Freire's view of pedagogy. By advancing this theory of liberation via making the illiterate literate, he runs the risk of being overly optimistic. Universalizing a problem (with a proposed solution) engenders the risk of subtle colonialization (Jackson, 2007). Nonliterate ways of knowing or producing knowledge are disregarded. This need not be. By engaging Indigenous cultures in the actual development of what is needed, rather than deciding what is required, we remove the privileging of one aspect of knowing and co-create a more inclusive higher education model (Taylor, 2008).

We need not even go abroad to find applicability of this approach. In Canada, studies have found a dearth of utility for secondary education. With the influx in part-time or temporal employment, many students are finding that they never use their degrees in a formal fashion (Grace, 2007). Here we have the question of whether increased education, formalized and consistent on a global level, is just another form of friendly oppression. Freire's approach can be understood as challenging these patterns in the workplace that are dictating educational goals. By educating self-directed and knowledge-constructing citizens, hegemony can be challenged effectively with critical thinking. It is the consciousness-raising that Critical Theorists argue is essential to bring about change via conflict or advocacy within the system (Payne, 2005).

There are some concerns raised regarding how an intellectual blind spot has developed in North America due to the buying into the notion that there is no viable alternative to capitalism (McLaren, 2003). Hence, all form of critical analysis have failed to examine this, as the demise of the former communist Eastern Bloc countries has created the notion that Marxist ideas had led to a failed experiment and that there are no alternatives. Paulo Freire is an example of the attempt to challenge these notions. There are alternatives. As our global economy seeks to gain an ever greater foothold in our lifeworld, this becomes an important reminder of how to resist.

Foucault is an important figure for social work education, as his ideas of power have relevance here. His role in contributing to education may best be explicated in looking at his conceptualization of knowledge itself. Knowledge is based on what has been privileged and what has not. The notion that history has functioned as a grand distiller of the best of what is objectively known about our world is exposed in Foucault's idea of archeology (Scheurich & McKenzie, 2005). All knowledge had to start somewhere. By "digging" for their origins, we find a past that defies the previous analysis. The illusion of the grand narrative and of a steady march of progress is exposed. Here we have the idea that, by introducing the subjectivist and relativist notions of ontology, we are not diminishing but enhancing what is known. Positivism tends to treat knowledge as rationalistic and reductionistic, but is not objective as it claims to (Fendler, 2004).

In genealogy, Foucault shows how previously unrelated concepts share common roots. By this rationale, it makes perfect sense to claim that social workers are related to other more overt agents of social control within the state. After all, social workers have emerged from within the system itself. They cannot be outside of it (Scheurich & McKenzie, 2005). Therefore, it is once again clear how important it is to be cognizant of how elusive knowledge truly is. By subscribing to a specific curriculum, we are not only exercising power over our students, we are unwittingly indoctrinating them into accepting a world as it is, rather than critically thinking for themselves about how things ought to be. This need not be a pessimistic prospect. One way of thinking of Foucault's concept of genealogy is to consider it a device by which to disrupt assumptions about status quo notions regarding the construction of the subject (Fendler, 2004). Foucault challenges us to examine the ways in which social constructions dominate our thinking in the classroom. It is the difference between teachers as legislators of an objective ontology versus as interpreters of a postmodern ontology.

How can such ideas take root in a social work classroom? A critical evaluation of history and how it is serving to reinforce perceptions and inequities can happen in any course taught for the discipline. It is an appreciation of the shades of gray, an appreciation of ambiguity, which can promote critical thinking. Or, as stated by Fendler (2004), "All ontological assumptions are products of particular historical circumstances and discursive interpretation" (p. 454). How we talk about what has occurred, shaped by our particular location of culture, gender, and socioeconomic status further reinforces an illusory perspective of a world that is "out there." By finding new ways of thinking, agency is promoted in the student. This sense of agency finds its way into praxis, as the real world is too complex for a simplified classroom curriculum to capture coherently (Taylor, 2008). Ultimately, if we employ a critical pedagogy, it is about embracing a third way of approaching knowledge—not from a technical or practical perspective but by an emancipatory orientation (McLaren, 2002).

It is important, however, to be aware of the inherent challenge in teaching a critical pedagogy. The classroom that emphasizes critical and reflective thinking in its focus will require a strong sense of self-awareness by the instructor. Jackson (2007) cautions that, even with Freire, we have a cultural blind spot. Our version of liberation is taught, as even instructors that aim to be more geared toward cognitive models that stress associational learning (prior knowledge or experience) change curriculum based on the faculty member's orientation (past experience, etc.) and don't explicitly involve the student either (Myers, 2008).

The learning environment

Learning can be conceptualized as the aggregate of sequential or linearly acquired information. This can be evaluated in the usual quantitative way via tests and grades given based on rubrics as final papers are evaluated. Alternatively, and perhaps based on contemporary ideas of how the brain actually operates—via association, not accumulation of information (Ashford et al., 2006), we would be looking at how the student constructs their framework of knowledge to get at the *quality* of learning achieved. This kind of learning could be understood as more hands-on in nature and approach.

A number of approaches can be employed to get at a deeper level of learning for students who may have very little direct knowledge or experience of populations they will serve as budding social workers. Heenan (2005) found that, by engaging students directly in a discussion about disability, it was possible to uncover stigma, preconceptions, and attitudes that they may not even have been aware of. By employing group discussions of norms and values, it was possible to get at underlying cultural stereotypes that predicate a biased worldview that students were holding. It is important to note that any feedback by the instructor be a reflection of tolerance and understanding. Seeking to challenge and see students grow, rather than to be cowed and embarrassed into adopting a more liberal worldview in line with what the instructor thinks (Lei, 2007). Simply put, if we want our students to become more tolerant and willing to suspend judgment, we must model this within the classroom environment.

Meyer (2007) found that including topics of international matters relevant to social work can be incorporated well in a "macro-practice" class. The seminar-style course emphasized a critical response to the readings along with electronically posting provocative questions relevant to both current events and community practice. Further, class time was dedicated toward identifying a current issue in the local community to respond to. By having students rally around this issue, they were encouraged to reflect on how global issues affected the issue in question. This kind of hands-on learning makes learning real to students (Meyer, 2007). The acting and reflecting on acting feedback loop encourages transformational learning.

Further approaches in teaching that appear promising include collaborative teaching. By employing interdisciplinary education, promoted by instructors from different disciplines within the same course, we can help students make new connections as well as learn in exciting and new ways. By co-teaching courses, students can see how a more realistic image of learning can emerge. Part of such an approach will need to include the modeling of new behavior in academia. A learning community of different disciplines where regular meetings focus on teaching in such a fashion is integral to this process (Inderbitzin & Storrs, 2008). By creating space for senior students to mentor junior students, we are further increasing the practice of what it means to be part of a greater learning community as well as reinforcing the practice of mentorship for social work students.

It is foolish to think that a critical and creative thinking-oriented curriculum can be easily implemented. The reality is that resistance is likely to occur. Fellow members of faculty may resist significant changes, as they struggle to keep up with all the demands of academic life. With the knowledge economy trying to meet the needs of a globalized economy, teaching and learning become increasingly commodified. Course offerings have become subject to evaluation criteria based on outcomes, despite the damage this does to students' self-concept, and increase attrition (Inderbitzin & Storrs, 2008). Teaching course loads have increased, while full-time status has decreased (Taylor, 2008). Compounding the reluctance to change to new paradigms of teaching may be the fear of the "bad student evaluation" if taking too many risks in the classroom (Inderbitzin & Storrs, 2008). Co-teaching a course has shown to improve dropout rates as well as higher achievement levels for students (Dugan & Letterman, 2008).

There are further advantages to collaborative teaching models. Students who struggle in interpersonal effectiveness skills are able to improve in this area, as they observe faculty collaboratively approach a given course (Dugan & Letterman, 2008). Students are able to increase their aptitude in viewing topical matters from alternate positions, as differences will invariably be evident in the classroom. A great amount of communication between faculty members is key to successful collaborative teaching. This is regardless of whether the classroom is co-taught or sequentially (Dugan & Letterman, 2008).

Power remains in the classroom and therefore it is essential that social work educators reflect on how students can speak into the learning process. One such area of potential can be student evaluations. Beyers (2008) explores the challenge of student feedback or evaluation. The problem is that they rarely have any meaningful value in shaping instructor performance. A number of reasons exist that challenge the value of this instrument. For instance, thoughtful reflections in evaluations are discouraged by the format. Generally, student evaluations tend to measure affective rather than cognitive features of the classroom. Furthermore, it has been found that usually little thought is given to these, as they are anonymous and ungraded. Myers (2008) found that part of the problem lies in the divergence of goals for students and faculty. Instructors generally aim to enhance learning and thinking processes, while students focus on affective and individual progress. "[T]he instructor prioritizes critical thinking and mastery of discipline content and the students prioritize career preparation, scientific reasoning, personal development, and art and cultural appreciation. Although the effect of the different relative priorities for any one goal may be medium, the cumulative effect of instructor–student differences across all the learning goals may be quite large" (p. 52).

Essentially what is of greatest concern here is that regardless of the intentions of the instructor, the gulf between them and the student body need to be acknowledged and dealt with. We may want to engage students in ways that enhances critical thinking and advances social justice. Our students will be concerned about career, income, student debts, and more. These realities will shape expectations of what education can provide and perceptions of what the instructor ought to be doing in the classroom.

Myers (2008) offers some ideas about how to address the challenging gulf between students and faculty. If we approach formative assessment in such a way that the student body is seen as the greatest untapped resource, we promote greater student satisfaction and learning. A collaborative approach, where faculty learns alongside the student emphasizes a democratic pedagogy. It is apparent that increased student–faculty contact has favorable learning outcomes. Hence one suggestion is for a committee or collaborative community of scholars, students, and administrators to meet with the express purpose of addressing improvements in the classroom and curriculum development.

Social work has reproduced and validated hegemonic worldviews that have been harmful to vulnerable sectors of society. While Cindy Blackstock (2009) makes the case related to child welfare in Canada, this is not the only domain of practice. Poole et al. (2012) claim that social work's allegiance to the medical model has normalized sanist aggression such as validating pathologizing labels. This raises the valid question of whether because of this privileging of medical concepts of madness we are even able to engage in anti-sanist social work. Poole et al. (2012) express concern in what is increasing evidence being found of social work discourses where references to diagnosis in classification seemed to suggest more of a medicalization of mental illness. This frequently excludes service users in that they're not recognized as legitimate producers of knowledge. Social work educators are challenged to engage in mental health courses from a critical or anti-oppressive stance. Further arguments are made that the next step in mental health education should be the challenging of sanism by involving people in the mad community in social work research and education. They argue that alternative histories need to be told that expose students to the mad movement, the struggle that continues to address the unequal power inherent in the psychiatric mental health system.

Brown (2016) raises the alarm of the creeping effect of neoliberalism via the new management approach in education. The academic institutions themselves increasingly reflect the free market, with precarious employees (i.e. sessional instructors) who struggle to eke out an existence, unable to find the space to contribute to scholarship. The neoliberal notion of education for employment further diminishes a depth and breadth in education that is sorely needed. For example, the focus on current aptitudes that find resonance in the working world makes the inclusion of history less relevant. This disappearing value in history as a course or way of looking at the world leads to less insight and makes the here and now more "real." Learning history has the potential of giving us greater capacity to see outside of hegemony and become more critical of the world and of social work.

While Brown (2016) is addressing the structural concerns of neoliberalization on social work education, I am unpacking the form of education itself in social work—both to resist the trends but also to find a way of teaching that communicates the anarchic nature of education itself—a liberatory experience. The following will be a brief summary of the main ideas of education in anarchist writings.

Anarchism and education

If we reflect on anarchism and its general tenets, it may appear that we are at an impasse. If education inherently reproduces and reifies power and hierarchical relations, how can anarchy apply? This is an important point to consider, for if teaching cannot be done without authority, is the realm of education unable to model anarchism? Does the student need to undergo a process of oppression via education before they can experience or appreciate antiauthoritarian ideas? Some may even think that permissive parenting is the negative example of child rearing that supports the failure of anarchism to be a useful construct when it comes to the development of children in their environment.

Certainly, it is possible to point to earlier examples in social work education, already raised in this chapter, to address power and authority in the classroom that can put to rest some of the concerns raised above. However, I would argue that the main issue remains vexing for both a critical pedagogy approach to social work education and anarchist educational ideas. How can education be engaged in a way that avoids the "power over" conundrum? The following will be a summary of some of the main ideas related to anarchism and education. At its conclusion, ways to explore the application to social work education will be discussed.

To begin, there are certainly areas of agreement between critical pedagogy and anarchist thought. Emma Goldman, a significant American anarchist thinker, held beliefs about education that prompted her to found a school in the United States, based on Spanish anarchist-educator Francisco Ferrer's Modern School (Marshall, 2010). Writing at the turn of the 20th century, she had a view about education that echoed critical pedagogy. She would refer to the educational system of her time as being the introduction of predigested food that robs students of the ability to engage creatively with their own learning (Goldman, 1906). "Goldman saw existing schools as drilling the young into absolute uniformity by compulsory mental feeding. The social purpose of the libertarian Modern School on the other hand was 'to develop the individual through knowledge and the free play of characteristic traits, so that he may become a social being'" (Marshall, 2010, p. 405). This kind of learning involves the abolition of rules and regulations. Educators should hence find ways to facilitate the child finding their own voice. New ideas ought to be engaged with from a position of understanding and sympathy. Interestingly, Goldman believed strongly that sex education should be a part of this—to see the beauty and centrality of this aspect of the human condition.

A contemporary of Goldman, French anarchist Sébastien Faure offered his own ideas about a libertarian education. He imagined children to be morally neutral at their birth. Education then, has the potential to influence the moral compass in profound ways. Strict discipline weakens the moral fiber and creates distrust as a hierarchical domination of the pupil ensues. He describes rather a relationship between teacher and student as a friendship on equal footing. The construct where choices are binary—reward or punishment—makes for a dangerous form of person who is willing to obey and perform acts of malice at the orders of authority.

> grey, drab, colourless, insipid beings bereft of all determination, passion or personality; a slavish, cowardly, sheepish breed, incapable of manly or sublime deeds, the execution of which presupposes and requires a dose of liveliness, fire, independence and enthusiasm, but instead one perfectly capable of cruelty and abjection, especially in circumstances where personal accountability is eclipsed by mob activity. (Faure, 1910, p. 2)

He describes a form of teaching where risk is involved on the part of the educator. A graduated guardianship which involves challenging the child with the myriad of perspectives and challenges along the way so that this becomes cultivated—the facility to encounter and challenge their own dangers along the way toward emancipation via the method of self-teaching. In effect, one can see the cultivation of critical thinking as key to the foundation of an anarchist pedagogy.

A key idea of Faure is leading by example. If you want children to mature without a violent heart, do not use force to rear them. Modeling what we want to see in our students is the best way to teach. Chinese philosopher Wu Zhihui (1908) contributes to this idea when he viewed education as revolution. These two things ought not be treated as separate ideas. Without confronting truth and morality via education, any grand revolution devolves into mere rebellion, as the passions are stoked without engaging thought. What this means in practice is that if we are educated on morality over the appeal only to individual rights, we are better able to engage in a moral life, able to set aside our own rights in favor of a better community and world.

According to George Cairncross (1971), the educational system is a process of conditioning citizens to accept the state as an unquestioning authority. One could take his concerns to relate to how places of learning are sites for engendering hegemony for democracy as it is currently practiced, where majority rule dictates action, and minorities must abide by this status quo. In the classroom then, the indoctrination of such norms is lived out—the student who succeeds is praised while the one who fails is made aware, sometimes painfully, in front of their peers that they have not. This reflects the larger societal principal of competition, where someone has to win over another. Put another way, to win, someone else has to lose.

What Cairncross then makes of the whole game of certification or the accomplishing of degrees, in general, is of note. If indoctrination via education leads to participation in the process of compliance, the awarding of degrees then would mean that authority can trust that those who have this distinction are trustworthy to perpetuate the ongoing project of democracy as conceived by the state. After all, the state is responsible for laying out what is appropriate education starting in childhood. He offers another view of education that is less dystopian, offering a hopeful perspective instead.

> Short of revolution, education is the only way that a society can be changed from within. Adults, as much as children, have to be educated to the idea of a new society for the old one to be superseded. A society that considers itself and its values to be responsible and just, is not likely of its own volition, to countenance a change in its structure through the educational system (p. 2).

This kind of approach to education must reconcile with the way resistance in the classroom is currently perceived. He makes the case that students who rebel are rarely understood but rather cast as disorderly, problematic, and in need of correction. The system or structure is not examined as the problem. The student is.

Matt Hern (2003) draws on history to make his point about education. Drawing from Platonic roots, a national universal educational system has been emerging since the Enlightenment era. What initially had been in the hands of the church in Europe, shifts to being under the control of the state. He refers to Napoleon as an adopter of this notion, so much even that he centralized education and took complete control over France's educational system. In fact, universities were designed with strict ideological control, a common uniform, and a regimented system of authority in the likeness of the military. Prussia, upon being defeated by France, revised its educational system, as it was believed that this would promote the cohesion and facility of the Prussian army to become more effective in future conflicts.

> To that end Prussian educational theorists devised a model for schooling, built around centrally controlled curriculums, constant fragmentation of days into changing classes at the sound of a bell, obedience and teacher-directed classroom groupings. At the heart of the system though was the primacy of the State, and that children both belonged to and were the responsibility of the State. (p. 3)

It was this Prussian version of state controlled, mandatory education that appealed and led the Massachusetts schools to form. A number of years later, in the 1880s, schools from elementary to junior high had become common across the United States, as had teachers' colleges to staff these public services. Canada was a bit less organized in the national rollout of mandatory education. By the end of WWII, however, this had become a universal standard as well.

If we take the supposition of the state's role in education as a given, it makes sense to consider as Hern (2003) does, the voices of opposition. Referring to early anarchist philosopher William Godwin, Hern expressed concern about how the state uses education to entrench its power structure within the minds of the young. He viewed education at its best when it is the pursuit of truth and justice which the state has subverted through their particular political interests. He takes these ideas further when calling for reflection on what is learning versus teaching (Hern, 1998). If we see learning as a natural expression of how we develop, teaching in its current iteration is more treatment than a learning process. Students are made to accept a specific set of concepts which they must demonstrate they can recall. It is counter to the concept of learning, which occurs by engaging the natural curiosity of students to explore their world. Furthermore, he calls for localized education that is reflexive, adapting to the interests, learning styles, and realities of students and communities. He ends on a cautionary note of how the current school system sets us all up to accept the notion of being under surveillance, which reduces the ability to think for ourselves and have agency in the world. A compelling point is made by Hern (1998) that we assume a monoculture when we expect the only standard for success to be school-related. The trades and other areas of knowledge get left behind which may be robbing some students of being able to explore and celebrate their unique aptitudes and learning styles. Challenging these assumptions of education versus learning can open up the discourse for addressing what, at heart, is a bad culture being validated by a public school system.

> The implications of schools reverberate throughout our culture, and it is plainly clear that an ecological society cannot bear the burden that schools place on our kids, families and communities. They are crude constructions for a world that has been exposed as unethical and unsustainable. (Hern, 1998, p. 11)

The anarchist zine collective Research and Destroy (2009) make the case that much of the criticisms leveled at education hold true when looking at the institutions of higher education. Universities reify obedience, along with rising debt loads, while students look forward to a bleak future in areas of employment fairly similar to the ones they have to participate in to afford the cost of a commodified educational system. Ivory tower hierarchies reproduce the meritocracy myth.

> The underlings are only too happy to play apprentice to the masters, unable to do the math indicating that nine-tenths of us will teach 4 courses every semester to pad the paychecks of the one-tenth who sustain the fiction that we can all be the one. Of course I will be the star, I will get the tenure-track job in a large city and move into a newly gentrified neighborhood. (p. 4–5)

Furthermore, they argue, the university is beholden to capitalism, as it has held the position of preparing a work force for the changing needs of industry. Now the crisis of education is recast in light of an economic system that needs fewer trained workers than ever before. Going back in time to the 1960s, where universities were the hotbeds of radical movements, is not an option, given the diminishing value for university education and the failures of that movement to connect anti-capitalist critique abroad (like Vietnam) with issues related to the working class, such as domestic oppression due to capital.

Reddy (2018) appeals for de-schooling approaches as a form of counter-education. Here there is reference to how education is not neutral, but rather is the blurring of process and product, especially in capitalist societies, like the United States. "[C]onflating schooling with the acquisition of knowledge, and mistaking the acquisition of skills with their just, equitable, and even emancipatory utilization . . . the educational system in a capitalist society is geared toward class stratification and the maintenance of class privilege through capitalist exploitation" (p. 125). Reddy refers to the writing of Austrian philosopher Ivan Illich, to raise the alarm that education is one of the stations in life that serve to reduce individuals to passive clients versus autonomous agents and that this results in a perception of medical treatment confused with health care and "social work for the improvement of community life, police protection for safety, military poise for national security, the rat race for productive work." (Ivan Illich, Deschooling society (2002), as cited in Reddy (2018) pp. 125–126).

Given the current structures around the financing of education in a capitalist society, a form of indentured servitude is created by soaring higher education costs and their attendant student debt loads. What this results in is a population that is losing autonomy, as they are needing to seek employment in order to pay off the debt of getting a post-secondary degree that they needed to get a job in the first place. Reddy's advice to students here is to find ways to continue to tap into struggles for social justice while balancing the demands of modern life. In effect, Reddy is talking about subversion—of poaching from the system while appearing to represent in order to engage in guerilla tactics to redistribute what has been privatized—education and knowledge and thus be contributing to abolition by helping underserved communities in the process.

Anatol Dniester (2017) chronicles the damage to students who are the commodity in capitalist educational society. The emergence of "cram schools," whose sole function is to prepare students for the increasingly more competitive world of university entrance examinations, has contributed to an environment that has harmed students' mental health, even leading to suicide. Noting UK statistics, this has now even led to a number of calls for mental health-related support due to school stress for children under the age of 11. In South Korea, "entrance exam war" has been understood to contribute to the second highest cause of death in teenagers aged 10–19 via suicide. Referring to projections of a future where up to 80% of society may be unemployed due to downsizing and automatization, the point is made that the competition for the best grades and the corresponding job will only increase under capitalism.

Dniester (2017) sees the use of standardized tests of knowledge in education as inherently unjust. Given diverse experiences growing up in different families and cultures, let alone differing learning styles, such an experience only serves to communicate to students that some people are better than others. This is at the heart of promoting hierarchies, which leads to future exploitation and dispossession. Arguing that the ruling elites never act altruistically, it would be foolish to assume that public education is anything but indoctrination into the existing world order. This can be best considered when thinking about the way education is regulated. If children are to be educated in an apolitical environment, why does government have such a strong hold on the curriculum? The expectation is that upon leaving high school, the adult has lost the faculty to question authority and has been conditioned to accept society as it is, not how it should be.

Education in a capitalist world is a commodity. The acceleration that occurs with the profit motive is that all aspects, including students themselves, are exploited.

> Schools and universities are marketed as brands or as shops, where anyone can buy whatever they desire. In this case, it is college degrees, prestige and a head start into a successful profession. Under capitalism, learning is secondary in the process of education. To attract as many students as possible, universities have huge spending on building lavish sports facilities, student accommodation and communal areas. (Dniester, 2017, p. 8)

Furthermore, the rising cost of textbooks is a clear indication that making a profit off education has become problematic. Students are spending up to 20% of their total cost for university on these resources. One could make the case that if education is becoming less available to all due to the financial impact of such a pursuit, it is a lie to refer to equal access for all. This is even more true if one is unable to leave an impoverished school, as those who can afford to send their child to a private school can.

> Without qualified teachers, resources or career advice, success is a privilege for the wealthy. This education system proved to be very efficient in creating an unequal society, where a few oligarchs accumulate wealth, while the living standards of the majority are in a steady decline. As such, the education industry assumed a new role—the divider of our society. Families with more resources can afford to send their children to private schools, creating a deep income segregation from the beginnings of the children's lives. (Dniester, 2017, p. 9)

In effect, the cuts to education as well as the rising cost for post-secondary opportunity make sense when viewed from the perspective of a ruling class. During a time where manufacturing is looking for a cheaper workforce by leaving the country, a nation must find ways to retain this industry. Dniester

(2017) notes that it's no coincidence that during this time education becomes de-emphasized to ensure a new group of workers that are only able to access jobs in a sector that is currently in need of employees who are unable to demand a higher wage given their low qualifications. If this doesn't work, the institution of student loans, administered again by the state, ensures that students are obligated to take less desirable, low paying jobs to pay on the debt. Essentially, he sees education as a tool of the state to ensure control by all the mechanisms described above.

Conclusion/discussion

Any new paradigm of education in social work needs to be aware of the discipline's role in perpetuating oppression in the name of client care. Structural Social Work theory would argue that, in our quest to be seen as legitimate, we have reinforced hegemony as an agent of social control (Mullaly, 2007; Payne, 2005). Feminist critique has aimed to expose how clinical labels have served to undermine legitimate issues of political, social, and economic subordination. By giving labels their prognostic power, real issues around our social reality are ignored and reinforced (Martin, 2003). Furthermore, feminist theory has contributed greatly to challenge even those approaches aimed at challenging hegemony that themselves omit consideration of oppressed groups. Social workers need to be aware of the power to oppress an explanation of behavior can provide. It is our awareness of our position in society, the expert position we occupy, that necessitates a greater obligation to ensuring we share power, not try to wield it with beneficence.

Further challenges to the profession lie in the realities of a global marketplace. Oppression is experienced globally while our consumer-driven economy seeks to blur national boundaries with policies aimed at protecting corporations and harming not only the environment but citizens of our world (Ferguson & Lavallette, 2005). According to some, education as an institution itself, has been under attack (Taylor, 2008). By creating professional degrees and aiming at the international market, education has become a commodity, where critical reflection and thought has been co-opted by measurable targets of indoctrination. Oppression becomes carefully preserved. Since social work aims to be a professional degree, this has additional ramifications. By developing rigidly prescriptive curriculum, we run the risk of under-emphasizing the adult learner as a dynamic actor in the field of education and practice.

What these ideas in anarchist education offer are new ways to think about both learning and revolution. The cards are stacked against us, they say. Our children go on a daily basis to an institution where they are treated until they accept a view of the world that does not brook dissent. I am reminded of Bookchin's (Marshall, 2010, p. 605) reference to the structure or state in our minds. If we are to be effective as social workers opposing oppression, we need to think about how we are educators, so we do not reproduce the same oppression.

Critical pedagogue, Henry Giroux (2021) refers to a phenomenon he calls "Pandemic Pedagogy." The neoliberal influence on education has made society vulnerable to fascist ideologies as our capacity for critically reflecting and developing a historical consciousness have been undermined. He argues that critical pedagogy is needed to help us have the tools to resist and to desire and imagine a better world. Conversely, the pandemic pedagogy is described as a process that includes the relentless work done by right-wing media during the COVID-19 pandemic. Here there is scorn for science or any truth as fake news, and reactionary, authoritarian solutions that legitimate discrimination and racism are the foundations of a dystopian worldview. This is where we must create a rupture of common sense. "Such a rupture should be one that embraces historical memory, rejects the normalization of fascist principles, and opens a space for imagining alternative worlds that can be brought into being" (p. 136). Smith (2020) argues that social work education needs to increase student's capacity for discomfort, to affectively confront their privilege. Decolonizing the classroom requires confronting such difficult topics as racism, where students who are experiencing oppression can work through the anger and pain that they experience on a daily basis. The social work educator is compelled to consider how to ensure there is space without seeking to regulate or control this as an important part of how to decolonize the classroom.

> Any process of working toward Decoloniality or anti-racism must include attention to the affective dimension of the experience of being in the position of the oppressed and the oppressor . . . Students discover the validity of anger at their own experiences of racist oppression and racially stratified socioeconomic inequality. Rather than having to minimize, control

and "soften" their own emotional responses, these kinds of exercises allow for a cathartic expression of what is often repressed emotional pain. (p. 409)

Yellow Bird and Clarke make a compelling case in "Decolonizing Pathways towards Integrative Healing in Social Work" (2020). Decolonizing social work requires confronting, decentering and dismantling conventional ideas within mainstream social work as they have contributed to the oppression and harm done to Indigenous Peoples as well as other communities. In fact, they argue that even radical approaches such as anti-oppressive, critical, feminist, structural and anti-racist social work practices, are unable to directly confront decolonization as they are the products of settler based perspectives (p. 165). My impression of their argument is that, by opening up the curriculum to Indigenous ways of knowing, the hegemonic western canon is challenged, its perch lost as the foundational knowledge and understanding of social work itself. Furthermore, I am seeing a case being made by these authors that if social work were to truly adopt the idea of healing from a context-rich, holistic perspective, we must depart from individualized and compartmentalized notions of care-the settler colonial mindset. This includes viewing ourselves as a part of the natural world, not above or beyond it. Those of us who are social work educators with unearned privilege, need to do our own work (Briese & Menzel, 2020). We need to admit to our bias, which shapes and reifies the dominant status quo if we don't engage in this practice that forces us to confront our own privilege.

Henry Giroux's contribution to a critical pedagogy for social work deserves further reflection in that he brings in the idea of hope (Morley & Ablett, 2020). In fact, such a radical hope that imagines a better future is a direct threat to the neoliberal present. By refusing the static model of simply downloading information to that which engages the student in the discourse of critical thinking, an educated hope emerges, or, a kind of "militant utopianism" (Giroux in Morley & Ablett, p. 209). According to Noble (2020), cultural critic, educator, and activist bell hooks would concur, that "A pedagogy that denounces all systems of domination creates a sense of hope" (p. 506). This means that we don't just raise the consciousness of social work students. We need to engage in exploring fully and deeply what needs to be done about it. This implicitly communicates a sense of hope, that real change is possible, if we do this work together in our classrooms, field placements, and ultimately our areas of practice.

This can be taken further when reflecting on a shared experience of learning that promotes creativity, curiosity, and trust that develops when dogmatic views of knowledge are abandoned.

Social workers need to engage with the painful questions regarding their own discipline. How much does a rigid view about our knowledge base benefit those we help, and how does it become the graveyard of new ideas? If we defend a fixed definition of a profession, are we not by default conserving an ideal, hence becoming conservative in the process ourselves? The project of professionalization, while laudable from the perspective of ensuring this degree can be relevant in diverse fields of practice, can also become static, oppressive, and fatalistic. By attaching itself to a present world order, it always will need to define itself in contrast to it. The result is that while appearing to work against oppressive systems, it is dependent on their existence to remain relevant. Hence, the system is never the true object to overcome or destroy. Anarchists' views of education could be offering a different opportunity. Knowledge that is emancipatory is good, and anarchist theories of learning move us beyond paradigms of hierarchies that need to protect and advance their hegemony. Together they can help social work think of itself, as well as the way we teach about it, toward a world that promotes students that are free to contribute to an ever-growing pool of what we know. We are all better for it.

References

Agger, B. (2006). *Critical social theories: An introduction* (2nd ed.). Paradigm Publishers.

Ashford, J. B., LeCroy, C. W., & Lortie, K. L. (2006). *Human behavior in the social environment: A multidimensional perspective* (3rd ed.). Brooks/Cole.

Beyers, C. (2008, Spring). The hermeneutics of student evaluations. *College Teaching*, 56(2), 102–106.

Blanchot, M., & Foucault, M. (1987). *Foucault Blanchot*. Zone Books.

Blackstock, C. (2009). The occasional evil of angels: Learning from the experiences of Aboriginal peoples and social work. *First Peoples Child & Family Review*, 4(1), 28–37. Retrieved from https://fpcfr.com/index.php/FPCFR/article/view/74

Briese, J., & Menzel, K. (2020). No more Blacks in the back: Adding more than a 'splash' of black into social education and practice by drawing on the works of Aileen Moreton-Robinson and others who contribute to Indigenous Standpoint Theory. In C. Morley, P. Ablett, C. Noble, & S. Cowden (Eds.), *The Routledge handbook of critical pedagogies for social work* (pp. 375–387). Routledge.

Brown, C. (2016). The constraints of neo-liberal new managerialism in social work education. *Canadian Social Work Review*, 33(1).

Cairncross, G. (1971). Education and the democratic myth. *Freedom, 32*. Reprinted in and scanned from: Contemporary Anarchism, edited by Terry M. Perlin (Transaction Books, New Brunswick, 1979, p. 203 ff) theanarchistlibrary.org

Clarke, K., & Yellow Bird, M. (2020). *Decolonizing pathways towards integrative healing in social work*. Routledge.

Dniester, A. (2017). *Inside the capitalist education system*. The Anarchist Library. theanarchistlibrary.org

Dugan, K., & Letterman, M. (2008, Winter). Student appraisals of collaborative teaching. *College Education, 56*(1), 11–15.

Faure, S. (1910). *Libertarian education*. The Anarchist Library. theanarchistlibrary.org

Fendler, L. (2004). Praxis and agency in Foucault's historiography. *Studies in Philosophy and Education, 23*, 445–466.

Ferguson, I., & Lavallette, M. (2005). Another world is possible: Social work and the struggle for social justice. In I. Ferguson, M. Lavalette, & E. Whitmore (Eds.), *Globalization, global justice, and social work* (pp. 207–223). Routledge.

Fook, J. (2002). Theorizing from Practice: Towards an Inclusive Approach for Social Work Research. *Qualitative Social Work, 1*(1), 79–95. https://doi.org/10.1177/147332500200100106

Freire, P. (2004). Pedagogy of the oppressed. In L. Heldke & P. O'Connor, (Eds.), *Oppression, privilege, and resistance: Theoretical perspectives on racism, sexism, and heterosexism* (pp. 5–23). McGraw-Hill.

Giroux. H. (2021). *Race, politics, and pandemic pedagogy: Education in a time of crisis*. Bloomsbury.

Goffman, E. (1961). *Asylums: Essays on the social situation of mental patients and other inmates*. Anchor Books.

Goldman. E. (1906). *The child and its enemies*. https://theanarchistlibrary.org/library/emma-goldman-the-child-and-its-enemies

Grace, A. (2007). Envisioning a critical social pedagogy of learning and work in a contemporary culture of cyclical lifelong learning. *Studies in Continuing Education, 29*(1), 85–103.

Haight, W., & Taylor, E. (2007). *Human behavior for social work practice: A delvelopmental-ecological framework*. Chicago, IL: Lyceum.

Heenan, D. (2005). Challenging stereotypes surrounding disability and promoting anti-oppressive practice: Some reflections on teaching social work students in Northern Ireland. *Social Work Education, 24*(5), 495–510.

Hern, M. (1998). *The promise of deschooling*. The Anarchist Library. http://www.theanarchistlibrary.org

Hern, M. (2003). *The emergence of compulsory schooling and anarchist resistance*. The Anarchist Library. http://www.theanarchistlibrary.org

Inderbitzin, M., & Storrs, D. (2008). Mediating the conflict between transformative pedagogy and bureaucratic practice. *College Teaching, 56*(1), 47–52.

Ives, N., Denov, M., & Sussman, T. (2020). *Introduction to social work in Canada: Histories, context, practices* (2nd ed.). Oxford University Press.

Jackson, S. (2007). Freire re-viewed. *Educational Theory, 57*(2), 199–213.

Jennissen, T., & Lundy, C. (2011). *One hundred years of social work*. Wilfrid Laurier University Press.

Jupp, V. (2005). Issues of power in social work practice in mental health services for people from black and minority ethnic groups. *Critical Social Work, 6*(1).

Kamberelis, G., & Dimitriadis, G. (2005). Focus groups: Strategic articulations of pedagogy, politics, and inquiry. In N. K. Denzin, & Y. S. Lincoln (Eds.), *The Sage handbook of qualitative research* (pp. 887–908). Sage.

Kincheloe, J., & McLaren, P. (2005). Rethinking critical theory and qualitative research. In N. K. Denzin & Y. S. Lincoln (Eds.), *The Sage handbook of qualitative research* (pp. 303–342). Thousand Oaks: Sage.

Lei, S. (2007). Factors changing attitudes of graduate school students toward an introductory research methodology course. *Education, 128*(4), 667–685.

Leonard, P. (2001). The future of critical social work in uncertain conditions. *Critical Social Work,* 2(1).

Marshall, P. (2010). *Demanding the impossible: A history of anarchism.* PM Press.

Martin, J. (2003). Mental health: Rethinking practices with women. In J. Allan, B. Pease, & L. Briskman (Eds.), *Critical social work: An introduction to theories and practices* (pp. 155–169). Allen & Unwin.

Morris, P. M. (2008). Reinterpreting Abraham Flexner's Speech, "Is Social Work a Profession?": Its Meaning and Influence on the Field's Early Professional Development. *Social Service Review, 82*(1), 29–60. https://doi.org/10.1086/529399

McLaren, P. (2002). Critical pedagogy: A look at the major concepts. In A. Darder et al. (Eds.), *The critical pedagogy reader* (pp. 69–96). Routlege/Falmer.

McLaren, P. (2003). Critical pedagogy and class struggle in the age of neoliberal globalization: Notes from history's underside. *Democracy & Nature,* 9(1).

Meyer, M. (2007). Globalization and social work education: Evaluation of student learning in a macro practice class. *Social Work Education, 26*(3), 247–260.

Morley, C., & Ablett, P. (2020). Henry Giroux's vision of critical pedagogy: Educating social work activists for radical democracy. In C. Morley, P. Ablett, C. Noble, & S. Cowden (Eds.), *The Routledge handbook of critical pedagogies for social work* (pp. 201–212). Routledge.

Mullaly, B. (2007). *The new structural social work.* Oxford University Press.

Myers, C. (2008, Winter). Divergence in learning goal priorities between college students and their faculty. *College Education, 56*(1), 53–58.

Noble, C. (2020). bell hooks trilogy: Pedagogy for social work supervision. In C. Morley, P. Ablett, C. Noble, & S. Cowden (Eds.), *The Routledge handbook of critical pedagogies for social work* (pp. 501–511). Routledge.

Parton, N., & O'Byrne, P. (2000). What do we mean by constructive social work? *Critical Social Work,* 1(2).

Payne, M. (2005). *Modern social work theory* (3rd ed.). Lyceum Books.

Pease, B. (2003). Rethinking the relationship between the self and society. In J. Allan, B. Pease, & L. Briskman (Eds.), *Critical social work: An introduction to theories and practices* (pp. 187–201). Allen & Unwin.

Poole, J., Jivraj, T., Arslanian, A., Bellows, K., Chiasson, S., Hakimy, H., Pasini, J., & Reid, J. (2012). Sanism, 'mental health,' and social work/education: A review and call to action. *Intersectionalities: A Global Journal of Social Work Analysis, Research, Polity, and Practice,* (1) https://doi.org/10.32920/21751490.v1

Prilleltensky, I. (1994). *The morals and politics of psychology: Psychological discourse and the status quo.* State University of New York Press.

Reddy, S. K. (2018). We don't need no education: Deschooling as an abolitionist practice. *Abolishing Carceral Society,* (1), 124–133.

Research and Destroy. (2009). *Communique from an absent future: The terminus of student life*. The Anarchist Library. http://www.theanarchistlibrary.org
Scheurich, J., & McKenzie, K. (2005). Foucault's methodologies: Archaeology and genealogy. In N. K. Denzin & Y. S. Lincoln (Eds.), *The Sage handbook of qualitative research* (pp. 841–869). Sage.
Smith, L. H. (2020). Frantz Fanon's revolutionary contribution: An attitude of decoloniality as critical pedagogy for social work. In C. Morley, P. Ablett, C. Noble, & S. Cowden (Eds.), *The Routledge handbook of critical pedagogies for social work* (pp. 399–411). Routledge.
Tannenbaum, N., & Reisch, M. (2001). From charitable volunteers to architects of social welfare: A brief history of social work. https://ssw.umich.edu/about/history/brief-history-of-social-work
Taylor, P. (2008). Higher education curricula for human and social development. In Global University Network For Innovation (Eds.), *Higher education in the world 3: Higher education: New challenges and emerging roles for human and social development* (pp. 89–101). Palgrave/Macmillan.
Zhihui, W. (1908). Education as revolution. In R. Graham (Ed.), *Anarchism: A Documentary History of Libertarian Ideas; Volume One: From Anarchy to Anarchism (300 CE to 1939)*. http://www.theanarchistlibrary.org

Chapter questions

1. What has been your greatest surprise or frustration about university education? How did it differ from high school?
2. What stood out in this chapter regarding education? Does it change how you would educate others?
3. Have you been a part of consciousness raising work? What did it look like? If you could design your own learning environment, would it be similar to ideas from this chapter? How would it differ and why?

7

Mutual aid and the way forward

Ideas and implications for social work practice

I find alien invasion movies a suitable way to start this chapter. A story about humanity under threat tends to be the general trend of each of these movies. Their trailers are evocative (as they are wont to be, after all, the spectacle is supposed to result in ticket sales) in showing the destruction of our world. Alien overlords are seen attacking the Western Seaboard, blowing up the Eiffel Tower, and subjugating the entire human race. The buildup in these trailers inevitably show pockets of resistance to this alien threat. The message is explicit: see how humanity resists domination and oppression.

What usually follows in these invasion flicks, is how humanity rallies and puts aside their differences to combat this overwhelming threat. This is the portion of the stories I tend to find the most interesting. On some level, perhaps I yearn for such a world, where we can dispense with the artificial constraints of made-up borders—both of land as well as the mind. The problem with these movies, however, is that they do not go beyond the inevitable victory of humanity. Do we need a threat greater than ourselves to come together? What happens afterward?

This chapter seeks to engage with the idea of mutual aid. A foundational notion for many anarchists, this is not a foreign concept to social work either (Shulman, 2016; Steinberg, 2010). What may be a challenge is to go beyond the notion and to challenge assumptions that seem to be made about the nature of society. Ruling authority is usually legitimated by notions of a humanity that will eat its young if left without supervision. In such a position, the development of a collective responsibility and care via mutual aid is assumed hence to be something that we teach or train communities to learn and come to see the benefits of.

Anarchists reject such a bleak view of ourselves. Returning to the movie theater and its womb-like comforts, staring at the spectacle of the world uniting against the alien antagonists, I believe that it isn't all misdirection. What if it is *in extremis* that our true natures emerge? What if the negative perceptions of society without rules are created? The real fiction isn't spaceships and laser bolts but the idea that collective self-governance would collapse under our flawed and selfish motivations.

When teaching Human Behaviour and the Environment, we review both Piaget and the spiritual analogue by Fowler that posits a notion of morality that first requires supervision before internalization (Zastrow & Kirst-Ashman, 2016)—Such ideas reinforce the idea that, at our base, we are incapable of empathy, care, and collective action—at least not before training and direction by an authority figure, parent or otherwise.

Something interesting happened as I was preparing for a class lecture to conclude a course on clinical practice. I was intrigued by references in our textbook about fostering mutual aid in group work (Shulman, 2016). Given my growing interest in anarchism, the same term continued to emerge. While the balance of this book has sought to draw connections between these two—social work and anarchism—I wonder if perhaps this concept can ultimately cement a relationship.

In preparing for the aforementioned lecture, I came across the idea of "elite panic" (Clarke & Chess, 2008). In essence, those in authority panic when a crisis that threatens society looms. It is their actions in relation to the fears they hold that result in chaos. In *A Paradise Built in Hell*, Rebecca Solnit (2010) paints a different picture. Here, stories are told of when communities, such as San Francisco after the earthquake in 1906, were able to engage in mutual aid. Communities were mobilizing to help families look for buried loved ones. Businesses who were already looking at writing off their inventory as a total loss, collaborated to make their food and other resources available. The people of San Francisco, in the midst of the most terrible experience of their lives, were able to transcend their atomized existence and rally as a collective. Solnit (2010) writes compellingly of further disasters where the innate capacity for mutual aid emerges. Such stories run counter to when authorities seek to intervene—dispatching police and the military, shooting "looters," and enforcing relief efforts that are regimented and signal a deep distrust in the capacity of civilians to care for each other fully and freely.

The following will be a summary of key ideas, both in anarchism and in social work, as to what constitutes mutual aid. Furthermore, mutual aid is looked at with the question of what conditions are needed for this to become possible. Finally, looking for ways to connect social work and anarchist ideas related to this phenomenon constitutes the discussion around what anarchist social work could be.

Before we go too far afield, I want to thank Dr Michael Yellow Bird (personal communication, June 14, 2021), for his insight as well as patience in discussing this topic with me. It is important that we don't dismiss the reality of in-group and out-group phenomena. Discrimination and othering are powerful ways of reinforcing differences and disrupting mutual aid. If, at the center, we are all hardwired to be a community that is greater than the sum of its parts, then racism and other forms of discrimination must be confronted. While other chapters engage with this topic more fully, it is important that we do not lose sight of the pernicious and odious influence of racism and all the other "isms" that serve to divide and justify oppression. It is my belief that these forces are the product of ongoing narratives that serve to justify power and authority. The entire project of expansion, of colonization, needed a narrative that would justify the splintering of any potential for collective identification, for the natural practice of mutual aid—hence narratives of difference that justified hierarchy and domination. When I think of anarchist ideas about how borders have been internalized, I am reminded of Harsha Walia (2021). Even the way we conceptualize the term "refugee" is carefully constructed to privilege and benefit those who either look like us or, in the Cold War, are fleeing an ideology we are against. Economic or ecological refugees from Black, Indigenous and People of Color (BIPOC) destinations are othered, incarcerated, and made illegal. Such ideas are not natural but require intentional construction by a state that needs to legitimize its own existence.

Mutual aid

I recall when I first discovered my love for the field of social work. Oddly enough, it took me to psychology first. As part of my liberal arts degree, I took Social Psychology. I was fascinated by the idea that we are shaped by social forces and that groups can be understood based on theories from this field of knowledge. Invariably, studies that described a dark essential human nature became the focus: The Stanford Prison Experiment, the Milgram Study, and the fate of poor Kitty Genovese. At the time, it was becoming clear to me, that the field of psychology was reporting and validating what Hobbes claimed about the short and brutish life without a sovereign or state to protect via their authority (Graeber & Wengrow, 2021; Knuttila, 1992). We need supervision, as we not only will do terrible things if left unattended but in the hands of ruthless leaders, we will also fall prey to our base natures and commit terrible acts upon each other.

Since then, I have come to appreciate the influence of the environment on the human condition. As a social worker, I believe in the healing work that can happen when people are supported in their social spheres by others such as family, friends, and community. Furthermore, since questions have been asked about the aforementioned either in their methods or in their findings or both (e.g. the Stanford Prison Experiment (Perry, 2018) and the Milgram Study (Haslam & Reicher, 2014), it is even more important to challenge the claims that they were making about our shared humanity.

A short brutish life: Challenges to mutual aid

It is fair for the reader to be skeptical of the assumptions behind mutual aid. One could argue that it is naïve to believe in the essential goodness of humanity; there certainly is enough evidence of genocide and the horrors of war to challenge this narrative. As stated earlier, my own encounter with social psychology included stories that seemed to validate this idea. "Bystander indifference" is a "pervasive psychological theory" (Hardie, 2010, p. 337) influenced by the tragic story local news story of Kitty Genovese (Hardie, 2010). A diffusion of social responsibility is posited where we tend to become apathetic when it is unclear who is in charge. The case of Kitty Genovese is used to illustrate how a whole community failed to call the police as she was stalked, assaulted, and ultimately killed by an assailant. Many neighbors had heard her cries but did not intervene. This particular story has launched many papers and books on the subject, and one could argue or make the case that we are not essentially Good Samaritans. What if this is not the whole story?

First of all, the events may not have been described correctly (Kitty Genovese, revised, 2007). The initial news story referred to three attacks by the assailant and no actions taken by the 38 residents that were home at the time. In fact, there were two attacks, and a neighbor did call the police after the first assault. At this time, Kitty's movements became difficult to track, as she had managed to get behind a building to a foyer. It is probable that neighbors would not have been able to see her. The second attack likely occurred without neighbors being aware. In fact, witnesses to this terrible event would later claim that, given the time of night, they had assumed this was a lover's quarrel that had spilled out from a local pub. It wasn't apathy but confusion and uncertainty of what was happening that may be a more likely explanation of events. That said, attempts to call the police had been made.

Writer Jim Rasenberger (2006) goes further to challenge how the mainstream media reported the story. The 38 residents of Kitty's Genovese's neighborhood were targeted for their failure to help as she cried for anyone to notice. In fact, news specials dedicated airtime to reflect on how apathetic Americans were, reflecting an increasingly amoral modern society. Rasenberger claims that the story is wrong from the beginning. The number of witnesses was likely an exaggeration, given the urban geography impeding the ability to hear or see clearly what was happening. Rasenberger argues it was most likely six or seven, not 38 people, that would have been witnesses at the time. It is also important to know how this story emerged in the first place. A young editor got a tip about this crime. The picture of a cold and uncaring New York neighborhood was false. In fact, aside from evidence that calls to the police had taken place, efforts to care for poor Kitty Genovese by her neighbors, as she lay dying, exist as well.

We may sometimes reflect on how science, even social sciences, can fall prey to our expectations or assumptions about the world we live in. The case in point above is to illustrate how our expectations of our collective humanity have been shaped by an idea that may not stand scrutiny. There is compelling evidence to suggest that we may be better than we think, especially if not compelled by the organized violence of the state. The remaining portion of this chapter will engage with the concept of mutual aid. There are connections between mutual aid and social work which will be explored as well.

Anarchism and mutual aid

Mutual aid as a key ingredient of anarchist thought and practice has been attributed to the Russian anarchist geographer Petr Kropotkin and his attempts to do so via his geographical discoveries (Day, 2005; Marshall, 2010; Van Meter, 2017). During a time when Darwin's ideas were being seized upon to justify a survival of the fittest ideology, he would pen his book, *Mutual Aid*. Social Darwinism is based on the idea that evolution favors the strong and that the weak wither as an evolutionary footnote at best.

Hence, he echoed this approach, looking to the physical world to construct an analogue for human behavior grounded in science. The case he makes in his work is to essentially disprove what has been said about evolution itself. It isn't the individual animal that succeeds but a collective response to the threat encountered in nature (Kropotkin, 2017). In fact, he argues that the tendency to sacrifice one's own finite existence for the good of others is instinctual. To put it plainly, mutual aid is an essential ingredient for survival. Finn (2021) refers to the analogy of being in a lifeboat as a refutation of the misunderstood, banal "survival of the fittest" adage attached to social Darwinism. In effect, people risking, even sacrificing, themselves for people they do not know, and for no material gain, is inherently how he sees mutual aid as challenging how survival as a species is to be understood.

Other anarchists have built off this argument and expanded, both in terms of the value of this practice and the pragmatics of its utility. Some have incorporated notions of a prefiguration (of anarchist futures) by the practice of mutual aid in the here and now (e.g. Laursen, 2021). Others have, especially during COVID, pointed out that this form of aid is best as it builds community while avoiding the condescension and disempowerment of charity-based approaches (Firth, 2022). Some have made the connection that mutual aid has roots in groups like the Quakers, themselves having learnt this practice from Indigenous groups in so-called North America (Graeber, 2004).

There are various ways that mutual aid has been understood in anarchism. By no means exhaustive, the following are illustrations of the ways that anarchism has described the importance of this practice and idea.

War & Mutual Aid

For example, several attempts have been made to unpack the idea of mutual aid during WWII. Romande Anarchist Federation in 1939 wrote how mutual aid can be seen as an antidote for going to war. In fact, competition is not the problem; if practiced in the spirit of seeking to improve everyone's lot in life, it can be a step toward a future free of war. They make a compelling argument in dispelling the aspersion or dismissal of such ideas as "utopian." "But, accepting this criticism implies despairing of ever realizing a truly human life, and forces people to remain attached to the worst forms of degradation and death" (Romande Anarchist Federation, 2009, p. 13). The Korean anarchists, writing in 1945 and having experienced the harsh conditions of

Japanese occupation, articulated a position of needing to practice mutual aid "not only must we overthrow Japanese imperialism, but also eradicate the internal evils of lack of freedom, inequality, and mutual antagonism. In their place we must lay a foundation of mutual aid, upon which to build a new society based on freedom and equality" ("The Korean anarchist manifesto," 2009, p. 38). In some ways, this can be understood not as prefiguration but as inoculation from future colonization being as successful in occupation and domination of the Korean people as the Japanese had been. Leftist philosopher Paul Goodman (2009), writing in 1945, argues that a new form of idolatry is at work which mutual aid can combat. He warns of a kind of "sociolotry," or the idolatry of society being supported by new technologies and formally organized societal structures that inhibit our desire for insurrection and promote the good life. "What is being suggested is that our disgust or concern is muted as our general living standard is being supported by industrialization" (p. 53).

Ultimately, mutual aid is seen here as a way to break free of this malaise. Goodman speaks of a form of mutual aid which has distinct features, such as mutual encouragement and care. He believed that the best form of mutual aid association is of the small group variety, as members need to be face-to-face to maximize the benefits. This then gets developed further into more progressive interactions with others, essentially building up the threads of mutual aid from the ground up.

A year later, in 1946, Alex Comfort, British scientist and anarchist (and author of the *Joy of Sex*), writes of peace and disobedience, where mutual aid is key (Comfort, 2009a). Again, the idea here is that mutual aid is not predicated on the notion of prefiguration, but rather as a way to prepare—that all war is bad—and that war is not an unhappy accident but is always planned and based on policy. Hence, as war is a totalizing force that tends to "subvert all existing social organizations, to sweep away its makers rather than to maintain their power" (p. 58), there are hence three duties one must hold to: to resist, to educate, and to build mutual aid. In fact, Comfort argues that the building of mutual aid is the way to survive the fall of western society to tyranny. Given the timing of when he was writing these words, it is clear that the specter of fascism remained in his thoughts throughout.

Alex Comfort (2009b) elaborates on how he imagines the practice of mutual aid in surviving tyranny when writing about art and social responsibility. In fact, the harbinger of insanity or madness, as he sees it in the late stage of empire, is the death of mutual aid itself.

> At a definite point in the history of every civilization, and shortly before its economic peak, there occurs a transfer of civic obligation, from the community based on mutual aid to the society based upon common irresponsibility. It manifests itself as an industrial revolution, a megalopolitan development of the city . . . and thereafter the barbarian revolution has taken place, and the actions of that society are irresponsible, and its members insane. (p. 105)

Essentially, our collective morality is undermined when the structures of the state and imperial aspiration take over. A nation can go to war and kill others, which is the ultimate insanity, as we collectively abdicate all responsibility. However, Comfort also sees the seed for futures in the ongoing alcoves of resistance within mutual aid. Rather than prefiguring a future, it is about ensuring that the future will have these seeds to work with.

> The weak are inheriting the earth . . . They are taxed, killed, frightened, conscripted, swindled . . . the gangs of good citizens drive them like sheep . . . Their sane moments are ultimately decisive. Their clinging among the wreckage to mutual aid perpetuates civilization . . . The woman who fails to fuse a shell securely, the clerk who does not look a second time at a pass . . . are acting as members and soldiers of the community of the weak, the greatest conspiracy in history, which is ceaseless. (pp. 110–111)

Italian anarchist and author, Marie Louise Berneri, in 1949 writes of mutual aid in the context of reclaiming a connection to each other that goes beyond the divisions of class and nation. "Loyalty to the state often demands the negation of the feeling of solidarity and mutual aid which naturally exists between men [sic]" (2009, p. 80). Through the logic of the state, a code of conduct is developed which governs the relationships we have with each other. In so doing, a split or compartmentalization emerges where we are courteous and friendly to our fellow citizens, but can be cruel or indifferent to the plight of others. "[H]e loves peace at home but carries out the most ruthless wars abroad" (p. 80).

Italian architect and anarchist, Giancarlo DeCarlo (2009)—after serving in the Italian anti-fascist resistance—writes of mutual aid in 1948. His idea is that mutual aid ought to be a feature of efforts to setting up tenant collectives not necessarily as prefigurative but rather as parallel structures in opposition to the state.

> We cannot count on the state's financial assistance... For this reason the financing must also be autonomous, arising from local circumstance based as far as possible on the mutual aid of the members of the collective, contributing money, in hours of work, in produce, and demanding assistance from those who at present have in their hands the wealth that properly belongs to the community. (p. 98)

To illustrate his position, he refers to the squatting movements that occurred in England post WWI and in Italy post WWII. In particular, it is in Messina, Italy, for example, that the archbishop's mansion was occupied in such a way. He notes how this mansion, consisting of 3,000 rooms, stood empty while people were homeless and desperate. Occupation of this space was a form of mutual aid in his view. Further, he believed that rent strikes where tenants refuse to pay rent as a group and refuse to move was a legitimate form of direct action in the spirit of mutual aid and resistance.

Mutual Aid & the Buereaucracy of the state

British political scientist, Geoffrey Ostergaard (2009), wrote in 1954 about a managerial revolution. He articulates the view that the British Fabian movement has harmed the socialist project in that it has mainstreamed notions of responsibility for the poor. These then are patronizing and paternal via the existing system of bureaucratization and governance—a socialism fit for the middle class to which Fabian socialists tend to belong. In effect, the structures that are created by Fabian socialism disrupt the natural state of being which would include mutual aid. Ostergaard laments how social efficiency via managerial administration and its associated bureaucratic mechanisms runs the risk of reducing socialism to mere social engineering and, "making it a task, once political power has been achieved, not for the ordinary stupid mortal but for the super-intelligent administrator armed with facts and figures which had been provided by diligent research" (2009, p. 156). People are being managed for their own good, and a national minimum standard of living is set for the people. Thus, the process of state socialism creates a smoke screen with "the public interest" wielded as a construct to hide the true capitalists that benefit from such a process at the top.

Between 1957 and 1962, French anarchist collective, Noir et Rouge (2009) further caution how the state subverts mutual aid via a series of strategies.

This includes employing church, army, and political parties to pit people against each other with strategies such as bureaucracy, hierarchy, and the drumbeat of war. Instead of binding them together in solidarity, cooperation, and the practice of mutual aid, the state employs essentially a divide and conquer approach to society by disrupting natural structures of cooperation, solidarity, and mutual aid.

Mutual Aid vs the State

In 1962, British anarchist and writer, Nicolas Walter (2009) described mutual aid as part of a larger effort. Along with civil disobedience and education, mutual aid is part of direct action to challenge what he called the "warfare state" (p. 205). Whereas fellow Brit, art historian, and anarchist Herbert Read (2009) would write during the 1940's about the intrinsic value of mutual aid. He would add that mutual aid is the center of anarchism by way of defining the extremes. Essentially, the moderate approach compared to the liberal veneration of the individual versus the totalitarianism of the collective in communist or state socialist ideas. In effect mutual aid as practice illustrates the anarchist belief that society can be organized on a cooperative basis—free of enforcement or dictates from a state. He goes as far as to suggest that mutual aid and the spirit behind it (of love) are best captured in the Sermon on the Mount.

Why do we give up mutual aid and default to the authority of the state? Cuban anarchist Jacobo Prince (2009) would argue that it is in part because organizing and mutual aid is work. It takes commitment and dedication to create and maintain. "The broad masses, including the most enlightened and idealistic persons among them, paid a very high price for their attachment to that magical formula that promised to spare them the great exertions and mutual aid required to organize, from the bottom up, a genuinely free, fraternal, socialist society" (p. 304).

In contrast, American philosopher David Thoreau Wieck (2009) suggests that mutual aid is part of a natural tendency being suppressed by the state. It is our tacit acceptance of current structures that needs to be usurped or disrupted, as we articulate a return to a more natural state where the capacity for mutual aid emerges once more. "Men [sic] possess a natural tendency to solidarity, to cooperation. This tendency our social institutions check and even suppress. Let men [sic] rid themselves of these constraints, and we will come into our biological heritage of mutual aid" (p. 231).

Journalist and author, Eric Laursen, in describing the state as a hostile operating system (2021) claims that mutual aid had been practiced over 150 years ago in communities where this was then subsumed under the state or absorbed by it. What is key for social work may be in how he argues this process was hijacked by the state. Essentially it began to create, "social insurance and welfare programs that borrowed from and effectively absorbed the practices of mutual aid that had long existed in traditional communities and were being adapted by members of the new urban working class for the industrial age" (p. 209). The question that needs to be confronted here is whether the new urban working class are social workers, supporting a bureaucratic, now neoliberal, welfare state.

Laursen (2021) takes this idea further when discussing "core identity groups" in his book which are the recipients of privilege. The bastardized version of mutual aid—now the modern welfare system—is inherently inequal in distribution and tends to privilege the "core identity group" versus marginalized groups. Furthermore, any state-inherited institution (i.e. former mutual aid systems) that carries the seeds of resistance must be controlled and surveilled. As a social worker, this may sound like the tendency by the state to control social services via reporting requirements and auditing mechanisms.

In contrast to the state, Laursen's idea of mutual aid takes shape in how he refers to grassroots activist, prison abolitionist, and scholar, Mariam Kaba who, during the COVID-19 pandemic described mutual aid as a path that cannot be predicted. A process leading to more projects and opportunities simultaneously, while people who were responding to the collective nightmare of health emergencies, lockdown, and associated isolation were reaching out to others in need. She sees this as the grist for a future mill of political action and community development (p. 211). Perhaps it is in these perspectives that the state sees the danger of a world where they are no longer necessary.

Regardless of the state's attempts at what Rhiannon Firth (2022) refers to as recuperation (the taking over of mutual aid), Laursen (2021) points to present examples where mutual aid formed the basis of community. From Russian anarchists (e.g. Tolstoy) to current anarchist thinkers, there is the tendency to seek to learn from those who are or always have been practicing a kind of anarchist living based on the principle of mutual aid. In Russia, it was the peasant communities post WWI that managed to live in this way. In South America he points to examples such as Bolivia, where Evo Morales rose to prominence by employing centuries-old traditional governance in the

Andes. "The Presidency of Evo Morales Ayma drew its organising strength from the *ayllus* (italics in original), a centuries-old Andean form of community that includes rotating leadership, an ethic built on mutual aid" (p. 214).

What Wieck may have described as insidious suppression, Taylor, writing in 1976, sees as more of a blunt assault by the state to destroy altruism (2009). He approaches this argument by referencing Kropotkin and his work, *Mutual Aid* (2009), to illustrate how the state has destroyed altruism. By taking up the functions of local mutual aid, welfare and so on are now in the hands of the state. This process heightens individualism, and altruism ceases to be practiced, witnessed, or experienced. This is connected to how Kropotkin identifies the process of the state during the late 15th century. States or proto-states would systematically eliminate mutual aid institutions at the local level (Day, 2017, p. 122). In doing so, they would enhance dependency on the state for the functions that mutual aid would have provided. This then results in creating and fostering an individualism that prefers to be free of the burden of collective practices in mutual aid (Wieck, 2009). What deserves further comment is how experiential learning is implicit in this argument. If we cannot experience the joy of mutual aid, we are less likely to discover and practice it.

Mutual aid vs Ideas of the nation (state)

Academic and activist Harsha Walia (2013) sees the plight of refugees and immigrants and the colonized and dispossessed as a way to understand mutual aid. Key is how she is able to see mutual aid as a path to connection between diverse groups of dispossessed and oppressed peoples. She argues that it is because of the fallout from neoliberalism via free trade agreements, that the plight of the undocumented is a shared suffering from the same forces that dispossessed, displaced, and colonized others. In sum, she makes the point that mutual aid is at work in how organizations such as No One Is Illegal are working to ensure their activism does not infringe or interfere with Indigenous groups seeking their liberation from the settler state. This shared solidarity is illustrated as she refers to immigrant and refugee groups meeting with Indigenous land defenders blockading extractive capitalists in British Columbia. Further examples include delegations in Montreal of non-status Algerians who met with Mohawk groups who in turn have participated in actions opposing deportations.

Graham (2013) would agree that the fault lies with nations and borders and what has disrupted mutual aid are the divisive notions of nations, race, and colonization. In fact, he refers to examples such as African anarchists, who "have sought to build upon the precolonial history of people living without States in egalitarian communities, particularly in light of the disastrous consequences of colonialism and the division of Africa into nation States whose borders were arbitrarily set by the former colonial powers (p. 575). Kurdish anarchists also see their own tribal traditions reflected in anarchist ideas of a decentralized approach to organizing. Their sympathy with anarchist rejection of nations states which have tried to control them has predisposed them to "the development of a community assembly movement drawing on the ideas of Murray Bookchin" (p. 575).

It is clear that Graham makes the argument that mutual aid, as a force that helps the common people survive the difficult and oppressive life under capitalism, is always there, ready to be used as a life-affirming practice. By engaging in these acts of resistance and care, the potential for a better world is coexisting within and alongside the oppressive shadow of the state.

Racial perspectives on Mutual Aid

Extending the racial perspectives on mutual aid, the Afrofuturist Abolitionists of the Americas (2019) write about how the ongoing exploitation by capital has a deeply racist nature. Black and brown bodies are bombed, as resources are extracted from Africa and the Middle East in order to continue to drive this project. It continues despite Black representation in media or politics, as the majority of BIPOC continue to experience violent oppression and exploitation—both in other countries and in North America. This is echoed by Black anarchist and writer, William C. Anderson (2021) who notes that the Black experience of fascism in America is unique. "We know what fascism is because it's there on the faces of our killers. Surviving this all is one thing, but moving beyond that to claim our right to be liberated and safe is another" (p. 35).

The Afrofuturist Abolitionists of the Americas (2019) echo the ideas of building strong communities as parallel structures (to the state) and the promotion of mutual aid systems. Key is a mutual aid that is distinct, and indeed different, from charity.

Mutual Aid is a voluntary reciprocal exchange of resources and services for the mutual benefit of everyone. Mutual aid, as opposed to charity, does not imply moral superiority of the giver over the receiver. Examples include organizing and benefitting from food drives, donating clothing or money directly to those in need, financial advice, tutoring, child-care, help navigating social services, and community defense networks, to name a few. Mutual Aid is based on the principle of investing in our communities now, for a return later. Under capitalism, the person who offers aid today may be the person who needs Aid tomorrow. Strong communities practice mutual aid. (p. 4)

They call for an Asset Based Community Development (ABCD) model that cultivates a particular kind of mutual aid. Like a strength-based perspective of communities, it is the idea that aid does not come from outside but rather a closed system. Communities that practice this form of self-governance are parallel structures that no longer rely on the state and hence reduce its impact and import.

Anderson (2021), by reminding us of the Black Panther's motto of 'Survival Pending Revolution', conceptualizes mutual aid that taps into existing forms of such survival already underway. By partnering with these efforts, the reaction to current conditions of Black oppression under capitalism can foster community but stresses the importance to view these efforts as transitional in nature, connected to a greater vision of transformative change. Along with this idea is the concern of the co-optation of radical ideas of transformation, such as abolition, which due to the increasing popularity of such ideas, is ever present.

Black Flag Sydney (2021) echo the concerns of co-optation where mutual aid is reduced to mere charity and defanged of its political orientation and aims. By writing that they are against mutual aid, they are not opposed to the idea but the action. In today's society, the reciprocity in mutual aid disappears or is less accentuated, and the distinction between charity and mutual aid collapses. One explanation they offer for this phenomenon has to do with how capitalism conditions or shapes our minds. This results in seeing mutual aid as a practice predicated on conditional exchanges for a specific purpose. It is in effect a functional activity, divorced of the culture that takes time to develop in mutual aid networks. Hence, mutual aid is primarily practiced as a form of service provision.

From a practical standpoint, the more developed a mutual aid organization becomes, the more it needs to depoliticize itself in order to access resources. Black Flag Sydney argues that this is seen in how Non Governmental Organizations (NGO) must frame a refugee crisis in humanitarian terms rather than the result of calculated political maneuvers involving war, the exploitation of neoliberal corporations, and so on. Doing this allows NGOs to tap into a broader array of philanthropic resources. This is captured well when reflecting on how to engage in mutual aid to address food insecurity. Essentially, if you are seeking to move food from the surplus of the grocery store to the people, you will likely not criticize the supermarket in how it underpays its staff.

From a class perspective, this results in shifting from raising working class consciousness and finding their own empowerment to the community as the focus with pleas for donations—effectively an illustration of how mutual aid groups depoliticize the process (Black Flag Sydney, 2021). They make the case that social work practice has been involved in this defanging process, even impacting those who had originally been Black Panthers.

> Whilst the label "mutual aid" is new, the practice of leftists engaging in social work is not; such activities were a mainstay of the many American New Left groups of the 60s and 70s. For the Black Panthers—romanticised by an enormous section of the left—the network of social support organisations they had built up like breakfast programmes and schools led, in part, to the integration of many Panthers into liberal-democratic electoral politics. (p. 6)

Ultimately the main point here is to return to the concept of mutual aid. What this means is that the practice of mutual aid was never to be bedfellows with capital to solve problems. The improvement of material (and other) conditions should not be ends but means. In other words, in contrast to what DeCarlo (2009) and the Afrofuturist Abolitionists of the Americas (2019) are saying about mutual aid—as the building of community power through parallel structures that avoids the work of dismantling or abolishing capitalism itself—real mutual aid, according to Black Flag Sydney (2021), is about keeping that focus beyond the immediate needs being addressed. In some ways, this concern—of practice removing real motivation for change—can be found in the Structural Social Work critique of social work practice as well (Mullaly, 2007).

Indigenous anarchist Regan de Loggans (2020) echoes similar sentiments as they pertain to the practice of mutual aid. They argue that mutual aid is essentially impossible for capitalism to practice. All capitalism can do is to engage in temporary relocation via philanthropy, also known as charity. In fact, the aspect of time is key to distinguish between charity and true mutual aid. A momentary action or response is charity. Long-term investment in the living breathing web of community is mutual aid.

While Anderson (2021) argues that Black communities have always practiced mutual aid in North America as a necessary practice of survival, de Loggans points to a larger, Indigenous project. They make the case that Mutual Aid has been co-opted by anarcho-communists, White scholars who risk erasing the long-standing tradition by Indigenous cultures who have practiced this since time immemorial. This point is further expanded on in the final chapter of this book, as Indigenous ways of knowing and Indigenous anarchisms deserve consideration and amplification in any work having to do with resistance to colonization and the White supremacist system that dominates all our lives.

Regan de Loggans' views on mutual aid include some further elaboration, especially in how it operates in contrast to the reductionist or even as Firth (2022) cautions, the recuperation of these movements. First, they caution that one must avoid the reciprocity trap. Once this begins, a kind of tit for tat takes over. In fact, de Loggans would argue that this can lead to a valuing of labor itself then. The fact is that some of the labor in mutual aid is emotional—such as caring or mentoring of the young by elders for example.

> We also do not measure things based in equal reciprocity, we do not need to practice payment or profit. In fact, we SHOULD NOT practice profit or payment. Mutual aid is not done from the kindness of our hearts (though that helps), it is done because we respect people's autonomous lives and want our communities to thrive. No one is expected to "pay" for anything, and there will be many unequal knowledge shares that are practiced, AND THAT'S OK. Stop viewing all actions as transactions or as tit for tat. We provide for the greater good and because we can and want to. (de Loggans, 2020, p. 4)

As has already been stated in this chapter, there is a tradition of mutual aid that precedes formal (Western) writings on the subject. While in no way exhaustive, the following is a sampling of Indigenous understandings of mutual aid that reflect this reality and deserve recognition.

Indigenous frameworks for mutual aid

Indigenous scholar Glen Couthard (2008) notes that Frantz Fanon's ideas can help us understand how mutuality is undermined via the politics of recognition. In effect, the acceptance of a non-mutual form of recognition (despite and maybe because of the desire of Indigenous nations seeking recognition) produces an internalized alienation of the self by the colonized in that they have to accept the "equal" merit of a settler state in order to be granted recognition (p. 194). Hence it is a good reminder of how mutuality (and its relationship to mutual aid) needs to be considerate of intersectionality and positionality of the subject (for each and all involved), or we reproduce oppression in the name of mutual aid. Enough examples exist, according to Couthard, of the tacit acceptance of "White justice," which privileges settlers and the internalization of this is for Indigenous peoples to assume that courts of law will be even or impartial in their actions.

Basically, "the liberal discourse of recognition has been limited and constrained by the state, politicians, corporations and the courts in ways that pose no fundamental challenge to the colonial relationship" (p. 195). Ultimately, by resisting colonial constructions (including of the Indigenous self/collective) and prefiguring an alternative to the colonial present, Indigenous ways offer not only the promise of Indigenous resurgence but also a model for living without or beyond imperialism. Here we have examples of Indigenous thinking that parallels that of anarchist ideas of a form of mutual aid that prefigures a reality without and beyond the state.

Mutual Aid and Harm Reduction

Mutual aid has another connection to social work by way of harm reduction. Faculty member at Memorial University School of Social Work, activist, and anarchist scholar, Christopher B. R. Smith (2012) writes about how a specific form of mutual aid has been defanged by capitalism. "Harm reduction" has been associated with anarchism in that it has origins in mutual aid and was practiced when the government failed to address suffering by people deemed lesser in society. Back in the 80s, hippies and anarchists illegally distributed clean syringes to drug users to combat HIV/AIDS.

Harm reduction then, is grounded in the same idea of mutual aid with anarchism at the root. When public health organizations sought to institutionalize harm reduction into public policy, they essentially defanged it. Smith (2012) argues that we need to reconnect harm reduction to ideas of anarchism in order to return it to it's potential as a liberatory and empowering force.

> The core values of anarchism are reflected in many elements of the founding philosophy—if not always the actual practice—of harm reduction. Growing out of the oppositional spirit of the movement, harm reduction discourse might therefore be seen as a disguised language developed to describe an emergent anarchist model of care for capitalism's most oppressed, yet symptomatic victims. (p. 8)

Human nature and the anarchist ideal

Key to much of the discussion around mutual aid is the idea of human nature itself. As has been evident, anarchists tend to have a more optimistic view of the human condition. Anarchist anthropologist, David Graeber, in his coauthored book, *The Dawn of Everything* (Graeber & Wengrow, 2021) makes a compelling case for reinvestigating what we assume to know about our collective past. Returning to the short and brutish nature of early civilization, they argue that such an account of our past is due to faulty and irresponsible scholarship. In fact, archaeological finds have been documented that challenge this narrative, where it is apparent that people who ought to have not passed the evolutionary imperative of survival of the fittest are buried with great care and affection by a loving community. Such evidence seems to suggest that, as Kropotkin had claimed so long ago, mutual aid was present in evolution and in fact can be discovered in our own bones.

David Graeber and Andrej Grubacic (2020) illustrate this further by referring to the Huron-Wendat statesman Kondiaronk and his critique of European society in the 1680s. A French colonizer by the name of Lahontan wrote a book documenting conversations with Kondiaronk which shaped the way future enlightenment scholars would frame their thinking of society into the 18th century. The ideas of enlightened western society were challenged to such a degree that Adam Smith had to invent notions of social evolution to refute them. The idea of capital and property needed to be recast as rational and enlightened aspects of modern civilization. Essentially, Kondiaronk asks why settlers are seeking private property and wealth accumulation since these ideas create the conditions that make people behave in ways that make coercion necessary.

While the threat of Indigenous critique is rationalized away by enlightenment writers, Graeber and Grubacic argue that Kropotkin sought to challenge the evolutionary theories that become arguments to support this bleak and brutish view of human nature. They point out that Herbert Spencer's term "survival of the fittest" ultimately is to blame for Darwin's use of it which has provided cover for genocide and colonization ever since. As previously stated, Kropotkin refutes these ideas by using his own observations, and the work of other Russian zoologists, to argue that natural selection is the product of cooperation, not competition. Key to Graeber and Grubacic's argument is how notions of mutual aid are undermined by paradigms of science that reinforce the hegemony of capital. Essentially, the point is being made that Darwinian science was hijacked by market place liberals. That it was based onon the absurdity of a hypercompetitive mindset—not on an objective idea of nature as it had claimed.

It is compelling to point to nature as proof of one's own ideology being validated. As will be discussed further in the conclusion, this can go both ways and may not be the best argument in favor of mutual aid. However, as is becoming more evident, with global climate change, geo-political unrest, and economic uncertainty, fascism is mounting a comeback. Along with this ideology of hate, the return of pseudoscience to validate White supremacy is of increasing concern. One could argue that the formation of sociobiology and evolutionary psychology are attempts to counter Kropotkin's view of mutual aid in nature and to bring back the Darwinian justifications that validate capitalism and the use of organized violence via the state to uphold "order."

Given these concerns then, it is important to note how the left handled mutual aid and specifically Kropotkin's work on this (Graeber & Grubacic, 2020). They largely ignored or ridiculed him versus trying to challenge his notions, as they worked to legitimate the state—although much of the modern welfare state is the product of mutual aid groups and the formalizing of these structures via the modern state. This is important to note as even in Germany, Bismark admitted to creating the welfare system so that Germans wouldn't turn to socialism. Again, this resonates when considering

Rhiannon Firth's (2022) concerns about mutual aid and the recuperation of these movements by the state.

While leftists in government sought to incorporate mutual aid into top-down vanguardist parties, it may be tempting to assume that this was representative of what people in society were wanting. Graeber and Grubacic (2020) argue that this is a faulty assumption. In fact, between 1900 and 1917, the common people, or working class, were more on board with libertarian Marxist and anarchist ideas for socialism. This only changed after the Russian Revolution where the vanguardist Marxist–Leninist model gained popularity due to its apparent success.

It is easy to assume that most anarchist writers view Marx negatively, given the history of discord and attempts by Marxists to dismiss anarchists as crackpot utopians. Graeber and Grubacic (2020) instead offer a way to find common cause toward bringing back mutual aid as a key ingredient in making our lives collectively better for all. In effect, by connecting Kropotkin to Marx the authors argue that this is the way to then help us discover a mutual aid that is always present, even among the cracks of labour-alienating capitalist production.

What this would require is for modern social theories, including Marxist approaches, to reconsider the ideas of cooperation, altruism, generosity, and so on as legitimate factors versus some kind of bourgeoise affectation. In fact, Graeber (2004) makes the argument, by referring to the writings of revolutionary socialist anthropologist Marcel Mauss—himself a nephew of Emile Durkheim—and his critique of Lenin's imposition of the market economy in Russia. Graeber makes the claim that the origin of all contracts lies in communism. In fact, he engages with the anthropological record to challenge assumptions of what pre-capitalism societies were like. He rejects the idea of a barter system but rather argues that most "economies" were gift economies, "in which the distinctions we now make between interest and altruism, person and property, freedom and obligation, simply did not exist" (p. 17).

Why does this matter to mutual aid? Because, in effect, mutual aid challenges existing notions in the marketplace of receiving something for something. While later in this chapter more will be unpacked on the significance of mutual aid as a counter or even anti-hegemonic practice, the idea of gift economies, as presented by Graeber (2004) has merit. Gift economies and mutual aid have much in common in that they are not predicated on an immediate obligatory exchange. De-commodifying all goods and dispensing with money entirely doesn't result in a variation of the same theme but an entirely different one, where what is given is given freely as you would do too—once, or if able to. In fact, Graeber offers an intriguing idea related to gift economies: the entrepreneur cannot gain wealth in this system but rather can only excel at giving it all away. Finally, returning to Durkheim's notion of anomie, of alienation, he suggests that mutual aid is the inverse. By practicing, we decrease our alienation as we reconnect more with each other.

Perhaps another way to examine mutual aid as a legitimate approach to living a better life for all can be found in the geopolitical context of the now. Graeber and Grubacic (2020) point to current geopolitical movements, where a resurgence of ideas from Kropotkin and Bookchin are finding connection to cultural practices and ideas within Kurdish society such as in Rojava. Social ecology ideas are finding traction there as mutual aid is lived out in resistance to the state right now.

Echoing what other writers have found during our global pandemic, Graeber and Grubacic (2020) argue that the Global North is experiencing a new appreciation for the concepts around mutual aid due to the social movements such as Black Lives Matter (BLM) that is driving the need for a new way of engaging with each other. Even the mainstream media is discussing these ideas as legitimate approaches during the pandemic.

The politics of the now: Mutual aid and the pandemic

By now it is clear that much of this book was written as the pandemic began. Throughout this process, I kept wondering how anarchism would be practiced during a global shutdown. The following are such responses: how mutual aid is practiced during this difficult time.

Jun and Lance (2020) point to the dismal failure of the US administration during COVID as the reason why the anarchist response is a fitting case study of mutual aid. According to social movement theory, the spontaneous advent of a social movement is unrealistic. Generally, movements emerge from existing networks. According to these authors, the (Washington) DC chapter of BLM is a fitting illustration as a case in point. This group was formed initially as a response to police violence but has since expanded to address gentrification and domestic violence. It was this DC chapter of BLM that practiced mutual aid during the darkest days of the pandemic. Another example is how Serve Your Youth, an organization aimed at working with disadvantaged youth via sports, was able to pivot when everything got shuttered and to leverage their social capital in these communities to do effective outreach.

The DC Mutual Aid Network had been so successful in their work, going on grocery runs for vulnerable people such as senior citizens, addressing food insecurity issues for at-risk children, that the DC government had started referring to them on their government website as a legitimate resource (Jun & Lance, 2020). Of course, this does not mean that any real material support was provided by the state in this case.

> Mutual aid—solidarity, free cooperation—is a core concept of anarchist thought. It is the principle around which just social organization must be built. To embrace mutual aid as the sole legitimate organizing principle of society is to reject the institutionalization of any means of coercion, or of violence and the threat of violence. It is to embrace the idea that we can cooperatively reason with one another, and thereby instantiate our common inclination to build a society that benefits all without instituting any sort of hierarchy that functions to enforce such arrangements. (p. 6)

According to Jun and Lance (2020), the DC Mutual Aid position is that solidarity and cooperation are a kind of mutual aid which is not charity. The community is doing the work during the pandemic, including the risky tasks such as delivering groceries to potentially sick community members or doctors coming out of retirement. Furthermore, they argue that this is predicated on the reality that systems of governance were not acting fast enough and that communities hence had to rely on each other. In some ways, this illustrates what Solnit (2010) is saying when it comes to how disasters show us the true potential for care, cooperation, and mutual aid.

One could argue that mutual aid is only fine and good until a reason to stop someone who is harmful to the group emerges. Jun and Lance argue that the idea of only an essential goodness in people that needs to be unearthed is indeed utopian. Referencing Kropotkin, they claim that,

> Just as the nature and development of biological species results from the tension between competing inclinations toward mutual struggle and mutual aid, so, too, is human personality constituted by the conflict between sociability and individual processes of self-development. From the outset, human beings inhabit a reality that is shaped by a struggle between diametrically opposed forces, both internal and external (Kropotkin 1924, 24). Far

from being founded on any essentialized conception of human nature, the ethical significance of solidarity, cooperation, and mutual aid is itself a reflection of this struggle (Kropotkin. 2002, 119–20). (p. 7)

This does not mean that the use of force (for some anarchists) where this may be necessary (e.g. to stop a homicide, sexual assault) invalidates the principle of mutual aid. The removal from the community of those who seek to harm it and are unwilling to change behavior is not equivalent to invoking a form of policing. Jun and Lance argue that law enforcement is constituted on the use of force as an organizing principle of society. It is not the exception but the rule for police to use force and must be rejected. Communities need to organize based on mutual care and cooperation as the basis for a healthy alternative to the current status quo.

Finally, they argue that the anarchist ideas that could get us out of the ethical morass of humanism can be found in mutual aid. One of the critiques of Humanist ethics is that if we seek to maximize an individual's freedom, what do we do if it requires the violation of another's (Dolgoff, et al. 2012)? In mutual aid, according to Jun and Lance (2020), one is not free as an individual unless others are too. It is in connection and solidarity with others that real freedom emerges as a reality for all. This includes the principle of localism—in how the preference is to privilege local communities to handle their own affairs.

> Localism is another core idea that emerges from many currents of anarchist thought: the idea that whenever possible, decisions should be left up to local communities. This is both a principle that supports democracy and freedom—if there is no compelling reason to require uniformity, then it would be an assault on freedom to require all communities to act in the same manner—as well as an epistemic principle. Local communities know best what their own needs are, what local conditions are relevant to meeting those needs, and what social conditions and historical associations will constrain just solutions. (p. 10)

As already suggested, Rhiannon Firth (2022), in writing about mutual aid and radical action, would agree with many of the perspectives already shared about mutual aid. However, she notes that we must acknowledge that "[t]he rise of the state is a violent process of dispossession, enclosure and destruction of communal folk knowledge [that] has been echoed and developed from feminist, ecological and decolonial standpoints" (p 76). Furthermore, she notes that some anarchist and libertarian Marxist writers have described the state as not just imposing outside control but actively promoting an internal state of psychological alienation. In effect, the totalizing effect of state power is made evident in how our minds have been influenced to see ourselves only as self-interested individuals.

Firth (2022) takes this idea further in that she would argue that what is happening is that people have gotten to the point where they relate to each other through a performance. A false self that is the product of internalized oppression and results in relations predicated on personal advantage. The selfish motive disrupts any potential for solidarity and mutuality. Community organizing then, is a way to ward off state interference as these associations find ways to care for each other instead. There is real potential for social work to connect to this idea. Pointing to Indigenous notions of the individual, as reported by Nurit Bird-David, in contrast to western frameworks makes this plain. In her discovery of an oil-in-water sociology as practiced by a Nayaka forest-dwelling group in South India, she states that,

> Individuals are conceived to be already whole, yet they are able to join and coalesce with other individuals in the way that drops of oil and water amalgamate into a greater drop. She contrasts this to English society in sociology, where individuals are understood to be rational, unique and autonomous individuals, yet in a sense are incomplete. (p. 78)

This has implications for social work as well. Firth critiques self-change approaches that emphasize the idea of resilience. By focusing on individual survival and promoting strength to persevere, we are submitting to a framing of the world that promotes personal accountability and de-emphasizes collective action and solidarity in the face of the external violence of the state. Key to mutual aid is also to recognize that we need to be aware that the needs of others are different than one's own. Moralizing judgments about this have no place in true mutual aid as a practice (p. 83).

At the heart of her book, *Disaster Capitalism* (Firth, 2022) is the story of how mutual aid is successful when the state is not. While Occupy Wall Street was based on the frustration with neoliberal economic policies and failing banks, mutual aid was being practiced. Networks were cultivated that continued past the end of this spectacular grassroots action. When Hurricane Sandy devastated New York, these networks were actively engaged in bringing relief to people suffering in the aftermath of this natural disaster, with Occupy Sandy as its new moniker. While NGO's and the Federal Emergency Management System (FEMA) struggled to respond, real and pragmatic help was underway. Around 60,000 volunteers and $1.36 million in donations were deployed to great effect. People self-organized via anarchist principles, where volunteers would show up and plug into whatever was needed. The speed at which people could directly get involved ensured that help was arriving faster than even the Red Cross could organize. These self-organized groups included medics, construction workers, legal aid volunteers, experienced kitchen staff, and more. Interestingly, Firth illustrates how the principle of locality pays off in practice. "The size of hierarchical organizations means that they were not in touch with communities' needs in the same way as Occupy Sandy, which has local connections" (p. 102). In fact, one volunteer that she interviewed remarked that it was obvious that the Red Cross had supplies, but did not know where or how to deploy food to communities effectively.

Returning to how internalized oppression can impact the flourishing of true mutual aid, Firth cautions against recuperation by the state. While the Department of Homeland Security (DHS) applauded the mutual aid on the ground during Hurricane Sandy, it took the shape of praising the plucky nature of resilience, of not needing to rely on the state. Essentially, the neoliberal gaze encouraging a return to casting people as deserving and undeserving all over again. What is so important about mutual aid is that it seeks to challenge assumptions that charity leaves in place. In fact, Firth (2022) argues that people will refuse needed help due to the mental conditioning under capitalism. No one gets something without something else expected in return. Mutual aid disrupts this thought process, as it is never truly apolitical. The very idea of helping without conditions is anathema to a worldview based on owing others and being in their "debt." If we want to reach those on the margins with real impact, mutual aid may be a more effective way to reach those who truly need it. "Mutual aid and disaster relief disrupts neoliberal certainties about individualism, competitiveness and selfishness by showing that cooperative being in relating are not only possible and desirable, but in fact already exist and are an effective way to solve problems" (p. 105).

When it comes to the COVID-19 pandemic, it is important to remind the reader of the many currents of anarchism. What this means is that responses to this global disaster were not universal for anarchists. Some saw lockdown, getting vaccinated, and observing public health mandates as harm reduction while others viewed this as dystopian and the work of the state to engage in totalitarianism (Firth, 2022). What this means is that in mutual aid there are no easy or pre-cooked solutions. If anarchist groups are consistent in their ideological approach, they must work within groups and networks that aren't necessarily anarchist at all. In fact, Firth found that activists talked about the challenge of working with volunteers from across the political spectrum. For instance, middle-class folks saw their own worldview as apolitical and hence were baffled by some of the nonhierarchical organizing. On the other side, concerns are held in tension with how to reach consensus that doesn't devolve into countless decision-making sessions without any meaningful action.

Similar to Occupy Sandy, in the UK, the government engaged in recuperation when mutual aid emerged (Firth, 2020). While some of the action was material support, such as organizing food supplies and delivering to people in need, other efforts included using technology such as Skype or Zoom to check in on vulnerable neighbors and offer emotional support. The UK government framed all efforts as proof that government reliance is less necessary than good community-based mutual aid efforts. Over time efforts at recuperation included more formal approaches to help, including the expectation that those doing the helping must provide government identification and pass criminal record checks under the guise of transparency and accountability. This then results in excluding "many people from ever 'helping' and permanently relegates them to 'helped' status—that is, people such as refugees and asylum seekers, convicts on probation, people awaiting trial" (p. 153). Mutual aid then, is always in tension between attempts to recuperate by the state, sometimes by disregarding its political nature or by reorganizing into hierarchical structures of organization. However, Firth maintains the view that anarchist ideas such as the social principle are always present and, even when mutual aid arises spontaneously, have this potential to be lived out in practice.

Firth (2022) turns to Rebecca Solnit's thesis about disasters to further support ideas of mutual aid as a natural state of society. That it is- the intrusive attempts at control by the state that interferes with this natural state of an emergent practice of mutual aid when disaster strikes. Disasters have the potential to disrupt these institutions, resulting in the reappearance of the social principle. To further explore this idea, it is helpful to look at the problem with "elite panic" and Solnit's work, *A Paradise Built in Hell*.

Elite panic

Our past and our present, then, are held by those in power who hold to a different narrative about the human condition. Writer, historian, and activist, Rebecca Solnit (2010) writes evocatively of a world where mutual aid is a feature and not the bug. The reason why we do not see this clearly, in part, is due to the idea of "elite panic."

By showing the reader numerous examples of when disaster strikes, she builds a case for how people in crisis will come together in the spontaneous practice of mutual aid. Disaster studies have found that panic is actually a relatively uncommon reaction to crisis (Clarke & Chess, 2008). In fact, Solnit (2010) documents how recovery efforts after earthquakes are underway in an organized and voluntary fashion well before the authorities can deploy their professional resources to the site. After 9/11, it was informal networks on the scene that were distributing food, helping locate loved ones, and providing material support from outside of the radius of the Twin Tower attacks. When the government moved in, these networks were disrupted, despite their effectiveness at meeting a very real need on the ground.

It isn't people then, but those in authority who will panic (Clarke & Chess, 2008). It is their actions that compound the misery experienced by those at ground zero. There are some in sociology that argue that the likelihood of panic in the public due to disaster is so low that it may cease to exist as a legitimate argument. So why does this persist? Clarke and Chess, as well as Solnit suggest that it is largely ideological. It supports a view of the world which legitimizes the current structures and their authority. Furthermore, as stated at the outset, authority and their panic shapes how they view "the people." The argument has been made that the elite-policy makers and planners act as if the public's response to disaster is worse than the disaster itself. In fact, it may explain why the public will frequently be kept out of the loop, receiving only the most rudimentary information all delivered in soothing tones. Elite panic then, is when authorities will deploy law enforcement or the military due to the belief that the masses will riot. The result can be as drastic as people who are sharing food unconditionally being forced to accept regimented food relief that is controlled by military personnel (Solnit, 2010). This can be further compounded by the elites distrusting the people and providing incomplete or vague information, which understandably increases the anxiety of those kept in the dark (Clarke & Chess, 2008). As a case in point, they note how, in the aftermath of Hurricane Katrina, misinformation by the Governor of the state increased confusion and harm due to her own panic.

> Blanco's reaction was a case of elite panic, with non-trivial consequences. Misinformed about conditions on the ground and overly fearful of the loss of property, officials turned resources away from rescue in New Orleans. Elites responding after Katrina were disconnected from non-elites and obviously fearful of them. Further, their actions and inactions created greater danger for others. (p. 1004)

Another feature of how the image of the panicked masses stampeding is maintained lies in our own perceptions. Clarke and Chess (2008) point to the tendency to describe a harrowing event in terms of our own emotional distress and panic, but upon further investigation, it is discovered that much of our actions involve caring for others. Our own perceptions of the crisis shape what we believe happened versus what objectively took place. What I believe is important to note is how our very structures of authority and hierarchy increase the danger posed here. Individual panic could be managed by a group, to provide support, a reframe and, in short, mutual aid. If the individual in panic has extensive power and authority, the hierarchical relations atomizing individual experience could lead to significant harm to communities and society itself.

Social work and mutual aid

Social work has its own relationship with mutual aid. Shulman (2016) explicitly describes mutual aid as something he identifies as signaling that the group work is successful. While some textbooks tend to talk about norms and how deviance in the group is sanctioned by the group (see Toseland & Rivas, 2012), Shulman unpacks mutual aid where it is apparent that the group sets the tone and pace at which members attend and care for each other. It is in fact telling how this framing of the ideal group dynamic can be understood as a natural state of being. Referring to Schwartz' article from 1961, he notes that, "the potential for mutual aid exists in any group, but simply bringing people together does not guarantee that it will emerge" (p. 371). Barriers exist such as prior experiences by members of the group, as does the framing of self-interest in attending the group based on one's own personal problems and agendas. This is expected and creates the argument for why a helping professional such as a social worker is there to help facilitate this group process. Mutual aid, then, emerges from the work being done to unblock the members of the group in order that the healing can begin which, paradoxically, can be found in the helping of each other. This contrasts with ideas of healing coming from personal reflection and working on one's own issues exclusively. What is key for the facilitator of the group is to do their own self-reflection to ensure their own past experiences do not negatively impact the group's work.

Shulman identifies several processes that can facilitate the emergence of mutual aid in groups that are worth noting. Sharing data can take the form of hearing others describe their challenges and being able to learn as well as identify with what is being shared. It can also be straightforward sharing of ideas that have been tried and tested by members. The dialectical process is where, due to the environment of the mutual aid group, members can test ideas that the group can respond to. In effect, members are sharing a thesis and antithesis as they seek to develop their own synthesis. While Shulman refers to taboo areas throughout his excellent textbook, in mutual aid there is the potential to challenge the dominant narratives or norms that make it difficult to challenge hegemonic thinking. In a mutual aid group, members can risk talking about topics that are socially sanctioned as taboos. "one member may take the first risk, directly or indirectly, that leads the group into a difficult area of discussion ... [this]allows the more fearful and reluctant members to watch as the taboo is violated" (p. 375). Interestingly enough, Shulman argues that different leaders can emerge depending on the taboo which echoes anarchist ideas of no fixed leadership but certainly respect given to those with greater experience or expertise in a given area (Marshall, 2010). Similar to how Mullaly (2007) talks about the process toward raising consciousness, Shulman refers to the all-in-the-same boat phenomenon which emerges as members of the group take risks to share feelings and beliefs that may have previously been sources of shame and internalized oppression. By discovering that others have these ideas and feelings, their validity is challenged in powerful ways. Shulman would see the group facilitator as encouraging these connections as the group coheres. Along with this process emerges the development of a universal perspective which he would argue can sometimes be the most powerful therapeutic experience in group work.

As the group culture coheres, mutual support emerges (Shulman, 2016). This is in part due to the deep empathy that can happen as members of the group are able to connect with and identify what others are sharing on a different, more intimate level than the group facilitator. "As group members understand the feelings of the others, without judging them harshly, they begin to accept their own feelings in new ways" (p. 377). This is only possible if the group includes a mutual demand in mutual aid. In other words, the group learns to care for each other but also holds the expectation that members of the group rise to the occasion and do the same. "Mutual demand, integrated with mutual support, can be a powerful force for change" (p. 379). Interestingly, by participating in mutual aid wherein members help others, it has a beneficial aspect to the individual members themselves. Aside from the catharsis that may be a component of helping others, it is a way to engage in problem solving in new ways. Helping others see their problems is usually easier than seeing our own, which can lead to new insights as well. Again, similar to Structural Social Work's (Mullaly, 2007) approach to raising consciousness, the strength in numbers phenomenon is where the group can exercise its power. As a challenge to feeling small and alone, this connection can facilitate a courage and commitment to speak truth to power (Shulman, 2016).

Writing a textbook with fellow social work academic, Alex Gitterman (Gitterman & Shulman, 2005) on mutual aid groups, Shulman further expands on his view of how they can be important to the healing of the marginalized. They argue that mutual aid approaches to group work help, for example, people who experienced sexual violence to get in touch with their rage, which is being covered up by the experience of depression and feelings of helplessness. The idea emerges that social workers help members and the group engage in mutual aid by making demands to do the difficult work, to practice and model empathy, and to reach for what is being shared, which facilitates both the member asking for help and the group providing it. By arguing that groups are microcosms of a larger society, Gitterman and Shulman raise an interesting premise: perhaps we are all being prevented from connecting at the level of mutual aid and could benefit from work to unpack this further.

Keys to how social work can contribute to facilitating mutual aid can be found in these ideas. While it may be a concern that experts take over, this need not be the case. Social workers can see their role as facilitating the unfolding of a group process that leaves the group to no longer need the intervention of the expert. The challenges may lie in how we have all been conditioned not to see the benefits of mutual aid. Perhaps our skills in facilitating group work can be applied with principles based on how to help the group identify and remove barriers to the flourishing of mutual aid.

While Mullaly (2007) doesn't explicitly refer to the practice of mutual aid in consciousness raising directly, a few references do seem to lend credence, as already stated, to the idea of mutual aid in practice. Similar to Shulman (2016), he describes the consciousness-raising process, especially when working with oppressed groups, as being helpful as it allows members of shared experiences of oppression to self-define a new identity beyond the one imposed upon them. Key to Structural Social Work is the challenging of a false consciousness, or internalized oppression, Anti-Oppressive Practice (AOP) theorists have suggested, via a group process. It is about facilitating a solidarity that ought to be the focus of social workers practicing from this approach.

Structural Social Workers have a unique challenge of trying to facilitate consciousness raising while managing the tension of the expert role which must be de-emphasized. For a group to become aware of their oppression, they need to find their own perspectives and belief in their own self-determination (Mullaly, 2007). However, "This does not mean that the structural social worker will not introduce new ideas or challenge beliefs held by the service user. Rather, the political education process takes the form of a dialogue where both the social worker and the service user assume roles of mutual sharing and learning" (p. 304). To do this effectively, the social worker needs to practice social or structural empathy, which involves being able to empathize with the service user's perception of their worldview and their feelings and perceptions that they have of the world.

What may strike the reader as challenging here, may be the concern of unequal power dynamics in such a group process. While the structural social worker may profess to center the perspectives of those who are in the group, a theoretical perspective is shaping the encounter. It may be good modeling to demonstrate how new boundaries are practiced, where self-disclosure is greater by the social worker than in perhaps more conservative approaches. However, it may still seem like the assumption that others are less sophisticated in naming their own experiences of oppression is a form of paternalism. Similar to how Marx assumed that the proletariat needed to be made aware of their own alienation, justifying a vanguard to benevolently guide the unwashed masses to their own better future (Marshall, 2010). However, there are differences as Mullaly(2007) argues that one needs to help others lean into the pieces of awareness already present of their own structural oppression. Perhaps another way would be to say that it is about helping others find the language to validate and articulate their oppression in order to facilitate momentum for emancipatory practice. Furthermore, he is explicit that, when a true mutual aid group is forming, the social worker takes great care to not step into a position of leadership. "They should not violate the social work value of self-determination by attempting to lead them" (p. 311). In fact, key to collectivization is to help facilitate the development of mutual aid groups, noting that in some cases, these collectives have managed to build their own social services within the larger structures of professional networks.

Structural social work offers interesting ways to contribute to the idea of mutual aid. Aside from group work, individual encounters with members of oppressed groups can be opportunities to use clinical skills such as reframing how someone understands their own behaviors within larger structural contexts. Seeing how one's own conduct may be a source of shame or material used to blame oneself for failure—in part connected to social forces and hegemonic thinking—can be emancipatory. Ultimately, this approach to social work practice has potential to find common cause with ideas of anarchism. After all, "Consciousness-raising can only occur within the context of a non-authoritarian relationship" (p. 318).

Muskat et al (2020) echo these ideas on their paper about the experiences of group workers in their field of practice. In fact, the therapeutic strategies outlined by Shulman (2016) are identical to these authors' definition for facilitating mutual aid. Mutual aid is identified as a concept which is a principle of actions with mutual or reciprocal benefit. Interestingly, here we have reference both to mutual aid as an organizing framework for social work in group work and acknowledgment that origins of mutual aid can be traced back to the anarchist Kropotkin in the early 20th century. The authors make it plain that the practice of mutual aid is hoped to promote a society that values cooperation and altruism for mutual survival. In fact, they argue that regardless of the purpose of the group, mutual aid emerges—referring to the idea that this is a need that emerges by virtue of the group process. This interactive process, where individuals are helped and help each other, ultimately leads to a stronger group as a whole.

Individual health can also improve in people who practice mutual aid (Muskat et al., 2020). According to studies on this topic, stress is ameliorated as are notable improvements in physical and psychological health when people participate in mutual aid work. However, Muskat et al. would support concerns about the role of professionals, as groups led by these tend to be less likely to bloom into full mutual aid models and more likely to employ more traditional approaches (counseling, etc.). Furthermore, group cohesion tends to be higher in groups that are peer-run. In contrast, however, the authors claim that for social work group practice, mutual aid has been seen as the central ingredient for good outcomes in group work.

van Breda (2018), by referencing a traditional South African idea, finds cultural resonance to the concept of mutual aid. Ubuntu refers to the idea of the personhood of the self as it is expressed in connection with others or rather a "humanness between people within community" (p. 2). While this concept has been used to describe mutual aid, van Breda sees potential for a decolonization of social work practice as well. van Breda suggests that, while little has been said about Ubuntu in the social work literature, it tends to focus on using this idea rather more as a descriptive term for the need to have connection and solidarity. Ubuntu has more to offer in social work theory. This construct has a history of being meaningfully attached as an asset in helping families and youth be resilient in African societies. In fact, it can help guide communities in how they respond to disaster, echoing what anarchist literature has claimed about mutual aid as well (see Firth, 2022, Solnit, 2010). The potential in Ubuntu lies in how it can go beyond what Person In Environment (PIE) does, which still focuses on the individual (in the environment) and that it is the lifeworld of community where real potential can be found. Notably, Ubuntu also de-emphasizes hierarchy in that all—child, parent, grandparent—are equal in the Ubuntu framework. This contributes to social justice as Ubuntu promotes reciprocity and selflessness. Contrary to the west and its neoliberal framework, Ubuntu values interdependence, not independence. Just as some anarchist authors reflect on why mutual aid, if naturally occurring does not emerge more frequently, van Breda argues that the fragmentation of communities is the product of genocide, colonization, and apartheid. He laments the colonizing gaze, as western approaches to child welfare and social work are about helping the child be an individual and succeed on their own. The result is that this is harmful in Africa in that children are not able to integrate into their culture and are seen by the culture as being morally off or wayward, as they do not have the approach of Ubuntu (interconnection versus independence) instilled by their child welfare experience. This has profound implications for culturally safe social work practice and the role that fostering mutual aid through culturally appropriate lenses can have on our work. To be clear, Ubuntu is more than what mutual aid has been described as so far. It includes collective interdependence beyond western, temporal understandings of family and community. Ubuntu includes an ethic of considering both living, ancestral, and future family members as part of the collective. By including the physical world in that the environment is an integral part of Ubuntu, one can see connections to North American Indigenous ways of knowing as well.

> From an African perspective, however, all generations (including past and future) are currently present, and thus ownership does not pass through the generations, but is currently held by all generations simultaneously ... the earth is only temporarily in one's direct physical care; we are not owners, but caretakers. (van Breda, 2018, p. 445)

For van Breda, this includes the settler or colonial experience, where our own reckoning with our ancestors needs to be part of the work as we seek to be part of a new connection with the world and others. There are three concepts to Ubuntu that can help us reframe these connections to ourselves and the natural world. First, there is the understanding of a universal connection to others. Ubuntu, if practiced with this perspective, has the potential to reverse or prevent othering as we are all connected to each other, regardless of nation, race, and so on. Next, understanding our ancestral connection matters in Ubuntu. It is seeing our ancestors and our future generations as existing alongside us rather than as abstractions of a misty past and unknown future. Doing so moves us all into a space where we must act according to these connections rather than nihilistically embracing only our present moment. Finally, viewing the earth as a partner in our living—as valid as any other member of our transnational, past, and present community—has the potential to challenge current exploitative, capitalist approaches to dealing with the environment.

Eiler and D'Angelo (2020) credit Kropotkin for advancing the idea of mutual aid as well. To be clear, they acknowledge that he didn't invent this, as various forms of mutual aid have existed in non-White societies for millennia. Of course, not necessarily always defined as mutual aid per se, but as complicated webs of exchange. More recently, the concept of mutual aid has been developed further from intersectional approaches that add depth and breadth from feminist and disability rights perspectives. They raise the argument that disability issues remain entrenched in a capitalist framework. When the frame of reference is on access to productivity (for people identified as disabled) such a conceptualization of value remains a validation of the status quo. By continuing to focus on productivity, similar to the chapter on work in this book (see chapter 3), the centering of White, productive men remains the standard to aspire to.

There is no illusion here to the problem of social work practice in that it has a history of focusing on function over cause (Eiler & D'Angelo, 2020). Social work has a history of pragmatism that leaves the structural conditions untouched. Furthermore, from a perspective of disability rights and justice, social work tends to reproduce oppression by following the medical model and its administrative functions which reinforce power dynamics. Again, the point is made that this is not the only path for social work to take. Social workers have the potential to reproduce oppression or to work from the inside to help change the system. While the authors are not explicitly anarchist, they argue that this orientation to mutual aid has the potential to meet a greater need which the state alone has not been able to address.

Eiler and D'Angelo note that one way of to think of mutual aid is that it basically is the practice of social work with groups but in the real world. They argue that the cultivation of mutual aid can bridge the gap between micro, mezzo, and macro practice. In fact, social workers can help self-help groups develop mutual aid by facilitating group processes and offering to help in organizing or tracking priorities. Key is to avoid stepping into any function or position of leadership. The setting of goals and agendas must not be appropriated by the social worker but firmly located and lead by people with lived experience. Again, returning to anarchist ideas, the authors credit this literature in helping to develop practices for organizing that emphasize and employ an anti-capitalist, nonhierarchical lens. Ultimately, Eiler and D'Angelo argue for more, "concerted efforts to engage in mutual aid and mobilization efforts with people with disabilities [that] need to be made by social workers, and such efforts need to be reflected in the literature" (p. 13). In fact, COVID has highlighted even further, due to the poor responses by government, the need and effectiveness of mutual aid networks. Social workers are encouraged to engage with these systems alongside (not leading) outgroups (such as those identified as disabled) toward a better world without capitalism.

Social work academic, Dominique Moyse Steinberg (2010), is explicit in arguing that group work is mutual aid when it is truly working as it should.

In fact, she makes the case that mutual aid practice is best practice for social workers doing group work.

> It is a process through which people (1) develop collaborative, supportive, and trustworthy relationships; (2) identify and use existing strengths and/ or to develop new ones; and (3) work together toward individual and/or collective psychosocial goals, which reflects the very essence of social work with groups as I understand it. Thus, in my mind to catalyze mutual aid and to engage in group work are synonymous. (p. 54)

Steinberg (2010) argues that mutual aid, while emerging in the sociological consciousness via Kropotkin, has been a hallmark of social work group practice as far back as the early 70s. What I find significant is how she ties mutual aid to the social work stalwart, the strengths-based perspective. How people take care of themselves and each other in crisis and under oppressive conditions can be harnessed through the group process as individuals learn to take care of each other via the emergence of mutual aid in group practice and beyond. In fact, one of her descriptions of mutual aid makes this explicit in the best way.

> In group work it is the presence of strengths that sets the stage for the helping process (why and how it should take place and how it can benefit individual members and the whole group) and that makes mutual aid (the discovery and exchange of strengths) possible. (pp. 55–56)

As social workers, we are to see people as more than their problems. A holistic appreciation of human beings opens up the potential for mutual aid. In group work, social workers can facilitate how members can learn to practice a helping of others that builds on their strengths rather than their deficits. Finally, she points to anti-oppressive approaches in social work as finding resonance with concepts related to mutual aid. In fact, for group work to be effective, an anti-oppressive focus is integral. Members of groups need to have a voice as they develop their own capacity to care for and help each other. By doing this well, the evidence of effectiveness becomes self-evident. Mutual aid in group work can only be present when it is truly effective. By definition therefore, according to Steinberg (2010), it passes the evidence-based practice metrics.

Rosenwald and Baird (2020) concur in that mutual aid for trauma-informed group work is a welcome paradigm shift away from authoritarian models. Key in such an approach is the relationship between group members and a shared common problems framework that members must work together to solve. While referring to Gitterman and Shulman and their group dynamics (already explored in this chapter), a few notable reflections in their work to facilitate trauma-informed group stood out in the practice of mutual aid. For instance, the all-in-the-same-boat phenomenon is referred to as a form of solidarity that is generated due to group member's growing awareness that they are not alone in what they think, feel, and other aspects of personal traumatic experience. In their work, they found that the dialectical process was an effective way to work through or tolerate disagreement in a group while the developing of a universal perspective is in effect a consciousness-raising activity.

According to Rosenwald and Baird (2020) there is evidence showing that mutual aid is an effective treatment for trauma in that it promotes healing via instilling hope, strengthening and enhancing self-esteem and resilience, and "promoting a sense of control over one's environment" (p. 261). In fact, groups addressing trauma and PTSD post 9/11 that used mutual aid were the quintessential model of group work, regardless of size or function. By merging trauma-informed care with mutual aid models, Rosenwald and Baird argue that trust, transparency, peer support and mutuality are maximized. In effect, the mutual aid process can help create safe spaces for traumatized people to share their trauma narratives in the context of an environment of solidarity and support. Furthermore, the sharing of historical trauma narratives can create solidarity for the group as members realize that their stories, while unique, have universals in common and can help challenge features of structural harms that are fostering negative self-esteem. Perhaps it is the facilitation of peer support that is the best illustration of the therapeutic benefits of mutual aid.

According to Rosenwald and Baird (2020), the social worker in these interventions should facilitate a greater focus between members and less to the leader—in effect, seeking to change expectations of group work at the outset to facilitate mutual aid. The final destination for group work then is to ensure the leader is no longer in charge or even necessary. It is this skill set by the social worker that is integral to the promotion of true mutual aid.

Lind (2020) ponders how the all-in-the-same-boat phenomenon shaped her group work class. The development of such a shared solidarity in her experience created a significant form of mutual aid for students. As the world shut down, and new ways of connecting were explored through the class, students rose to the occasion. This prompted Lind to reflect on how crisis can bring out the worst or best in people. In this case, the best, as mutual aid emerged for the class.

Conclusion

Mutual aid as an idea has many potential avenues for how social work can be reconciled with anarchism. While social work has been accused of sanitizing capitalism, it has a history of activism as well. It does not need to be the case that a social worker intervenes and brings progress to a halt. We have a history in community organizing (Hick & Stokes, 2017; Kirst-Ashman & Hull, 2018) that further can add to the important practice of mutual aid. While mutual aid can be seen as a stumbling block in anarchism—a way to point to the naïve or utopian nature of its philosophy—it can also be seen as a refusal to submit to a kind of pessimism about the human condition.

Social work is about believing in people, in their capacities for growth and change. This belief ought to be at odds with the mainstream Hobbesian nightmare that is being used to justify the organized violence of the state. In mutual aid, I contend, that the various ideas brought forward by anarchism can find a resonance to social work practice.

It is important that we do not mistake a strategy for validation as the reason to dismiss the concept. Mutual aid is developed as a legitimate reality for humanity by appealing to nature for evidence. While compelling, it is important to recall Graeber and Grubacic's (2020) argument that social Darwinists have projected their preference for capitalism as a subjective screen by which to vet empirical data. The reverse could be said as well. Therefore, it may make sense to reconsider whether looking for scientific evidence in nature as a biological imperative is the best strategy to appeal for a humanity that practices mutual aid and cooperation versus self-interest and competition. There is a promise of the innate response by communities in moments of crisis that give hope for us all (e.g. Solnit, 2010; Firth, 2022).

Throughout this chapter, I hope it has become obvious to the reader that social work has a unique opportunity to help foster mutual aid. The concerns of social work, especially the legacy of harms in service to the state, need to be confronted. However, as the final chapter will further explore, we have an interesting challenge ahead. I continue to believe that the best work we can offer needs to be grounded in the sincere and compelling vision of seeking our own obsolescence. If we can unmake the reason for our existence, we are fundamentally bringing about the better world that anarchists are calling for. In practice, what this means is to make the implicit explicit. I agree with the social workers arguing for a form of mutual aid needing to emerge in group practice. However, rather than reflect on the progress a group can celebrate (e.g. a grief group and their growth in this regard) it would be good to be explicit about the techniques and strategies the group facilitator used to facilitate the emergence of mutual aid. If we seek to become obsolete, we need to pass on our knowledge of group facilitation to foster mutual aid. This need not be restricted to the micro and mezzo practice level but can come into play at the macro level as well.

One of the vexing issues with mutual aid is that it seems to require a utopian faith in humanity that just hasn't been true if history is any indication. While this chapter has illustrated some of the ideas seeming to confirm this idea in anarchist thought, there are some points deserving of reflection. First, there are the prior narratives generated by a scientific argument steeped in controversies. We must ask ourselves why we were so quick to believe and to turn around and be resistant to accept the critiques of this. Maybe we just want to believe that we are essentially malevolent individuals without authority because it appeals to a theology we embrace. Or the idea that our status quo is suspect is too upsetting to contemplate. Regardless, to dismiss mutual aid and its premise due to a claim of utopian essentialism is premature.

American academic and one of the founding members of the North American Anarchist Studies, Jesse Cohn (2013), finds old sources to make a new argument about mutual aid and the problem with human nature. He offers a new perspective of these writers to challenge a criticism of anarchism: If mutual aid and solidarity are natural aspects of the human condition, such an essentialism is defeated by all the atrocities humanity has been responsible for. Cohn counters with a review of the works of Bakunin and Kropotkin to show that their ideas are more than such a simplistic notion. In his view, both writers were expressing a social constructivist notion: that the capacity for mutual aid is present but that the opposite, a desire for individual power and domination are present as well. Firth (2022) would agree, in that there is an assumption of classical anarchist literature being tarred by the brush of essentialism. By referring to the ideas of Anthropologist Brian Morris as well as Linguist Davide Turcato, she makes the case that,

The classical anarchists anticipated the poststructural critique of productive power, for example in Kropotkin's analysis of the ways in which power produces institutions, propaganda, laws, ideologies and modes of resistance ... the anarchist tradition was never just an abstract ideal but a complex set of debates linked to real movement praxis. (p. 80)

In effect, mutual aid and its associated behaviors of altruism and the rejection of power over others, is present as a potentiality. We have the capacity for these things that can be built up—with collective will—a struggle to be produced for a better world for all.

In fact, Cohn connects to Kropotkin's ideas around mutual aid by pointing out that this Russian thinker emphasized that it is not enough to oppose authority and seek its unmaking, but that there is the need to build something better in its stead. This requires effort, conscious effort which necessitates a construction of the human condition that needs more than the removal of barriers to goodness (p. 438). What this means is that there is work to do, let's get to it.

References

Afrofuturist Abolitionists of the Americas. (2019). *Anti-capitalism, mutual aid, and asset-based community development* [zine]. https://theanarchistlibrary.org/library/afrof uturist-abolitionists-of-the-americas-anti-capitalism-mutual-aid-and-asset-based-community

Anderson, W. C. (2021). *The nation on no map: Black anarchism and abolition.* AK Press.

Berneri, M. L. (2009) Journey through utopia. In R. Graham (Ed.), *Anarchism: A documentary history of libertarian ideas. Volume 2: The emergence of the new anarchism (1939–1977)* (pp. 76–82). Black Rose Books.

Black Flag Sydney. (2021). *Socialism is not charity: Why we're against "Mutual Aid."* https://blackflagsydney.com/socialism-is-not-charity-why-were-against-mutual-aid/

Clarke, L., & Chess, C. (2008). Elites and panic: More to fear than fear itself. *Social Forces, 87*(2), 993–1014. https://doi-org.ezproxy.boothuc.ca/10.1353/sof.0.0155

Cohn, J. (2013). Anarchism and essentialism. In R. Graham (Ed.), *Anarchism: A documentary history of libertarian ideas. Volume 3: The new anarchism (1974–2012)* (pp. 434–446). Black Rose Books.

Comfort, A. (2009a). Peace and disobedience. In R. Graham (Ed.), *Anarchism: A documentary history of libertarian ideas. Volume 2: The emergence of the new anarchism. (1939–1977)* (pp. 56–60). Black Rose Books.

Comfort, A. (2009b). Art and social responsibility. In R. Graham (Ed.), *Anarchism: A documentary history of libertarian ideas. Volume 2: The emergence of the new anarchism (1939–1977)* (pp. 103–111). Black Rose Books.

Couthard, G. (2008). Beyond recognition: Indigenous self-determination as prefigurative practice. In L. B. Simpson (Ed.), *Lighting the eighth fire: The liberation, resurgence, and protection of Indigenous First Nations* (pp. 187–203). Arbeiter Ring Press.

Day, J. F. (2005). *Gramsci is dead: Anarchist currents in the newest social movements*. Between the Lines.

DeCarlo, G. (2009). Rebuilding community. In R. Graham (Ed.), *Anarchism: A documentary history of libertarian ideas. Volume 2: The emergence of the new anarchism. (1939–1977)* (pp. 95–100). Black Rose Books.

de Loggans, R. (2020). *Let's talk mutual aid*. https://theanarchistlibrary.org/library/deloggans-let-stalkmutualaid

Dolgoff, R., Harrington, D., & Lowenberg, F. (2012). *Ethical decisions for social work practice* (9th ed). Brookes/Cole.

Eiler, E. C., & D'Angelo, K. (2020). Tensions and connections between social work and anti-capitalist disability activism: Disability rights, disability justice, and implications for practice. *Journal of Community Practice, 28*(4), 356–372. doi: 10.1080/10705422.2020.1842278

Finn, M. (2021). *Debating anarchism: A history of actions, ideas, and movements*. Bloomsbury.

Firth, R. (2022). *Disaster anarchy: Mutual aid in radical action*. Pluto Press.

Gitterman, A., & Schulman, L. (2005). *Mutual aid groups, vulnerable and resilient populations, and the life cycle* (3rd ed.). Columbia University Press.

Goodman, P. (2009). Drawing the line. In R. Graham (Ed.), *Anarchism: A documentary history of libertarian ideas. Volume 2: The emergence of the new anarchism (1939–1977)* (pp. 42–56). Black Rose Books.

Graeber, D. (2004). *Fragments of an anarchist anthropology*. Prickly Paradigm Press.

Graeber, D., & Grubacic, A. (2020). *Introduction to mutual aid: An illuminated factor of evolution*. https://drive.google.com/file/d/1kGouNfYyzt2FwHUAx_KfFyqUKVN5Kzzg/view

Graeber, D., & Wengrow, D. (2021). *The dawn of everything: A new history of humanity*. Farrar Straus and Giroux.

Graham, R. (2013) Afterword: The anarchist current: Continuity and change in anarchist thought. In R. Graham (Ed.), *Anarchism: A documentary history of libertarian ideas. Volume 3: The new anarchism (1974–2012)* (pp. 475–584). Black Rose Books.

Goodman, P. (2009). Drawing the line. In R. Graham (Ed.), *Anarchism: A documentary history of libertarian ideas. Volume 2: The emergence of the new anarchism (1939–1977)* (pp. 42–56). Black Rose Books.

Hardie, M. (2010). Dead spots in the case of Kitty Genovese. *Australian Feminist Studies, 25*(65), 337–351. https://doi-org.10.1080/08164649.2010.504995

Haslam, S. A., & Reicher, S. (2014). Just obeying orders? *New Scientist, 223*(2986), 28–31. https://doi.org/10.1016/S0262-4079(14)61766-8

Hick, S., & Stokes, J. (2017). *Social work in Canada: An introduction* (4th ed.). Thompson Educational Publishing.

Jun, N., & Lance, M. (2020). Anarchist responses to a pandemic: The COVID-19 crisis as a case study in mutual aid. *Kennedy Institute of Ethics Journal, 30*(3/4). https://doi-org.ezproxy.boothuc.ca/10.1353/ken.2020.0019

Kirst-Ashman, K. K., & Hull, G. H. (2018). *Empowerment series: Generalist practice with organizations and communities* (7th ed.). Brooks & Cole.

Kitty Genovese, revised. (2007). The Wilson Quarterly *(1976-), 31*(1), 78–79. http://www.jstor.org/stable/45270339

Knutilla, M. (1992). *State theories: From liberalism to the challenge of feminism* (2nd ed.). Fernwood Publishing.

Korean anarchist manifesto. (2009). In R. Graham (Ed.), *Anarchism: A documentary history of libertarian ideas. Volume 2: The emergence of the new anarchism. (1939-1977)* (pp. 36–39). Black Rose Books.

Kropotkin, P. (2017/1902). *Mutual aid: A factor of evolution.* (A. Gouveia, Trans. & Ed.). CreateSpace Independent Publishing Platform.

Laursen, E. (2021). *The operating system: An anarchist theory of the modern state.* AK Press.

Lind, K. (2020). Mutual aid during a pandemic: A group work class example. *Social Work with Groups, 43*(4), 347–350. doi: 10.1080/01609513.2020.1790230

Marshall, P. (2010). *Demanding the impossible: A history of anarchism.* PM Press.

Mullaly, B. (2007). *The new structural social work.* Oxford University Press.

Muskat, B., Greenblatt, A., Garvin, C., Pelech, W., Cohen, C., Macgowan, M., & Roy, V. (2020) Group workers' experiences of mutual aid: Stories from the field. *Social Work with Groups, 43*(3), 241–256. doi: 10.1080/01609513.2019.1571470

Noir et Rouge. (2009). Resisting the nation state. In R. Graham (Ed.), *Anarchism: A documentary history of libertarian ideas. Volume 2: The emergence of the new anarchism. (1939-1977)* (pp. 170–182). Black Rose Books.

Ostergaard, G. (2009). The managerial revolution. In R. Graham (Ed.), *Anarchism: A documentary history of libertarian ideas. Volume 2: The emergence of the new anarchism. (1939-1977)* (pp. 153–157). Black Rose Books.

Perry, G. (2018). The evil inside us all. *New Scientist, 240*(3199), 39–41. https://doi.org/10.1016/S0262-4079(18)31849-9

Prince, J. (2009). Fighting for freedom. In R. Graham (Ed.), *Anarchism: A documentary history of libertarian ideas. Volume 2: The emergence of the new anarchism (1939-1977)* (pp. 299–304). Black Rose Books.

Rasenberger, J. (2006). Nightmare on Austin Street. *American Heritage,* 57(5), 65–266.

Romande Anarchist Federation. (2009). Coming to grips with war. In R. Graham (Ed.), *Anarchism: A documentary history of libertarian ideas. Volume 2: The emergence of the new anarchism. (1939-1977)* (pp. 12–17). Black Rose Books.

Rosenwald, M., & Baird, J. (2020) An integrated trauma informed, mutual aid model of group work. *Social Work with Groups, 43*(3), 257–271. doi: 10.1080/01609513.2019.1656145

Shulman, L. (2016). *The skills of helping individuals, families, groups, and communities* (8th ed.). Brooks/Cole.

Smith, C. B. R. (2012) Harm reduction as anarchist practice: A user's guide to capitalism and addiction in North America. *Critical Public Health, 22*(2). 209–221. doi: 10.1080/09581596.2011.611487

Solnit, R. (2010). *A paradise built in hell: The extraordinary communities that arise in disaster.* Penguin Books.

Steinberg, D. M. (2010). Mutual aid: A contribution to best-practice social work. *Social Work with Groups, 33*(1), 53–68. https://doi.org/10.1080/01609510903316389

Taylor, M. (2009). Anarchy, the state and cooperation. In R. Graham (Ed.), *Anarchism: A documentary history of libertarian ideas. Volume 2: The emergence of the new anarchism (1939-1977)* (pp. 385–390). Black Rose Books.

Toseland, R. W., & Rivas, R. F. (2012). *An introduction to group work practice* (7th ed). Allyn & Bacon.

van Breda, A. D. (2018). Resilience of vulnerable students transitioning into a South African university. *Higher Education, 75*(6), 1109–1124. https://doi.org/10.1007/s10734-017-0188-z

Van Meter, K. (2017). *Guerillas of desire: Notes on everyday resistance and organizing to make a revolution possible.* AK Press.

Walia, H. (2013). No one is illegal. In R. Graham (Ed.), *A documentary history of libertarian ideas. Volume 3: The new anarchism (1974–2012)* (pp. 404–412). Black Rose Books.

Walia, H. (2021). *Border and rule: Global migration, capitalism, and the rise of racist nationalism.* Fernwood Press.

Walter, N. (2009). Direct action and the new pacifism. In R. Graham (Ed.), *Anarchism: A documentary history of libertarian ideas. Volume 2: The emergence of the new anarchism (1939–1977)* (pp. 196–205). Black Rose Books.

Wieck, D. (2009). The realization of freedom. In R. Graham (Ed.), *Anarchism: A documentary history of libertarian ideas. Volume 2: The emergence of the new anarchism (1939–1977)* (pp. 227–233). Black Rose Books.

Zastrow, C. H., & Kirst-Ashman, K. K. (2016). *Understanding human behavior and the social environment.* Cengage Learning.

Chapter questions

1. Have you experienced mutual aid? What did it feel like?
2. Would you say that human nature is essentially good, bad, or neither? Did this chapter give you another perspective to consider?
3. This chapter suggests that we ought to make the implicit explicit, to help members of groups see the skills we used to facilitate mutual aid. What do you think?

8
Wither social work?

Reflections on the end of social work (and a world that needs it)

The purpose of this book is to take the reader to the source of a set of ideas—in this case, anarchism. While over the years there has been much work done to develop social work theory unique to this discipline, such as Humanist (Payne, 2011), Anti-oppressive (Wehbi & Parada, 2017), Structural (Hick et al., 2010; Mullaly, 2007), and Anti-privilege (see West & Mullaly, 2018), this book was not intended to provide similar results. It may be helpful to consider theory and employ this as a lens to guide critical analysis and practice. However, a prefab theory of social work removes the reader from a crucial step. We are seeing the final product of admittedly brilliant scholars developing their own synthesis from diverse source material. My intention is to expose the reader to the source material directly. My own connections that I draw between anarchism and social work I would present as illustrations of my own work, not a firm pronouncement of theory. In a lot of ways, the return to my invitation for this journey was not a mere device to hook the reader. I have struggled to reconcile my anarchist thinking with my social work education. My participation in social work practice has been a conscious attempt to find a way to reconcile these ideas. This meant fully embracing aspects of the field to reflect upon and reconsider. This work therefore is intended to get the reader to see the space of ideas and be invited to ponder the places of contact, the divergencies and new branches of thought that could come from considering anarchism for social work. This echoes my thoughts on anarchism as well, where there have been grave concerns raised about the hegemony of theory itself.

As I write this final chapter, I am struck by a conversation I had years ago with an academic colleague. He had read my dissertation, essentially a historical analysis of social work practice at a psychiatric institution and had asked me if the whole thing wasn't just "identity politics." At the time I was taken aback by this question. I am aware of the crisis of representation that social work has struggled with and wanted my research to contribute to a growing body of locating the discipline within a field of practice. Sometimes I have answered this question by saying that the constant ebb and flow of social problems, welfare reform, economic tides, geopolitical considerations, and so on, require a social work that is more quicksilver. In effect, its crisis is actually an illusion, a reaction to the conditions of our world.

Related to this idea, is the frequent assumption that social workers are unique in that they are always identifying this way. In other words, a social worker is the identity of the graduate—regardless of whether they're at work or not. The fact that social workers are encouraged with some regulatory or licensing bodies listing them as "non-practicing" reinforces this message. As the reader was able to see in the chapter on work (Chapter 3), we may need to reconsider this notion. Does indoctrination into social work as a complete identity foster a better world or does this promote a hegemony of its own, with ideological blinders? I find myself struggling with this idea. I am proud to call myself a social worker and have done my part to promote the profession, to teach the curriculum, and to defend the measures made to establish a foothold in the field of the helping professions. However, there is our dark legacy, such as the 60s Scoop and current realities of our power in child protection. In writing about social work and crime, I hope to have convinced the reader as well about the problems with being involved in areas of social or legal control.

If we claim to be a social worker at all times, what does this mean? If we look at this from curricular objectives, we can certainly outline distinctions that we would expect to find: a developed sense of the self, a commitment to human rights and social justice, and so on. I wonder if we are placing too much value on the concept of social work to define ourselves. Setting aside the problematic idea of fully defining ourselves by our work, it is also misleading to think that there is some universal definition of "social worker" that we can all either identify with or embody. Perhaps this is a remnant of modernity, or post-positivist thinking. Ontological certainty perhaps just outside the reach of current measurement. To illustrate, I will engage in the use of anecdote. During my time of study for my MSW in the United States, I encountered a professor who claimed to be politically conservative. I remember being baffled by this. I couldn't fathom how a conservative mindset could apply to social work. For this person, there was no disconnect. To me, it is difficult to not see politics as predicated on what we believe about human effort and achievement. How can someone educated as a social worker believe in residual welfare approaches based on thinking that poverty is the result of moral failure? Of course, Chapman and Withers (2019) would point out that politics and practice in social work do not have a history of clear lines of progressive vs conservative, radical vs liberal. Especially in the history of mainstream social work practice.

When it came to my education, we were trained in how to use the Diagnostic and Statistical Manual of Mental Disorders (DSM) to provide provisional psychiatric diagnoses. While we talked about the problem with medical model approaches to mental health, we learned about alternative evaluations and assessments. Ultimately, I was left with the impression that we need to know the tools being used by a way of thinking about the world that is problematic, but we use them anyway. The assumption was that our identification with social work would result in a less harmful application of diagnostic impressions.

I have since met many social workers who see their role as participating in the system and acknowledge its damaging impact but seek to reform it from within. Again, this can only be done by knowing enough about the system to operate from within. I return to the question of identification as a social worker. If social work can embrace ways of thinking about the world—be it political, psychological, ideological, and so on—that contribute to the suffering of those we believe we are helping, then we need to reflect on the implication. If liberal thought prevents meaningful change, how are we change agents? In *The End of Social Work*, Steve Burghardt (2020) notes that our profession needs to have a reality check. We have been unrealistic in revising history to cast the profession as instrumental in social change. Other factors, including labor organizing and civil rights movements and their leaders, must be considered as well. Burghardt claims that it is this incomplete revision of our own past that has created our current perception that we are increasingly losing power and effectiveness. He argues that in the past we partnered with others, in our relative powerlessness to bring about joint change that eclipsed our own narrow interests, and that we need to return to this again. Frankly, I appreciate this perspective. Social work has had power over vulnerable and marginalized people; this is not disputed. However, if we harnessed our efforts to partner with other relatively powerless groups for real meaningful change in the past, I have hope for a better future for all. Social work can be a part of this change.

However, if this book has done anything, I hope it is to challenge our idea of change. Incremental change may be tempting to engage in as social workers. After all, advocacy is taught to include a focus on policy analysis and policy making. Policy making can be understood as kind of reform. It assumes that the systems within which policy occurs can be rehabilitated or improved. Returning to the chapter on welfare systems (Chapter 2), any attempt to engage with the welfare system will be validating. Further, the character of liberalism is to perpetuate a false consciousness predicated on pluralism. Social workers in the field, and those directly impacted by welfare reforms, can attest to how inequality is reality in this present moment. Belief in a welfare reform that will be more humane is just softening the edges of capitalism.

The same point holds true for social work in the field of criminology. Existing beliefs about the causes of crime and their solutions are reaffirmed when social work collaborates within existing legal structures. Similar to welfare, we have the opportunity to work with people to help challenge internalized oppression, to make strange the assumptions about living under capitalism that blames victims. Going beyond the consciousness raising of existing social work theory, however, is needed. Defining ourselves as social workers continues to risk the entire project. To borrow from Rosa Luxembourg (2006), we need to consider reform or revolution.

As you have been reading this book, you may have discovered (hopefully) that anarchism is not so easy to define. There is a divergence of thought and a commitment to not privilege or usurp the idea of anarchism by one branch. What is common, however, is the conviction that all forms of authority, and hence associated hierarchy, are inherently damaging to the human condition. This makes it impossible to get lost in well-intentioned reforms that reproduce oppression in another guise. Of course, there is a difference in identification with an ideology versus a professional identity. What I ask is for the reader to reflect—is there a fallacy in thinking as a social worker at all times? Does full identification with a profession make anti-work claims, for instance, invisible as we valorize an occupation over what it means to be fully human? I am reminded of Poole et al. (2012), who write about how social work's participation in validating psychiatric labels participates in exclusionary practice, in sanism. People who have more relevant and direct experience with the given area of practice are excluded, as they do not have the representative authority of being a social worker.

It is my hope that this book stimulates discussion and reflection. I believe that considering anarchism can help social work avoid the challenges of being servants of government or any other form of authority. Both anarchism and social work have similar beginnings, as I have alluded to before. Both are responses to significant changes in the social world brought about by industrialization. Anarchism raised the alarm about the coming misery that would be the lot for many with the ascendancy of industrial capitalism. One could argue that social work emerged in the trenches of urban sprawl as an attempt to deal with the resulting misery. Both were present, if perhaps located in different positions. Anarchism and social work would want the misery to end and can find common ground here.

Social work has struggled to see itself as apart from capitalism. As the previous paragraph stated, it is a response to capitalism, hence connected. An explicit anti-capitalist approach can help challenge this, showing a new way for social work to function. Perhaps the very responses of social work can be exploited to amplify the awareness of the toxic impact of the status quo. In other words, our interventions, designed to help those who are oppressed, need to be elevated not as evidence of our effectiveness but rather as a way to point out how bad it has gotten and to engage, to network with other groups that would want to join a vision of a better world.

A colleague of mine rightfully asked whether I would include Indigenous ways of knowing in this book. At the outset you will note my hesitation. I am not Indigenous and would not want to claim to be able to represent ideas as if I have the right to do so. That said, it is compelling to think about Mino-Pimatisiwin, the Indigenous concept for what can be understood as the good life or the way to a good life (Hart, 2002). After all, if anything, anarchism seeks to ensure we are all able to experience the good life. My sole intention here is to unearth and expose ideas usually ignored or avoided by mainstream thought. There are many more voices that raise similar points. Indigenous thought has existed well before colonization and would have similar things to say about community, governance, and coexistence. These voices deserve attention and recognition, and I look forward to more conversation between and among people who share these ideas.

It is not possible to talk about anarchism without addressing decolonization in my view. Critiques of anarchism have been right in that there is a danger that we are once again privileging White male settlers and their voices. There are a number of thoughts that deserve further unpacking. First off, I want to reiterate that Indigenous ideas about land, about earth itself, are of paramount importance. As the chapter on the environment (Chapter 4) pointed out, we are all residents of a planet on fire. I agree with Naomi Klein's (2019) position that we need to partner with Indigenous land defenders. They have much to teach us on the sacred duty we have to our shared earth. I also want to reflect on what Craig Fortier (2017) notes about the history of poor relationships between anarchists and Indigenous people on Turtle Island. Decolonizing anarchism requires a willing spirit to be open to critique. We need to listen to those who have borne the brunt of empire, of colonization. Otherwise, we risk an ideological conviction that can become reactionary, oppressive, and guilty of reproducing hierarchies of domination.

I have tried to introduce the reader to a variety of anarchist thought and am aware that this has included a canon which includes a number of White, male thinkers. While anarchists insist that they reject "great men" there is a bread crumb trail leading away from a series of contributions made by writers whose work has been instrumental in advancing anarchist thought. That said, the point remains, Indigenous thought has predated many of the ideas presented by these authors. I am reminded of the Davids—Graeber and Wengrow (2021)—who document a history of just such ideas and ways of living by cultures that an arrogant west considered too primitive. Their writing on this subject shows how perplexing and even disconcerting these questions by so-called primitive interlocutors were in that they threatened a status quo view that was justifying their exploitation of the "new world." New anarchist contributions by Indigenous anarchists are further important contributions to challenging a current iteration of exploitation bolstered by a neoliberal marketplace. There are two further reflections that I hope can contribute to how anarchism and Indigenous worldviews can be allies in the ongoing fight with colonization and economic exploitation (currently in the guise of neoliberal capitalism). First, I want to return to Craig Fortier's (2017) work, *Unsettling the Commons*. His suggestion would be for non-Indigenous people (I would include the anarchist in this) to get to know the concept of "sovereignty." I found this concept, when recast from an Indigenous perspective, to be incredibly helpful. Anarchists may at times be quite concerned about national identities and their desire to abandon or transcend these, given the history of how such constructs have been used to harm and oppress in the name of patriotism. I am reminded of Gordon (2013) and his ambivalence about supporting a Palestinian state, given his anarchist position on national identity. It certainly is tempting to point to Walia (2021) and her recounting of bordering practices based on national identities to see the harms this creates. This is something I believe anarchists need to reflect on and accept if they are to be at all useful to the decolonizing project. To be clear, I find it incompatible to be an anarchist and to not oppose the state violence that continues to marginalize, and has tried to eliminate, Indigenous people around the world. We are simply going to have to accept, however, that we can never fully understand or identify with the experience, as non-Indigenous who have benefited and hold privilege due to the expanding empire of which we are citizens. We do not have a choice in the genesis of our membership, but we can collaborate and conspire with others, including Indigenous communities, that have never stopped resisting.

My second thought on the subject is a work in progress, as a through line for this book perhaps. If Indigenous voices have been raised throughout the colonization project, what is the point of revealing and considering anarchist writings? I do not mean to dismiss the valid concern that one could obscure or dismiss Indigenous thought and privilege the west again. But I do think there is a benefit to engaging with anarchist thought. In *Gramsci is Dead*, Richard J. F. Day (2005) argues that we have all been misled into thinking that Marx was the sole and most influential contributor to socialism. This book in part sought to challenge this notion and offer another perspective. But to the main point of my second thought, I kept imagining this behemoth or juggernaut that was the first Industrial Revolution ushering in a new age. Beneath its wheels, from inside the expanding empire, writings emerged that urged us to reconsider and to challenge our understanding of progress. The critiques were coming from inside the house, if you will, not from those experiencing the ravages of colonization at the boundaries of the settler state. This is where I can see further fruitful discussion—how those most impacted (e.g. Indigenous voices) and those from inside who sought to use their privilege (in the case of Kropotkin, an aristocrat with scientific credentials)—to challenge a rapacious burgeoning capitalist state with an alternative, a better world for all.

Now to a more traditional concluding chapter. It is generally expected that a book ends with a summary of all that has been discussed. Once this has been done, the author may indulge in some speculation about paths not yet taken or areas of the subject matter that did not find their way into this book. All of this is to say, I do believe that there are areas for further consideration when it comes to anarchism and social work practice. First, it is fairly obvious to me, that further work with Indigenous ways of knowing and anarchist thought are important in how they could inform social work. Given the significant role of social work in child welfare, there is further exploration possible (potentially related to the chapter on education, Chapter 6) that addresses anarchist ways of thinking about child development and the adult that challenges notions of authority and what is best for the child. In the area of gender and sexuality, anarchist thought has been active—including in the postmodern turn. Notions of queering anarchism can be a helpful discourse as social work seeks to find its place alongside further marginalized groups that have had to resist the androcentric gaze of the modern, White supremacist state. While some chapters were specific to a topic, it was intentional to illustrate ways to think of anarchism for social work; hence the chapters on supported employment and the law (Chapters 3 and 5, respectively). Further focus on how Mad activism, anarchism, and social work could help create new relationships and understandings of what it means to be active in this field of practice would be good to explore. What Black Lives Matter (BLM) has made clear over the last few years, is that there would be value in exploring how anti-racist practice (e.g. anti-oppressive practice, AOP) could be further supported by anarchist critique of racism, fascism (e.g. Antifa), and more. The following is a more complete, but certainly not exhaustive, reflection of directions for future work on anarchism and social work.

Anarchist-feminism and social work

I have referred to feminist theory and how this has shaped social work, as well as referenced anarchist-feminists (e.g. Emma Goldman, Ruth Kinna, L. Susan Brown) throughout. However, further work needs to be done to engage more deeply with anarchist-feminist perspectives. Anarchism itself has struggled with this. In fact, while anarchists like Bakunin supported gender equality, others such as Proudhon did not (Klito, 2005). This dissonance in anarchism is further illustrated in how the first Argentinian anarcho-feminist newspaper at the end of the 19th century was received by fellow anarchists (Anarcho, 2009). The newspaper was lauded by some but ran into conflict with other male anarchists, when critiquing how they continue to believe and behave according to patriarchal values.

Some have argued that anarchist-feminism itself emerged from the conviction that radical feminism is a kind of anarchy (Tanenbaum, 2016). As patriarchy itself is about hierarchical relations, where women and children are lesser humans or even property, radical feminism—it can be argued—is anarchism. However, this is where it is important to reflect on how early feminists differed from an anarchist vision. Perhaps this is best captured by how the work of anarchist-feminists, such as Emma Goldman, Voltairine DeCleyre, and others, can be seen as a feminism of the working class (Anarcho, 2009). This has profound implications in that it challenges the perception of first wave feminism and the fight for the vote. The anarchist-feminist view held that patriarchy and it's ending must be connected and be a part of a bigger fight against the hierarchies which are reinforced by social and economic classes. "It was not centred on educated middle-class women, whose feminism was dismissed as a [sic] "bourgeois" or "reformist" (Anarcho, 2009, p. 2). Emma Goldman, for example would dismiss the suffragette movement as mere symbolic efforts (Marshall, 2010, p. 406). Her vision of true emancipation had to be the full humanity of women. This didn't mean that she didn't believe in the right of women to vote, but that the right itself was without real-life value to bring about meaningful change.

The problem is that gender equality has seldom been the focus of anarchist movements and struggles (Klito, 2005). In fact, the potential in anarchist-feminism has been that it is the intersection of gender and capital that is crucial to critique. One can have a non-capitalist society that maintains dominant gender norms after all. Anarchist-feminism makes the important point that real anarchism has to unmake all hierarchies. The anarchist-feminist collective, Klito (2005), takes this further in that they argue that the essentialist perspective of gender itself needs to be deconstructed. That if we see male and female as socially constructed, we accept that what is considered "natural" male or female behaviors cannot therefore exist. Hence, reactions such as homophobia and transphobia are based on a failure to understand or accept this. This is an important distinction, as other radical feminist movements have at times struggled with accepting non-heteronormative groups.

de Heredia (2007) argues that it is anarchism's own insistence on including a focus on freedom in personal relationships that have opened it up to the possibility of an anarchist feminism. Tanenbaum (2016) claims that the first terms referring to what would later be called "anarcho-feminism" only emerged in the 1970's. Why this matters is because others have argued that efforts to claim further forms of anarchism are redundant as all hierarchies and their unmaking is encompassed in the general term of anarchism. However, this has tended not to turn out as issues such as are important to feminism disappear within a more general focus on traditional anarchist liberation struggles (de Heredia, 2007). In effect, we need to name it so that it does not get lost or dismissed. Anarcho-feminism can help prevent anarchist thought to deflate to the binaries of class and power. It can enhance the critique of power and its structures and enhance solidarity with all who are oppressed.

Ruth Kinna (2017) notes that the story of anarchism and feminism is a complicated one. She makes it clear that anarchism in general has failed to incorporate feminist writers in the canon. She concurs with the ongoing problem of anarchist movements and approaches having reproduced ongoing androcentrism and even misogynist thought and behavior. In another argument against essentialism, she unpacks the problematic behind framing feminism within waves, in effect emphasizing fragmented periods of time where prior radical theories are left behind in the illusion of progress. This includes the dismissal of stories of resistance, to male authority and domination, by women outside of academia and who are BIPOC, for example. In other words, it omits the reality of feminist resistance beyond the last 100 years of the anglocentric (and White) gaze. The same can be said for how anarchism has failed to consider the importance and relevance of feminism. Citing Marshall's summation ([2010] in Kinna, 2017, p. 13) of the impact Emma Goldman had on anarchism, Kinna refers to how he is describing her as someone whose anarchist-feminist ideas did not find an audience in her time among fellow anarchists. However, she would agree with Marshall that her influence has only grown over time.

What this all suggests to me, is that there is more work to be done. Anarchism has to continue to confront its tendency toward "Manarchism" (Kinna, 2017), which can be described as behaviors and actions that reflect an androcentric perspective that allows for "the adoption of aggressively cisgendered male predatory behaviors, uninvited protectionism premised on norms of dependency, sexual violence and the casual dismissal of gender politics" (p. 4). Furthermore, feminism, without an anarchist perspective, is more likely to engage in activism that misses intersectional realities and the dynamic interplay of such. In fact, there is a potential for anarchism and feminism to challenge and critique what may appear to be foundational places of struggle and are, instead, ways of validating the existing systems of oppression one is trying to gain privilege from within. Social work has been shaped by feminist theory. It would be worth considering how this could further be impacted by an engagement with anarchist-feminist theory in future works on the subject.

2SLGBTQIA+ people and anarchism and social work

With the postmodern turn, new ways of conceiving anarchist thought are emerging. The intersectional lens is giving us interesting and novel approaches to seeing a kind of anarchism that challenges the gender binary and previously held definitions of sexuality itself (e.g. Heckert, 2011). Given social work's interest in working with the marginalized and vulnerable, more can be done on this subject. With the rise of homo and transphobia around the world, it is unfortunately a timely and important topic. In fact, Heckert (2011) connects the post structural thoughts of Foucault, Deleuze, and Guattari to a postmodern anarchism that moves past the essentialism trap of representation and identification. In effect, challenging movements based on Marx that rely on an essential subject position, this new way of looking at anarchism and post structuralism, "rejects vanguardism and promotes an ethic of decentralized social action" (p. 198). This author struggles with how the alliances with a state, by seeking recognition or granting of rights for a particular out-group—such as in the case of Two-spirit, lesbian, gay, bisexual, transgender, queer and/or questioning, intersex, asexual, and additional orientations and gender identities (2SLGBTQIA+)—can become an implicit validation of the oppressive reality of said state. "I'm concerned, for example how to address the homonormativity which arises when gay and lesbian rights claims coincide with the racial politics of state\ capital\ Empire, for example" (Puar (2008), as cited in Heckart, 2011, p. 199).

The potential here is to explore further for ways that anarchist thought can help break through labels and identities attached to these for real liberation. In fact, Heckert (2011) offers a tantalizing glimpse when talking about the way Foucault's care of the self can be understood from an anarchist perspective. "When I feel less attached to the question of who I really am—activist or scholar, homosexual or bisexual—I find myself experiencing a deeper sense of connection with others" (p. 205). For social workers, there is room to reflect and grow as we engage with groups who have been marginalized due to our (or the state's pervasive labeling game downloaded into our worldviews) perceptions that define our relationships with them and the world.

Postmodern anarchism and social work

Todd May (2013) writes about how, contrary to Marxist approaches, anarchism is interested in exploring how the oppressed themselves define their experience. It eschews the politics of representation in favor of direct practice. In postmodern thought, this can include representation of ideals which can bring about a form of intellectual subordination. What this means is that any idea that rallies the masses is viewed with suspicion by anarchists. This lends itself well to intersectional critiques of modernity and opens up new ways of engaging in resistance to the state apparatuses that entrench submission. May (2011) connects this to the ideas of Deleuze and Guattari in how the state can exert control over our desires by constituting the subject through such devices as the Oedipus complex. We are conditioned to accept our identities by way of pathology. The inverse—to love the authority figure and to accept limitations on our desires—is the preferred condition of the loyal and obedient subject. Even in this, there is a binary which Deleuze and Guattari would likely reject in favor of "lines of escape" (as cited in May, 2011, p. 419). Other writers have returned to classic anarchist writers, such as Emma Goldman, to argue that their ideas were postmodern all along (e.g. Bertalan, 2011).

Indigenous ways of knowing: Decolonizing social work and anarchism

Further work is needed to engage with Indigenous ways of knowing, anarchism, and social work. While this book primarily sought to engage in anarchism more broadly, I have tried to refer to and include non-Caucasian perspectives as they pertain to ideas of anarchism. It would be wrong of me to claim that this was exhaustive and, frankly, would be beyond the scope of this book to do so. However, as I am reflecting on further areas for exploration, I believe it is necessary to return to Indigenous perspectives—both those who explicitly incorporate anarchism and those who are bringing ideas of Indigenous resistance and resurgence. Again, not to make the claim that I have done this thoroughly, but rather to introduce and reflect on paths still to be taken on these topics.

Indigenous anarchist Tawinikay (2021) offers an interesting perspective of how settlers and colonized could work together for a shared goal of liberation from the state. She calls out the trend of claiming Indigenous identity to be more relevant in the struggle, or various ways to escape the responsibility of being the settler, the colonizer. Tawinikay argues that anarchists need to do better to call out compatriots who engage in these tactics. She challenges the racist blood quantum concepts and argues for Indigeneity beyond blood and how kinship matters more. If you have a connection to the community versus some ancestry.com test results, this holds a greater meaning and value.

> This is not to say that anarchists have not fucked things up and lost relationships in other ways: by swooping in and ditching early, by not repping their own politics, by breathing way too much air, or simply not knowing much about the history of this land. They definitely have. But having to add "letting their friends play Indian" to that list feels like a real shame. Of all the settlers here on Turtle Island, anarchists have the most to offer Indigenous struggle and the closest shared vision of a decolonial future. I say this as both a Michif halfbreed and an anarchist. (p. 4)

Tawinikay makes the case that we, the settler need to sit with our mixed emotions, fight for land that is not ours and to accept the Indigenous rage that will be part of the struggle. To seek to escape for the siren song of an illusory, deeper solidarity by identifying as Indigenous is a form of theft and deception—you are letting yourself off the hook versus doing the difficult work with fellow settlers when owning your positionality. She acknowledges what I believe as well: we, the settler, have been colonized over millennia by our own process, having been alienated from the land and a spirituality that has been lost. This is important work but cannot imitate or appropriate Indigenous spirituality. Furthermore, this painful history of genetic gatekeeping has been about privileging White purity over Indigenous status. The fact that this is now shifting and that settlers want to claim advantages on this now is shameful and wrong. Given the politics involved in Indian status, she rejects these ideas as ultimately serving to validate a state which she rejects. Regarding our (settlers) own work, we need to re-engage with the land to disrupt or destroy our own ancestral alienation.

Tawinikay (2021) calls for a parallel process between settler anarchists and Indigenous people. Rather than default to guilt-ridden subservience to Indigenous groups—which again places the burden on Indigenous peoples to problem solve—anarchist settlers need to challenge their peers who are seeking to escape their whiteness and guilt with Indigenous self-identified claims (and thus also supporting the binary of western, individualism). We are called on to develop our own reasons for seeking the end of the state and a reason to defend the land (even if we have no claim to it).

Adopt your own reasons for defending the land or attacking the state, separate from your practice of support. Learn the real, unromantic history of colonization, complete with occasional Native complicity. Understand who you are and what your responsibilities are to the next generations. Gain confidence in communicating your own politics of anarchism to Native comrades. Don't allow your crew to adopt a politic that makes it valiant to be a victim, the kind that leads people to want to stack up oppressed identities in order to gain social power. And, most importantly, practice the self-assurance necessary to stop yearning for the approval of Indigenous land defenders. Understand yourself well enough to catch validation-seeking behaviours and be able to interrupt them and ground yourself in your own reasons for acting. (p. 11)

Tawinikay (2020) makes the case that Indigenous approaches are similar to anarchism in that one needs to recognize that we have to be accountable for what we say, and that knowledge comes out of the creative act of communities, the flattening of hierarchies thus and that that no one person is above others. Using the logic of anarchism, she argues that movements, such as Idle No More, have run their course and that the well-intentioned attempts to engage with the state and its laws is over. She argues that settler laws are illusory in their claim at being neutral or objective. Inevitably, the state will change the laws and rules to privilege its own status and agendas. The time for direct action, for the blockade, is now. While she makes it clear that settlers cannot escape their legacy and unearned privilege, settlers can get involved, using the "Two Row Wampum" argument: solidarity here is fighting your own battles to reclaim the commons together. Again, settlers cannot escape their legacy but build their own resistance toward that common goal, including land back for the Indigenous of Turtle Island while cultivating our own connection to the land.

While reconciliation is a construct much bandied about in North America, Tawinikay challenges the utility of this. She argues that decolonization is a better word, as it is about repealing the authority of the settler state and validating Indigenous worldviews previously dismissed or even suppressed. She challenges the way terms are used in that if you believe in a kind of liberal incrementalism where reconciliation is feasible, you are not supporting decolonization. In fact, if you believe in decolonization, it is a radical departure, as it requires departing from any relations with the state. According to Tawinikay (2018), this confusion that has resulted in an interchangeable use of the two terms is in some part due to how universities have employed them. In fact, if you engage in a reformist notion of reconciliation, you are submitting to the authority of the state in how it validates your ownership. Which means that it can turn around and take it all away as well. She argues that other forms of the state, be they communist or otherwise, are anathema to Indigenous worldviews, as they always require a form of organization that reproduces the settler state. Anarchism, according to her, is closest in approximating Indigenous ideas of governance and supporting Indigenous future sovereignty. Furthermore, anarchism and its refusal to believe that nation states are necessary, as well as that non-human beings should not be reduced to a value to humans under capitalism that extends to a stewardship (versus ownership) of land fits well with Indigenous worldviews.

> The thing is, I don't think settlers need to co-opt Indigenous worldviews or to start using our forms of governance. I really think anarchism can provide us with a political system parallel and harmonious. A set of ideas that can also allow for us to acknowledge the interdependence of the earth and to form new values based on that sacred connection. (p. 8)

I find myself agreeing with the idea that the path forward, wherein settlers can forge a parallel strategy grounded in anarchist ideas and ideals, is promising. This can achieve the same goal without running the risk of appropriation or passively waiting for directions from the colonized to avoid reproducing oppression. It still requires a humble acknowledgment of our history and accountability, but it avoids the trap of the binary of either co-opting Indigenous struggle or being useless. Again, I am reminded of my vision of anarchist currents. While newer writers have expanded horizons—from queer, BIPOC, and others—the legacy of the works of Kropotkin, Bakunin, and more recently Bookchin and Graeber are but a few examples of anarchist ideas being written from inside the settler/colonial experience. At the margins, as Indigenous resistance and resurgence is growing, there is a parallel of ideas and strategies that help bring about a better world for all.

Some anarchists may argue that voting is, at best, harm reduction. Indigenous Action (2020) make a compelling argument from an Indigenous anarchist perspective as to how dangerous this idea can be. In pointing to the legacy of attempts at assimilation of Indigenous peoples in the United States via the process of citizenship, voting becomes the validation of the settler state and subordinates the Indigenous to this apparatus. Indigenous Action

(2020) point to the Tribal Councils as evidence of this meddling and assimilation. Essentially, the US governance model is transposed into reserves with the imposition of Tribal Councils. Further, it gives cover for extractive capitalism to get access to the land via the voting process on Tribal Councils (see Crosby & Monaghan, 2018, who document how the Canadian settler state has done this time and again). Repeating a similar logic as philosopher Robert Wolff (1998) outlined in his book *In Defense of Anarchism*, representative democracy as it exists in the United States expects majority rule which, barring some extreme Indigenous population growth, will always mean that Indigenous people will always be in the minority and have to abide by the tyranny of the majority.

> No matter what you are led to believe by any politician seeking office, at the end of the day they are sworn to uphold an oath to the very system that was designed to destroy us and our ways of life ... A less harmful form of colonial occupation is fantasy. The process of colonial undoing will not occur by voting. You cannot decolonize the ballot. (Indigenous Action, 2020, p. 9–10)

There have been issues between anarchist and Indigenous groups that also need further discussion. For example, Insurgent-S (2003) argue that in some *petit* anarchist theory literature, the employment of the noble savage trope remains—which is problematic. They exhort anarchists to directly engage with Indigenous solidarity movements, not idealize them. However, they do still believe that it is possible to find common cause with anarchists to engage together in direct action and organizing against a common enemy, a shared struggle for liberation from the state.

Aragorn! (2005), articulates an Indigenous anarchism that is place based but he explains this as more complex than may be initially understood. Place could mean remaining in one place for one's whole life, or the seeking out of wooded areas, arid deserts in a nomadic fashion. Basically, whatever it is that one resonates with as the connection one has to place. In other words, a place-based anarchism that is Indigenous could seem to be nomadic or sedentary in appearance. Further, it requires a sense of life—that everything has spirit—even what one would in a western gaze see as only objects. He notes that Indigenous people have not been quick to adopt anarchism for several reasons—one being that it is another Western idea and that it is perhaps too far beyond the mainstream to have any relevance or interest to Indigenous people. However, another real and legitimate concern can be that anarchists may see race as a social construction that serves a purpose to divide and conquer the proletariat/lumpenproletariat -the whole racial capitalism argument. In such a perspective, Indigenous self-determination is undermined as it is misunderstood. Put another way, "The question that anarchists of all stripes have to answer for themselves is whether they are capable of dealing with the consequences of other people living in ways they find reprehensible" (p. 6).

Aragorn! (2005) raises an interesting and relevant critique in that there can be arrogance in anarchist ideas—as practiced by a group that is less interested in evangelism and more in getting internal agreement on ideas, language, and tactics. He rightly argues that anarchist critiques tend to be repetitive and say more about anarchism than the world being critiqued and that this can be a real turnoff, as Indigenous people see an insular sect versus a welcoming ally. However, he sees value in developing an Indigenous anarchism, but that this is still an early process and that there aren't any teachers or guides along the way.

In 2007, Aragorn! argued that perhaps the issue is less complex than we have made it. There was a time when a challenge had been issued to anarchists to cease focusing on their differences and come together with common cause, with unity of focus. This has been called "an anarchism without adjectives." He argues that the notion of ending the state and all authority may be naïve but that our daily actions to work to bring about change in the here and now (not some imagined or utopian future) is where real potential lies for anarchism. In effect, he exhorts us to engage in a naïveté toward each other that we reserve for the world: if we believe that thousands of years of indoctrination can be undone for a better world—that change is possible—why can't we have the same approach to each other?

Other Indigenous voices include the work of Leanne Betasamosake Simpson (2017) who introduces another way to think of Internationalism. Even from the theoretical lens, she acknowledges the utility of "Western liberatory theories" when grounded in Indigenous thought systems and Indigenous normativity. One can imagine that anarchism could fit here as well. She introduces a new international idea: Indigenous ways of knowing have always been international. She does this by noting how Indigenous worldviews include connections with plants and animals as a form of internationalism already—not necessarily requiring large geographic distances. How she approaches the inclusion or consideration of non-Indigenous thinkers is based on a series of questions such as, what is the source, context, and process by which these ideas were generated? Further, how was the scholar/writer's relationship to their own community as well as the dominant power structures? How will this sit with or fit with Indigenous thought? Will inclusion of these ideas replicate anti-blackness, transphobia, or any of the other coordinates of oppression? These questions need to be employed before such ideas can be incorporated. These are helpful ways for future scholarship—regardless of the social location of the scholar—to engage with ideas that are not part of one's own culture.

Regarding anti-capitalist organizing, her construction of internationalism fits with this idea as well as Indigenous resistance.

> This interests me because I see the dismantling of global capitalism as inseparable from the struggle for Indigenous sovereignty, self-determination, and nationhood because capitalism at its core is not just incompatible with core Indigenous values but has to violently shred the bodies who house those values in order to sustain itself. (p. 67)

Furthermore, she references an Indigenous woman from the 1860s, Michi Saagiig Nishnaabekwe, Nahnebahnwequay, who—after losing her Indian status for being married to a White man—met with the Quakers on the way to confront the Queen of England to address this injustice.

> The Quakers became part of a network of allies who existed outside of the dominant political landscape and forged a solidarity with his allies that gave her support and access to power she would not have had otherwise. (p. 68)

This is significant, given how Graeber and Wengrow (2021) credit the emergence of mutual aid from the Quakers, themselves having been taught by Indigenous people of Turtle Island. Simpson (2017) references Glen Coulthard (see Chapter 7 on mutual aid for more on his ideas) and his work to apply the politics of recognition from Frantz Fanon to the Indigenous struggle to argue for a reframing of resistance.

> The first tenet then of radical resurgent organizing is a refusal of state recognition as an organizing platform and mechanism for dismantling the systems of colonial domination. The second tenet requires us to refuse the state's framing of the issues we organize around. (p. 176)

Further, she argues it is crucial to do this as the state will always come up with solutions that validate, legitimate, and retrench its power. Again, the potential for anarchist ideas to find connection here are clear. According to Simpson (2017), Indigenous resurgent activism is broad—from giving talks and educating others to the building of breakfast programs that highlight Indigenous foods as well as participating in rotating blockades that prevent extractive capitalism from doing it's foul business. She notes three strands or approaches towards the state and it's political reality. The first is the rights-based approach, which would employ strategies based on policy making and be fought within the arenas of the courts and electoral politics. Second, the treaty-based approach similarly uses the legal mechanism of the state, in effect, beating the state at its own game. The third and final approach is a nationhood approach that seeks to dismiss the politics of recognition and rights-based politics and is focused on Indigenous resurgence which she argues is necessarily anti-capitalist in nature. I am intrigued by these ideas, as they can help us understand how resistance beyond the state can take shape. Anarchism can help explain why colonization has and continues to be ruthless in its quest to oppress and dominate while pretending at reconciliation. The real threat of Indigenous peoples involves how they are a clear and present danger to capitalism and the lies it tells about itself. These Indigenous societies call into question this laissez-faire existence for one that is more humane, loving, and sustainable to a world on fire. Finally, it is Simpson's evocative description of revolution that bears reflection. She describes it as taking on a form we haven't seen before and that it is the culmination of "the past and the future collapsing in on the present" (p. 247).

In contrast to Simpson, one could argue that Palmater (2020) represents more of a rights-based approach, especially given her pedigree as a lawyer. She notes that, for example, the issue of the Indian Act reflecting this challenge. On the one hand, in Canada, this is a racist legal document but the abolition of it has its own racist agenda. For example, she argues that Canadian Prime Minister, Justin Trudeau's father, argued for its abolition with the purpose of eliminating First Nation's rights (p. 216). However, she also challenges electoral politics as a hollow and merely symbolic approach to bringing about meaningful change-suggesting the adoption of the third approach as well.

> Voting in the oppressor's regime has, not surprisingly, failed to end oppression. Yet, those in power in Canada would have us believe that our power comes from voting for them, as if they represent our nations... Even today,

those who vote are voting for the party that will represent the next minister of Indian affairs. The political players are really secondary considerations given the complex construct of laws and policies and economic structures that exist to deny us our basic human rights, let alone our Aboriginal treaty rights ... First Nations voting in federal elections will not bring about the change we need. (pp. 222–223)

Inuk scholar Jackie Price (2008) shares that Indigenous governance models tend to be based on ideas that the reader would likely recognize as being similar to anarchist models. In Inuit governance in Nunavut, community leaders work with each other in respectful ways that keep the common member of the community in mind. Hierarchies are not considered here. What is different from anarchist organizing includes the spiritual dimension. Rules that govern relations are based in the spiritual world and, in effect, are a moral code of conduct that everyone is responsible to. These are called Maligait. Following these rules keeps the balance between people, animals, the spirit, and the physical world. Tellingly, Price refers to an Inuit on Rankin Island who explains that the problem with laws is that they are written down. Paper can be torn up and the law, in effect, vanishes. Maligait is in the heads of the Inuit. They will survive regardless of whether individual members of the community pass on. In effect, they have more integrity, durability, and are more binding as the community has integrated these rules for "what must get done" by all.

Settler-anarchist voices

While it is important to center Indigenous voices in future works exploring the intersections of anarchism and Indigenous thought, settler contributions to these conversations are instructive here as well. First, it is part of the ongoing discussion of the need for us settlers to do our own work that is important here. The following brief excursion into the literature by settlers, some explicitly anarchist, some less so, highlights some of the work being done in ways that try to avoid the pitfall of Indigenous appropriation. They are seeking to challenge the western mindset of anarchists—to support Indigenous resurgence in ways that can promote a greater solidarity—and, finally, to challenge our understanding of what solidarity can mean.

Anarchist settler, Adam Gary Lewis (2017) notes that, as has been seen with Occupy movements, the issue of stolen land needs to be addressed and dealt with, or there is the real risk of reproducing settler/colonial logics that also uphold the White supremacist system that make it so. He argues that by incorporating Indigenous theory and practice, it can help create prefigurative futures outside of the state and capitalism that places these ideas explicitly in order to be accountable to Indigenous people, lifeways, and laws. According to Lewis, the challenge may be in how anarchists resist any authority and do not submit. However, if we do not do so when it comes to the struggle on Turtle Island, we are no use to Indigenous resistance and we certainly are not allies in the struggle. Lewis argues anarchists need to—at least initially—voluntarily associate (borrowing from the anarchist idea of voluntary association) with Indigenous people. In doing so, voluntarily submitting to their laws and forms of governance is key. While this may seem controversial or even offensive for some anarchists, Lewis makes the case that our preconceived resistance is predicated on western, capitalist notions of laws and governance. Indigenous governance and law are grounded in nonhierarchical frameworks that assume a form of direct democracy that upon further examination ought to be complimentary to the ideas on this in anarchism. Similar to the way Tawinikay writes on this, he imagines futures of parallel communities in mutual coexistence where settlers are engaging in more overtly anarchist practice. However, this needs to be secondary to the primary aim of working with Indigenous people on their terms first.

> So anarchists might consider delegating authority, as it were, to Indigenous nations, in part because resurging Indigenous political systems are themselves anti-state and anti-capitalist, and share a number of affinities with anarchist ideas. This is one way that anarchists might adapt their general radical visions to the specific context of settler colonialism. (p. 6)

What Lewis (2017) is saying is that activists have treated the commons as an empty space rather than one that belongs to the Indigenous who have been dispossessed of it. Settler society will construct their legitimacy from the Locke approach of claiming Terra Nullius. Since "unused" equals unoccupied, this means that occupation is legitimate. This is then followed by narratives of settlers who are fleeing their own persecution and violence to "eclipse the violence against Indigenous people." (p. 10)

Lewis echoes my concern in even citing or referring to Indigenous writers for risk of appropriation and fundamentally misunderstanding the location. Essentially, it is the fact that there tends to be a privileged position that most anarchists occupy (unless one is Indigenous) which may contribute to misreading or misrepresenting the ideas of Indigenous writers. The perspective of colonization being driven by capitalism is incomplete according to Lewis. We need to consider Marx' point that a precursor is needed—primitive accumulation which dispossesses the regular peasant from their labor (and the enclosure of the commons) are preconditions. What this means is that we need to acknowledge that early colonization was essentially not capitalist. The expansion had to occur first before capitalistic relations could take place (p. 14).

He acknowledges that Coulthard (as cited in Lewis, 2017, p. 14) understands this best as he argues for reframing this process of proletarization (the dispossession of the worker from the work, and so on) to the colonizing context where it is dispossession (of the Indigenous) itself that is the precondition for successful colonization. He argues that Simpson's (as cited in Lewis, p. 14) reframe is integral—Indigenous people are not dissenting or resisting. This casts the whole encounter in a binary where we continue to engage in settler logic. The Indigenous are engaging in resurgence, a reclaiming of their own sovereignty and self-determination. This isn't a battle in which to "win" against the colonial state, which would bring it back to a kind of validation of the state in the first place. To resist against means it has authority that needs to be challenged after all. He makes an important point in that anarchism is richer as a result of having learned from Indigenous governance and struggles.

> Importantly, it is not Indigenous peoples who have drawn from anarchist forms of organization, but rather the other way around, with major anarchist theorists drawing from the Haudenosaunee confederacy or the struggles of the Zapatistas, for example. These points of contact, with anarcha-Indigenism as but one example, might be fruitful places to enact anarchist solidarity with Indigenous struggles now, with a view to deferring to Indigenous self-determination and autonomy in the future. (p. 19)

Ultimately the point is made that prefiguration itself—frequently employed by anarchists—needs to be decolonized. Indigenous resurgence is a form of prefiguration already in process. Any future reference to prefiguration by anarchists needs to defer to Indigenous laws and forms of practice on stolen land.

The prior idea fits well, in my view, with social work scholar, Elizabeth Carlson-Manthara and Indigenous scholar Gladys Rowe's book, *Living in Indigenous Sovereignty* (Carlson-Manthara & Rowe, 2021). Their book is an invitation to reflect and learn about how we can dispense with the White Savior complex and be open to learning from Indigenous people as we develop our own relationship to the land we occupy. I am also indebted to Elizabeth Carlson-Manthara for providing me with another resource to consider when it comes to the relationships between anarchists and Indigenous people (Personal Communication, November 23, 2022). Barker and Pickerill (2012) make the case that anarchists need to be aware of how their efforts can compound harm if not aware of Indigenous place-based ideas of resurgence. A series of questions can be asked by anarchists to ensure they are aware of this concern. For one, anarchists need to reflect on what a decolonized settler colonial society ought to look like. In this society, how would the decolonized settler identity engage in relationships with Indigenous peoples' and their places? "Answering these questions should be a primary goal of anarchist Settlers pursuing Indigenous solidarity; however, the pursuit is not so simple" (p. 1710). I can see benefits here in that, if anarchist groups can reproduce patriarchy and White privilege unwittingly, perhaps another boon to anarchism by Indigenous ways of knowing is to help anarchism be less unaware and more conscious about these dangers and engage to address them. This is made more explicit in how Barker and Pickerill (2012) note that Eurocentric views privilege time versus Indigenous worldviews that focus more on place as a frame of reference for history and the world. They argue that Indigenous people can help anarchists challenge their Romantic or Classical view of nature. There is a real failure in imagining nature as a pristine, unsoiled space as the Romantic view tends to emphasize or as a wilderness in need of domination, taming, and "civilizing," as in the Classical view. Both place humans at the center, which an Indigenous perspective seeks to challenge.

How anarchists can make their views more problematic can be seen in the implementation of autonomous zones. They aren't necessarily decolonized and hence may be erasing Indigenous realities. It is the ongoing dialogue between settler anarchists and Indigenous people that is key—always in flux and ever reconstituting relationships that are based on mutual respect (Barker & Pickerill, 2012). I would want to add that it is also necessary for anarchists to listen due to unequal power dynamics in play. Given the White supremacist structures privileging the White anarchist, we have an obligation to do so. When it comes to autonomous zones, which tend to be urban spaces, another suggestion for anarchists in organizing these spaces is to engage with Indigenous groups to get to know the "personality" of the place/space.

Finally, Barker and Pickerill (2012) make the point that failing and fear of failing are colonial mindsets. To decolonize means to risk making the mistakes and being a part of something larger than ourselves, seeing the effort to decolonize not as a burden to place at the feet of Indigenous people but to do this work ourselves while avoiding appropriation or co-optation.

> It is not the role of Indigenous activists to instruct Settler anarchists in the dynamics of colonization. It is not up to Indigenous peoples to decolonize Settler society. Rather, Settler anarchists must make the conceptual leap from a position of "anti-colonial solidarity" generally, to "decolonising affinities" specifically. (p. 1721)

Settler activist and sociologist Craig Fortier (2017) writes about the need to unsettle the commons which captures similar perspectives to those mentioned above. Some activists see inclusion for Indigenous peoples in a shared struggle but miss the very idea of sovereignty in the process. Thus they end up reproducing even the assimilationist agenda due to failure in understanding this difference. In fact, one could say that it is the ongoing engagement through discussion, debate, and conflict that the work toward building relationships based on solidarity as well as seeking consent that are key. He reiterates the notions that both Indigenous resurgence and antiauthoritarian struggles share affinities in how both oppose the legitimacy of the state. By referencing Leanne Simpson's (p. 79) idea of trans-motion, he helps give a glimpse of how Indigenous worldviews can help anarchists understand how to challenge the logic of the settler state itself. Essentially, she argues that the state as a centralized political structure is anathema to nature. The Nishnaabeg ways of being emphasize boundaries in the form of relationships which are always in flux, as this dynamic is more accurately a reflection of the natural world. Fortier argues that we need to unsettle—which is unsettling—our minds and intentions when we think about the commons and it's reclamation. There is a need to center and cultivate Indigenous views and perspectives as well as accountability. He argues that we need to challenge the static and complete notion of knowledge itself—knowledge ought to be more dynamic, incomplete, and relational. By being open and uncertain, we are allowing for an unsettled perspective of social movements as well as their goals. Further, he argues that apologizing (for colonization) is insufficient and that a shame or guilt-based approach seeks to only help the colonizer feel better. Accountability means to engage in a shared struggle toward undoing the systems that enable and continue to empower colonization in the first place. Returning to previous arguments, he argues that antiauthoritarian movements (that reject authority on principle) will need to get used to the idea of taking direction/valuing the authority of Indigenous people in these struggles.

As previously alluded to in this chapter, the most profound point Fortier (2017) raises in my opinion has to do with the way we think about the concept of sovereignty itself. Settlers tend to think of this idea in western terms, which implies rule. This likely is a significant part of the reason why anarchists may struggle with Indigenous governance. This is based on a failure to appreciate and understand Indigenous ways of knowing. Indigenous sovereignty is not counter-hegemonic but non-hegemonic. There is no state which is being influenced or is influencing others from a dominating position of authority here. "Indigenous sovereignty is articulated through relationality rather than domination. This relationality emphasizes interdependence between humans, animals, the natural world, the ancestors, and the cosmos" (p. 79). Finally anarchist scholar Rhiannon Firth (2022) cautions that any exclusion of the concept of gender in developing an anarchist Indigenous framework risks not only failing Indigenous women but any effort at anti-colonial, anti-capitalist action. In fact, she points to the secularization of religious tendencies in anarchist circles as resulting in the exclusion of feminized and Indigenous knowledge (p. 82).

Antifa and social work: New ideas on the politics of confrontation and advocacy

While "conflict theory" is introduced in human behavior and the social environment textbooks (Schriver, 2004; Zastrow & Kirst-Ashman, 2016), it is incomplete. For example, Zastrow and Kirst-Ashman (2016) argue that conflict theory is predicated on the assumption of scarcity. Competition for these scarce resources is assumed to be the basis for conflict. While they allow for some benefits to conflict, presumably civil rights reform, they argue that it tends to be critiqued for leading oppressed groups to consider revolt versus incremental, system-based reform. Anarchists may critique conflict theory based on the instrumental flavor of Marxism (reform versus revolution), but Antifa can teach us about the boundaries of debating ideas. We may believe that our efforts to listen and be empathetic opens others to change. There are ethical arguments for why a nonjudgmental stance is problematic. In writing about social work and ethical practice, Loewenberg et al. (2005) certainly point out the perils of such a stance. In effect, by listening nonjudgmentally to a domestic abuser, one runs the danger of communicating tacit endorsement or support of their actions. Antifa's uncompromising stance in the face of fascism may hold promise for social work to consider how we avoid becoming complicit with both side-ism. I think that, especially given this volatile and polarizing time, this is an urgent topic needing further focus. In fact, while I could point to places of convergence between anarchism and anti-fascism, anti-fascist activist and writer Shane Burley (2022) makes this case better, as he points to how mutual aid was a factor that was essential in maintaining anti-fascist action during the BLM uprisings after George Floyd's death (p. 12). Lavin (2022) notes that part of the reason that the media struggles to understand anti-fascist action is that their allegiance to institutions and the state makes it difficult to conceive of the concept of non-state actors, "individuals and collectives acting from no authority but their own desire for a better world" (p. 1).

As with anarchism, there are no fixed definitions when it comes to anti-fascist thinking. There are commonalities for sure. For example, some may argue that fascism is the result of capital defending itself as the contradictions of capitalism become too much to bear for an outraged public (Rappoport, 2019). Other voices have argued that fascism is independent of the proletariat; in fact, it is a force that at times will even garner support by targeting the global elites. Mathew N. Lyons (2022) argues that the idea of capitalism using fascism is too simplistic. "Just because someone hates the rich and wants to overthrow the government, don't assume they're progressive" (p. 21). The January 6 riot at the Capitol seems to be a case in point for this perspective.

Returning to the earlier point of ethical practice, perhaps anti-fascism can teach us ways to think about a response to hate that does not seek to model a virtue of active listening at all costs? A liberal debate in the marketplace of ideas, according to anti-fascists, only emboldens the hate. In fact, activist and scholar Mark Bray (2017) points to history and the rise of fascism as evidence of where reasoned debate and liberal politics enabled the rise of Nazism. He argues that free speech is never absolute and that anti-fascists are simply more overt about the political nature of their limitations—a group who argues for the destruction of others is not one worth debating but rather deplatforming or shutting down. History has shown how totalitarianism is enabled when good people allow the hateful rhetoric of White supremacy to hide behind free speech, after all.

Turning to the earlier chapter on the environment (see Chapter 4), another factor involves fascism itself. It may come as a surprise to some, but there is a history of fascism venerating the environment. Moore and Roberts (2022), in their book *The Rise of Ecofascism*, point to how even the Nazis engaged in an form of nature veneration that reflected their obsession with racial purity. Andreas Malm and the Zetkin Collective (2022) further note how right-wing governments—when unable to deny the climate catastrophe—will argue that keeping "the other" out of their country is going to keep their national, natural world pure and good. According to Moore and Roberts (2022), it is the feature of fascism to apply the anti-immigrant framework to any issue, regardless of how nonsensical this may seem. In fact, pointing to such horrors as the Christchurch mass killer's manifesto, one can see how this kind of rhetoric is used to justify racist violence. There is more work to be done in how to combat fascism as it appears on the rise, not only due to financial instability in the world brought on by a rampant capitalism's neoliberal turn but also as a result (and directly caused by extractive capitalism) of climate change. I believe social work needs to engage with how to address this concern to life itself. Those we claim we serve deserve our best efforts in this regard.

Anti-psychiatry: Madness, social work, and anarchism

Social work scholar, Bren LeFrancois (2022) raises an important point in how we need to become epistemic dissidents (p. 506). Both classical anarchists and social workers are being challenged to reconsider our ideas about knowledge itself and how we privilege the rational, enlightenment-era paradigms. By engaging with cultural, racial, and alternative reality perspectives (i.e. what has been deemed psychosis) as ways or forms of knowing, we are opening up new ways to understand our world. What I take from these ideas is that there is space here to discover how the overlap of Mad and anti-psychiatry movements, anarchism, and social work can bring about new ways of thinking about how our world has been shaped in regard to the sane/insane binary.

Critical psychologist and academic Isaac Prilleltensky argues that even problem definition is a political action. In choosing to frame things from the mental domain, the social domain and its contribution to the presenting concern remains unchallenged (Prilleltensky & Nelson, 2002). Furthermore, self-determination and autonomy as the standards for well-being can become problematic if they are the main values for a given society. In effect, if happiness equals personal success, it means that unhappiness is because of one's own personal failures. "In cases of misfortune, the conflation of self-determination with personal responsibility produces self-blame" (p. 28). Liberal individualist notions of personhood thus form the genus of pathology for the fields of psychology and psychiatry (Chapman, 2019). This idea of the unitary moral self with a binary notion of good and bad, responsible/irresponsible, and objectification originates in Eurocentric notions of the self. The potential of challenging these assumptions thus may have further potential to decolonize our concepts of mental health. As social workers, we can work to undermine these implicit assumptions of mental illness in our practice and beyond.

American psychologist, Bruce E. Levine (2022) searchingly asks if psychologists and psychiatrists are being asked to compel individuals to adjust to an inherently toxic world by the authorities in charge. Similarly, it is the biological theories (of etiology) that serve to distract us all from the environment—the societal ills driving behavioral maladaptation. Herein the uncomfortable truth may lie. Are we, the mental health experts, dispatched to "other" the dissenters, to make the dissident "crazy," so as to marginalize them? To silence their legitimate objections to a world that is mad? "Are mental health professionals undermining mutual aid and other forms of nonhierarchical organization and democracy?" (p. 188). In fact, he points to how, in the Soviet Union, dissidents were frequently diagnosed with a "sluggish schizophrenia" (p. 189) and hospitalized for this. The reason this is compelling is that the mental health professionals in the Soviet Union genuinely believed the dissidents were ill, as their status put them outside the boundaries of conventional thought and behavior. Of course we don't need to point to Soviet Russia as an example of how the state manufactures consent with psychiatric labels. "In 1805, Rush diagnosed those rebelling against the newly centralized federal authority as having an 'excess of the passion of liberty' that 'constituted a form of insanity,' which he labeled as the disease of anarchia" (p. 190). It is, of course, quite easy to point to how anarchism was dismissed in this fashion. However, some may say that this was long ago and not a reflection of modern society. In the 1960s, Black Power activists got swept up in this as well when their resistance to authority was coded as a form of schizophrenia, and they were hospitalized for this against their will. By questioning the validity of the neurotransmitter theory of mental illness, he asks why it is that the pharmaceutical industry and its medication regiments remain the most common form of intervention. Oftentimes this includes overprescribing to marginalized populations that do not have psychosis. How we construct difference is how we enforce hegemony. As social workers, we need to explore the ways this is done to help aid in the resistance against such oppression and control.

Social work and anarchism

This chapter would not be complete without acknowledging some of the good work already underway by fellow social workers in applying anarchist ideas. Bren LeFrancois (2022), in conceptualizing a social anarchist social work, challenges the field to consider ways to be a part of movements, where our power and authority are de-emphasized in favor of the mutual aid networks that are already present in places where we are practicing. They argue that Marxist, structural and anti-oppressive approaches have failed to separate social work from the state in any meaningful way. Moreover, they raise the concern that how the ongoing project of professionalization has harmed the very people we intend to be helpful toward. While working within systems may be necessary, they would urge us all to think of how to bring about a better world, beyond the state that seeks to address the communities' need for social and environmental justice.

> In anticipation of the eventual collapse of capitalism, social anarchist social workers may now begin to support the values, ideas and actions inherent to libertarian communitarianism, given the important emphasis in social work education and practice on community development. This includes collectively organizing alternatives to state care, as we develop beyond or in parallel to our current capitalist-directed welfare-state society. (p. 499)

I am further indebted to their conceptualization of the challenge of expert knowledge, particularly in the helping professions vis-à-vis our relationship with those we intend to help. It is not the knowledge or the knowledge holder that is the problem, per se. According to LeFrancois, our opposition as social workers needs to be to any group (nursing, psychiatry, social work, etc.) that wields the knowledge as a cudgel for compliance and dominance. When it is deployed as "shared acts of solidarity and support" (p. 500), and those impacted have the agency and desire to seek this information via informed choices, it is an asset to the greater cause for emancipation. Furthermore, an anarchist orientation to social work would question any coercive process which we ought to be rejecting to participate in. Involuntary mechanisms should be refused from an ethic of care grounded in antiauthoritarian arguments found, in part, in anarchist ideas. I concur further with their position that an anarchist approach to social work needs to include a decolonialism that refuses to participate in the nationalism that promotes othering, disenfranchising, and domination by the state. No one is illegal.

While it is encouraging that both LeFrancois and Mark Baldwin (2022) are included in the larger work *Critical Social Work Praxis*, he argues that anarchism has been informing social work already—it just hasn't been openly acknowledged or credited directly. I concur with his arguments that mutual aid is key for demonstrating that people can be helped without using authoritarian, coercive, and centralized means. He argues that people are inherently creative when control is returned to rather than wielded over them. Mutual aid in effect, is the playful path toward healing that social workers ought to get behind. I welcome his contribution to this fledgling idea that social work and anarchism can be combined, especially given the reality of our frequent positions of authority within systems of social control. What I find useful is ways to think about how, as a social worker, to model egalitarian relationships—not just with the ones we profess to help but also with each other inside these systems. For example, "an anarchist social worker will ask themselves whether their use of authority is justified, and, if so, what justifies it. Who gains and who loses by their use of this authority?" (p. 518). Furthermore, anarchism challenges social workers to conceive of people beyond the individual, atomized relations they observe. While I could argue that our ecological models need to address this, I cannot disagree with the critique that, in our daily practice, we may not be considering the elaborate connections in community, the way mutual aid is practiced already, and that there is more going on than the individualized, "presenting problem."

Baldwin challenges us to look at how to meet the need of others, not assess for their eligibility. The former supports agency and choice, the latter is about a neoliberal framing of resources. It is hence our ethical imperative to always be on the side of championing for what others need, not what the state has decided they deserve.

Anarchist social worker Martin S. Gilbert (2005) writes about how social work has been painted into a corner by Marxist critiques. Gilbert identifies how the critique of reform versus revolution has been championed by a left authoritarian Marxism. By addressing the harms caused by the contradictions of capital, we are stealing the momentum for meaningful change. He counters this from an anarchist perspective, noting that anarchist social work practitioners are addressing immediate needs in the short term so that those at the margins have the capacity to raise their heads and even contemplate action. By helping those at the margins with real, material issues, they can look to the horizons of new possibilities that daily survival makes impossible (pp. 10–11). This is an idea we will return to in the conclusion of this chapter.

Conclusion

Social work academic Steve Burghardt's (2020) critique of the profession is timely in his work *The End of Social Work*. He laments the loss of a sense of social justice in American social work. While schools continue to educate about human behavior and the social environment, macro practice has been receiving less and less attention. This has had several implications and consequences. For one, it has left social work graduates with less education about how to address the structural harms that are experienced as the contradictions of capitalism under neoliberalism accelerate suffering. Another feature, he argues, is how this has also resulted in a toothless self-soothing approach for how to avoid burnout. Mindfulness and other approaches that focus on the individual continue to reinforce an apolitical, individualist paradigm that leaves the social floor undisturbed.

> Today's discourse on working conditions has been supplanted by the professions focused on licensure and the professionals' responsibility for self-care as the primary ways to respond to worker burnout and work induced stress. The idea of the collective self-interest of the social worker that

animates the environmental, food justice, and immigrant struggles of today is literally not imagined, let alone acted upon. (p. 9)

What I find intriguing in his analysis is how he recasts our historical understanding of the profession of social work. We tend to view social work as heroic—even if the public does not recognize our status as essential workers and first responders during the pandemic—and we see our past as rife with stories of resistance and advocacy. We are and always have been at the front lines of civil rights reform and other human rights-related issues. Burghardt (2020) challenges this view. Our history is a revision, a kind of fiction that inflates our importance, the power, and the weight of our performance in past social justice movements. It is this inflated story of our past that is now a part of the reason why we appear so lost and ineffectual. It was never social work by itself but rather a collection of various groups that, along with a similar lack of status and influence, banded together with common cause. He points to Depression-era activism that saw worker's rights and tenant rights, being experienced by those engaged in these struggles, as one and the same. There was a solidarity in the past which is integral to thinking of the present moment. Intersectional experiences of oppression hence predate the terminology and give us a way to think about current struggles in what I would argue is for emancipation against the state, capitalism, and its current iteration in neoliberalism. This overestimation of the power of social work has resulted in students entering the field with an unrealistic sense of their own role in bringing about social justice. In effect, he is arguing that we are creating our own downfall as disenchanted social workers either settle for less or burn out and leave the field.

> When social work leaders ignore the political economy as a way to exaggerate workers' valuable contributions, we diminish the profession's stature and erode professionals' confidence about what they can do . . . Today, left without an analysis that situates social work within larger political, economic dynamics, social workers end up expected to somehow achieve the unachievable. (p. 29)

I think it is important to say that this critique by Burghardt (2020) does not mean to suggest that individual or even associations of social work aren't trying to engage in activist work. His comments are directed toward the profession as a whole, as professional associations tout legislative victories to advance the self-interest of social work over any meaningful collective action toward social justice in the world. He is making the case that it is impossible to practice without political considerations. Social needs are harmfully impacted by neoliberalism—parents are overworked, while kids are in pre- and post-school type daycare for parents to be able to do this. Precarity, job stress, and mounting debt have resulted in ever-increasing domestic violence and drug and alcohol abuse. Even if you want to remain apolitical in your practice, politics (under neoliberalism now) is not going to let you. Burghardt argues that if we want to help children and their families, we need to speak out and challenge the political economy that causes or exacerbates social problems.

Social workers are not immune to neoliberalism and its effects. Burghardt points to studies that show how many social workers are dissatisfied with their work and struggle with depression and burnout, which has to be impacting their work in adverse ways. He suggests that it is imperative for social workers to think of themselves as part of the struggle for emancipation from the current political system that is grinding us down.

> Social workers would serve themselves and their clients/community members far more effectively by militantly joining with them on fights over income inequality—including their own—than spending another guilt-ridden minute that they are even a partial cause of working and poor people's lack of militancy directed at neoliberalism. (p. 45)

Burghardt (2020) suggests that our thinking needs to change, beginning in the classroom. He calls for a return to anti-racist practice and to model and encourage self-regulation. By making the implicit explicit, we are learning how to self-monitor. First, it is in the classroom, where our dominance structures (i.e. the establishment of expectations for hierarchical relations, etc. as well as the unconscious use of unearned privilege and the baggage that comes with it) need to be observed, critiqued, and overcome.

While our historical consciousness may have been wrong about our power, we have also forgotten that social work theory exists in our past that can help us move forward with this effort. Burghardt (2020) illustrates this point by referring to how the concept of empowerment, a topic of controversy and derision, has been "whitewashed." Black professor Barbara Bryant Solomon in 1977 was writing about Black empowerment and how this seemed to be part of a larger effort to address the color-blind 1950s era practice model.

In fact, using the most recent social science literature available to her, she wrote about an approach that levels the playing field between client and practitioner.

> Her breakthrough was clear: Social workers had to know—and thus learned from—the poor Black people themselves before attempting any active intervention. Responding to the basic knowledge that White practitioners needed at the time, she also placed special emphasis on the variety of African Americans within the Black community. (p. 92)

By the 1980s, the term had been reduced, both conceptually and literally, to only "empowerment." The focus now being on personal self-care and change versus the ground-breaking and socially focused practice it was supposed to have been—a paradigm shift in the worker–client relationship. Burghardt (2020) accuses social work education in disappearing the work done by Black social work scholars. The reason? Their work is too specific in focus and can only be applied to other Black clients or issues related to racial discrimination and racism. Theory, according to the larger body of social work educators, needs to be more generalizable. Hence the work by White female academics with their problem-solving and person in environment approaches is more comfortable. Our own complicity in perpetuating White supremacy, by benefiting from the privilege we enjoy, remains unexplored.

I believe that it can be frustrating when looking at social problems and their genus without it leading to answers of how to respond. The challenge raised by progressive and radical approaches to social work can lead to a binary impasse. Either you ameliorate suffering as a helping professional and thus reduce the evidence of damage caused by our status quo, or you focus on the system and its structures for meaningful change for all. I think that this is a false dichotomy that prevents us from creatively engaging in future possibilities. Certainly, other writers above have articulated this in ways that give me hope (e.g. Burghardt, 2020; LeFrancois, 2022; Gilbert, 2005).

It may be true that direct action brought about by collective discontent has been the likely trajectory that both anarchism and Marxist thought have claimed. As social workers, what would it look like if both—direct helping and developing collective strategies for change—are possible? For this to be considered, I want to conclude this book by returning to my primary occupation: that of a teacher at an undergraduate BSW program. It is my hope that

I can help challenge us all to consider future possibilities for a better world together.

While preparing for my final class in a course that focused in part on group practice, I came across the concept of "elite panic." Emerging from this rabbit hole, I am surprised to discover that this concept has potential to lead a vision of another kind of clinical social work practice. As the class progressed, I was finding myself thinking about other ideas connected to clinical work. If mutual aid is the natural state of society in the face of crisis, and the goal of working in groups is to facilitate this process from unfolding, perhaps this connects further to what anarchism has been saying all along: the state is an artificial imposition on society, bolstered by a form of economics that privileges individual accumulation of wealth and power. This is contrary to the natural state of society; hence something has to give. We are told that the natural state is the individual and that deviations from this are pathology, and our pain and suffering are due to mental health problems rather than as a direct consequence of our artificial separation from each other.

It may be reasonable to ask then, what about individual work with people? How does this fit in with such logic? I recall in my Intro to Clinical Practice class always reviewing the idea that ultimately, it is about how well the individual feels understood and heard. Empathy is the culmination of this experience. It is the opposite of thinking about ourselves and the tuning into the other. Put another way, it is about the true experience of connection with someone else where the healing begins. As social workers, the social world/environment is our focus. We are in a unique position to consider how mutual aid has the potential to impact the environment of those we serve. I believe there is a potential for a better world of which we can be a part—not leading the charge, but coming alongside this revolutionary potential.

Returning to the proposal by Gilbert (2005, pp. 10–11), I am wondering if a fitting analogy for social work can be found at the heart of mass protests. During the civil unrest that resulted after the murder of George Floyd, images of clashes on the streets became common. We became witnesses to the horrors of far-right violence and police brutality. Another figure intrigued me throughout. Never in the spotlight—but always present—was the street medic, handing out supplies, treating injuries, and responding in what appeared to be a tireless struggle to ensure that those who were seeking to rise up had the resources to do so. I don't believe that anyone would question their motives by suggesting that their intervention prevents real change to be possible as they remove the evidence of the violence being transacted on the bodies of the protesters. In fact, it is the opposite. I would like to think that social work can take a page from this essential worker. Our contributions can amplify and bring about change, not alone, but connected to this larger world we are a part of.

Whether the reader is convinced that anarchism is the best way forward for social work or not, the research is compelling for greater equality in the world. Wilkinson and Picket (2009) in their ground-breaking work, *The Spirit Level* show how, when societies are more equal—on multiple measures, not only income—they are healthier. It is better for us to have greater equality in the world. In fact, these authors are able to point to other factors that can predict population health such as, "If—for instance—a country does badly on health, you can predict with some confidence that it will also imprison a larger proportion of its population, have more teenage pregnancies, lower literacy scores, more obesity, worse mental health, and so on" (pp. 173–174).

If this is the finding, then we, as social workers need to become more interested in how to increase equality and decrease hierarchies, as they are the ossified structures that validate inequality. Anarchism may be one way to explore how we can be part of this better world for all. As Wilkinson and Picket (2009) note, it is the practice of mutual aid that can improve population health. They argue that Hobbes got it wrong about the nature of humanity. Instead of valuing homogeny, it is our diversity and difference that are the real asset for survival.

> As well as the potential for conflict, human beings have a unique potential to be each other's best source of co-operation, learning, love and assistance of every kind . . . So important are these dimensions of social life that lack of friends and low social status are among the most important sources of chronic stress affecting the health of populations in rich countries today. (p. 201)

In order for us to be a part of the solution, I believe it is necessary to engage in the difficult work of reflecting how we contribute to being part of the problem. In my own engagement with anarchist ideas, I find myself questioning implicit assumptions about our practice. As already alluded to above, I wonder about how we valorize our identity in the first place. When we claim to be social workers, it tends to be a complete identification. We are always social workers, no matter if on the job or off. Our professional ethics, values, and so on are inculcated into our very being. While I understand the rationale, anarchism has helped me question if this is really in the best interest of our profession or even those we seek to help. Being a social worker, after all, is a professional designation, and, hence, there is the real risk of being totalized by an epistemology that reduces individual variance and communal models of identity. This is then replaced by identification with a community of professionals rather than fellow human beings. So, when we say we are always social workers, we are venerating the idea of identification via our occupation, by our work. If anything, it is my hope that the chapter on supported employment can make this strange. Our collective humanity is not advanced by this kind of identification. After all, our grand purpose ought to be to work for our own profession to become irrelevant. The end of social work as the sign of a newer, better humanity for all.

References

Anarcho. (2009 March 3). *No God, no boss, no husband: The world's first anarcha-feminist group*. Accessed January 29, 2021, www.anarchism.pageabode.com. www.theanarchistlibrary.org

Aragorn! (2005 Spring). *Locating an Indigenous anarchism*. Green Anarchy (19). Accessed April 22, 2009, www.greenanarchy.org. www.theanarchistlibrary.org

Aragorn! (2007). *Anarchy without road maps or adjectives*. https://theanarchistlibrary.org/library/aragorn-anarchy-without-road-maps-or-adjectives

Baldwin, M. (2022). Mutual aid, autonomy, and anti-authoritarianism: Building an anarchist social work practice. In S. S. Shaikh, B. A. LeFrancois, & T. Macias (Eds.), *Critical social work praxis* (pp. 515–531). Fernwood Press.

Barker, A., & Pickerill, J. (2012). Radicalizing relationships to and through shared geographies: Why anarchists need to understand indigenous connections to land and place. *Antipode, 44*, 1705–1725. 10.1111/j.1467-8330.2012.01031.x

Bertalan, H. (2011). When theories meet: Emma Goldman and 'post-anarchism'. In D. Rouselle & S. Evren (Eds.), *Post-anarchism: A reader* (pp. 208–230). Pluto Press.

Bray, M. (2017). *Antifa: The antifascist handbook*. Melville House Publishing.

Burghardt, S. (2020). *The end of social work: A defense of the social worker in times of transformation*. Cognella Academic Publishing.

Burley, S. (2022). What is antifascism? In S. Burley (Ed.), *No pasaran! Antifascist dispatches from a world in crisis* (pp. 5–18). AK Press.

Carlson-Manthara, E., & Rowe, G. (2021). *Living in Indigenous sovereignty*. Fernwood Press.

Chapman, C. (2019). Becoming perpetrator: How I came to accept restraining and confining disabled aboriginal children. In B. Burstow, B. A. LeFrancois, & S. Diamond (Eds.), *Psychiatry disrupted: Theorizing resistance and crafting the (r)evolution* (pp. 16–33). McGill-Queen's University Press.

Chapman, C., & Withers, A. J. (2019). *A violent history of benevolence: Interlocking oppression in the moral economies of social working*. University of Toronto Press.

Crosby, A., & Monaghan, J. (2018). *Policing Indigenous movements: Dissent and the security state*. Fernwood Press.

Day, R. F. (2005). *Gramsci is dead: Anarchist currents in the newest social movements*. Between the Lines.

de Heredia, M. I. (2007). *History and actuality of anarcha-feminism lessons from Spain*. A Feminist History Journal, [42]-56. https://theanarchistlibrary.org/library/marta-iniguez-de-heredia-history-and-actuality-of-anarcha-feminism-lessons-from-spain

Firth, R. (2022). *Disaster anarchy: Mutual aid and radical action*. Pluto Press.

Fortier, C. (2017). *Unsettling the commons: Social movements within, against, and beyond settler colonialism*. Arbeiter Ring Press.

Gilbert, M. S. (2005). An anarchist in social work. In M. S. Gilbert (Ed.), *Anarchists in social work: Known to the authorities* (pp. 7–32). Martin S. Gilbert.

Gordon, U. (2013). Israel, palestine, and anarchist dilemmas. In R. Graham (Ed.), *Anarchism: A documentary history of libertarian ideas: Vol 3: The new anarchism (1974–2012)* (pp. 135–138). Black Rose Books.

Graeber, D., & Wengrow, D. (2021). *The dawn of everything: A new history of humanity*. Farrar Straus and Giroux.

Hart, M. A. (2002). *Seeking mino-pimatisiwin: An Aboriginal approach to helping*. Fernwood Publishing.

Heckert, J. (2011). Sexuality as state form. In D. Rouselle & S. Evren (Eds.), *Post-anarchism: A reader* (pp. 195–207). Pluto Press.

Hick, S. F., Peters, H. I., Corner, T., & London, T. (2010). *Structural social work in action: Examples from practice*. Canadian Scholars' Press Inc.

Indigenous Action. (2020 February 5). *Voting is not harm reduction*. Indigenous Action. http://www.indigenousaction.org/voting-is-not-harm-reduction-an-indigenous-perspective/

Insurgent-S. (2003 November 24). *Colonization, self-government and self-determination in British Columbia*. https://theanarchistlibrary.org/library/insurgent-s-colonization-self-government-and-self-determination-in-british-columbia

Kinna, R. (2017). *Anarchism and feminism*. Accessed November 8, 2021, www.researchgate.net Published version in Nathan Jun (Ed.), Brill's Companion to Anarchism and Philosophy. www.theanarchistlibrary.org

Klein, N. (2019). *On fire: The burning case for a Green New Deal*. Knopf Canada.

Klito. (2005, March). *What's new under the black flag? Some thoughts on anti-sexism in the libertarian movement*. Accessed May 13, 2019, https://libcom.org/library/what's-new-under-black-flag-some-thoughts-anti-sexism-libertarian-movement

Lavin, T. (2022). On the uses and manifestations of antifascism. In S. Burley (Ed.), *No pasaran! Antifascist dispatches from a world in crisis* (pp. 1–3). AK Press.

LeFrancois, B. (2022). Social anarchist social work. In S. S. Shaikh, B. A. LeFrancois, & Macias, T. (Eds.), *Critical social work praxis* (pp. 497–514). Fernwood Press.

Levine, B. (2022). *A profession without reason: The crisis of contemporary psychiatry untangled and solved by Spinoza, free thinking, and radical enlightenment*. AK Press.

Lewis, A. G. (2017). Imagining autonomy on stolen land: Settler colonialism, anarchism, and the possibilities of decolonization? *Settler Colonial Studies*, 7(4), 474–495. doi: 10.1080/2201473X.2016.1241211.

Loewenberg, F. M., Dolgoff, R., & Harrington, D. (2005). *Ethical decisions for social work practice* (7th ed.). Brooks/Cole.

Luxembourg, R. (1908/2006). *Reform or revolution and other writings*. Dover Publications.

Lyons, M. N. (2022). Three way fight politics and the US far right. In S. Burley (Ed.), *No pasaran! Antifascist dispatches from a world in crisis* (pp. 20–41). AK Press.

Malm, A., & The Zetkin Collective. (2022). *White skin, Black fuel: On the danger of fossil fascism.* Verso.

Marshall, P. (2010). *Demanding the impossible: A history of anarchism.* PM Press.

May, T. (2013). Post-structuralism and anarchism. In R. Graham (Ed.), *Anarchism: A documentary history of libertarian ideas, Vol. 3: The new anarchism (1974–2012)* (pp. 413–423). Black Rose Books.

Moore, S., & Roberts, A. (2022). *The rise of ecofascism: Climate change and the far right.* Polity.

Mullaly, B., & West, J. (2018). *Challenging oppression and confronting privilege: A critical approach to anti-oppressive and anti-privilege theory and practice.* Oxford University Press.

Palmater, P. (2020). *Warrior life: Indigenous resistance and resurgence.* Fernwood Press.

Payne, M. (2011). *Humanistic social work.* Oxford University Press.

Poole, J., Jivraj, T., Arslanian, A., Bellows, K., Chiasson, S., Hakimy, H., Pasini, J., & Reid, J. (2012). Sanism, 'mental health,' and social work/education: A review and call to action. *Intersectionalities: A Global Journal of Social Work Analysis, Research, Polity, and Practice*, (1). https://doi.org/10.32920/21751490.v1

Price, J. (2008). Living Inuit governance in Nunavut. In L. B. Simpson (Ed.), *Lighting the eighth fire: The liberation, resurgence, and protection of Indigenous nations* (pp. 127–138). Arbeiter Ring Press.

Prilleltensky, I., & Nelson, G. (2002). *Doing psychology critically: Making a difference in diverse settings.* Palgrave Macmillan/Springer Nature.

Rappaport, C. (2019). Fascism. In S. Faure (Ed.), *The anarchist encyclopedia abridged.* (M. Abidore trans.). AK Press.

Schriver, J. M. (2004). *Human behavior and the social environment: Shifting paradigms in essential knowledge for social work practice.* Pearson Education.

Simpson, L. B. (2017). *As we have always done: Indigenous freedom through radical resistance.* University of Minnesota Press.

Tanenbaum, J. (2016). *To destroy domination in all forms: Anarcha-Feminist theory, organization, and action 1970–1978.* https://theanarchistlibrary.org/library/julia-tanenbaum-to-destroy-domination-in-all-forms

Tawinikay. (2018). Autonomously and with conviction: A Métis refusal of state-led reconciliation. Retrieved on 25th February 2021 from north-shore.info. theanarchistlibrary.org

Tawinikay. (2020 February 15). *Reconciliation is dead: A strategic proposal.* Accessed February 25, 2021, https://north-shore.info/2020/02/15/reconciliation-is-dead-a-strategic-proposal/

Tawinikay. (2021 April 12). *Settlers on the Red Road: A conversation on Indigeneity, belonging, and responsibility* (zine). Accessed April 22, 2021, https://north-shore.info/2021/04/12/settlers-on-the-red-road-a-conversation-on-indigeneity-belonging-and-responsibility

Walia, H. (2021). *Border & rule: Global migration, capitalism, and the rise of racist nationalism.* Fernwood Press.

Wehbi, S., & Parada, H. (Eds.). (2017). *Reimagining anti-oppression social work practice.* Canadian Scholars.

Wilkinson, R., & Picket, K. (2009). *The spirit level: Why equality is better for everyone.* Penguin Press.

Wolff, R. P. (1998). *In defense of anarchism*. University of California Press.
Zastrow, C. H., & Kirst-Ashman, K. K. (2016). *Understanding human behavior and the social environment* (10th ed.). Cengage Learning.

Chapter questions

1. This chapter focused on several topics for further discussion. Some received greater attention than others. What do you think? Was this valid?
2. Are there topics you would like to have seen covered that weren't mentioned? What would these be?
3. Reflect back on the first chapter and your reading experience. How has your understanding of anarchism changed? Do you think that there is potential for an anarchist social work? Why or why not?

Index

For the benefit of digital users, indexed terms that span two pages (e.g., 52–53) may, on occasion, appear on only one of those pages.

Adams, J., 17–18
advocates for the landscape, 74
affinity groups, 70
Afrofuturist Abolitionists of the Americas, 150–51, 152
Agent of Chaos (Spinrad), 87
altruism, 149
anarchism
    antiauthoritarian principle, 9–10, 23–24, 201, 210–11
    better world principle, 6
    class concepts, 24
    criminology, 24–25, 91–100
    critiques of, 196–97
    empowerment via, 5
    green, 63–69
    individuality/self-development, 28
    law enforcement views of, 5, 6, 24–25
    mutual aid principle, 159–160
    place-based, 196–97
    postmodern, 191–92
    property in the person, 48
    property is theft principle, 5, 12, 23, 27–28, 66, 91
    queering, 187–88
    reciprocal awareness principle, 28
    Sawatsky's background in, 7–8
    sovereignty principle, 5
    on the state, 22–28
    theory described, 4
    without adjectives, 197
anarcho-capitalist, 22–23
anarcho-feminism, 188–90
Anderson, W. C., 150
Antifa, 1, 205–7
anti-oppressive practice (AOP), 4, 106, 168

anti-psychiatry, 207–9
Aragorn!, 196–97
archaeology, 118
aristocracy, 20, 45, 46–47
Asset Based Community Development (ABCD) model, 151
Auschwitz, 74
Autonomie Magazin, 36–37
autonomous zones, 203–4
autonomy *vs.* collectivity, 23–24

Baird, J., 174
Baldwin, M., 210–11
Barclay, H., 26, 28
Barker, A., 203–4
battle for Seattle, 4
behavioral maladaptation, 207–9
Bentham, J., 87
Berlin, S., 107–8
Berneri, M. L., 145
Besthorn, F., 59–60
Beyers, C., 121–22
biodiversity, 59–60, 65
Bismarck, O. von, 156–57
Black, B., 41, 47–48
Black, Indigenous, and People of Color (BIPOC), 81, 85, 109, 140, 150. *See also* carceral system
Black codes, 83
Black Flag Sydney, 151–52
Black Lives Matter (BLM), 79, 158–59, 187–88, 205–6
Blackstock, C., 122–23
Bolsheviks, 27
Bookchin, M., 23, 63–65, 68–70, 132, 195

bourgeoisie, 20, 27–28, 40, 188–89
Bray, M., 206–7
breadwinner model, 75
Brown, L. S., 48–49, 123, 188
Burkhardt, S., 183, 211–14
Burley, S., 205–6
bystander indifference, 141–42

Cairncross, G., 125–26
Canadian Association of Social Workers (CASW), 79–80, 103
Cantine, H., 37–38, 49
capitalism
    critiques of, 5–6, 10–11, 73–74
    disability rights under, 171–72
    exploitation/oppression by, 3–4, 27–28, 30–31, 116, 128–32, 150, 171–72, 186–87
    humane capitalism, 58–59
    industrial, utilitarianism in, 21
    as nihilist, 63–66
    power relationships, 66–67, 118
    preservation of state via, 27–28, 67–68
    reform of, 65–66, 70–71, 118
    science under, 66–67
    terminology, 4
    Thatcher on, 5
    victim blaming, 66–67, 74, 184
    welfare state relationship to, 8–9
carceral system
    abolition of, 95, 100–3, 110
    allyship, 102
    anarchist criminology, 24–25, 91–100
    autonomy, 102, 106
    body cameras, 79–80
    boundaries, national interests, 89, 90, 99
    capitalism influences on, 86, 88, 93, 95–96, 100
    cheap labor pools, 81, 84, 107
    colonial legacies in, 89, 95, 99–100
    community-based solutions to, 94–95, 98, 101–2
    community damage via, 81, 88, 94
    community policing, 104–5
    crime prevention, 104
    dehumanization, 87, 89–90
    deschooling, 101–2
    drug offenders, 83–84, 100–1, 104
    executions, 86, 96–97
    for-profit industry, 84
    health impacts of, 92
    Indigenous peoples in, 87–90
    inmate statistics, 91–92
    mass incarcerations, 19, 80, 81, 86–87
    media role in, 81
    Othering, 83
    peacemaking criminology, 98
    police abolition/defunding, 79–80, 82
    police and crime, 81–91
    police killings, 89–90, 94
    political activism and, 89–90, 94
    power relationships, 86–87, 97–98
    privilege and, 80, 84
    property/wealth accumulation and, 95–96, 102
    public opinion/censure, 97
    public safety/for their own safety, 99
    racism/racial profiling, 80, 81–91, 104, 109
    reform/rehabilitation, 85–87, 97, 100–1
    religious connotations, 86–87
    resistance to, 98–99, 102, 106
    restorative justice, 102–3
    school-to-prison pipeline, 92–93
    social work advocacy in, 103–8
    state authority and, 85–86, 88–89, 93–95, 98
    unnatural deaths, 89–90
    white supremacy and, 82–84, 101
    women in, 85, 88–89
    youth offenders, 80, 88, 90–91, 105–7
Carlson-Manthara, E., 203
Carson, R., 59–60
Carter, A., 26–27
Charity Organization Societies (COS), 17–18
Chess, C., 164–65
CITE, 122–23
civil rights movement, 18
Clarke, L., 164–65
climate change, 57–63, 69, 71, 73–75, 207
Clinton, W. J., 83

Cohn, J., 176
collaborative teaching model, 121
colonial legacies
   in carceral system, 89, 95, 99–100
   in climate change, 60
   in education/training, 73–74, 89, 95, 117–18, 132
   Indigenous peoples, 202
   mutual aid, 150, 171
Comfort, A., 144–45
communism, 47–48, 157
community, belonging, 23, 25–26, 32–33, 58–59, 70, 143
Community Oriented Policing Services (COPS) program, 83
community policing, 104–5
conflict theory, 205–6
consciousness raising, 118, 133, 168
control. *See* social control
Coulthard, G., 154, 198, 202
COVID-19 pandemic, 36–37, 56–57, 132, 143, 148, 158–63
CrimethInc, 94, 101
critical theory, 3–4, 7, 116–17
Crosby, A., 88, 89
cultural heritage sites, 60–61

Dachau, 74
D'Angelo, K., 171–72
Darwinian evolution, 63, 142–43
Dauvé, G., 48
Davis, A. Y., 81–82, 84, 86, 87, 100–1
Dawn of Everything, The (Graeber), 155
Day, R. J. F., 187
DC Mutual Aid Network, 159
Debord, G., 3–4
DeCarlo, G., 145–46, 152
Declaration of the Rights of Man/Citizen, 21–22, 40
DeCleyre, V., 188–89
decolonization, 185–86, 192–200, 204
deforestation, 73–74
degrowth, 72–73
de Heredia, M. I., 189–90
Department of Homeland Security (DHS), 162
Derrida, J., 99

desertification, 60
dignity, 25, 32–33
Disaster Capitalism (Firth), 161–62
Dniester, A., 129–31
Dominelli, L., 60–62
drought, 60
dualism, 65
Dubler, J., 86–87
Dubois, W. E. B., 17–18

eco-communities, 65
eco-fascism, 73–74
ecological model, 57–58
eco-terrorism, 74
education, training
   agency/autonomy, 119–20, 128–29
   analysis skills, 61–62, 118–19
   anarchist principles of, 123–31, 132, 213–15
   capitalism influences, 128–31
   certification/degrees, 126
   challenges in implementation, 121, 131–32
   co-construction in, 117–19, 124–25
   collaborative teaching model, 121, 124–25
   colonial legacies in, 73–74, 89, 95, 117–18, 132
   consciousness raising, 25, 118, 133, 168–9, 184
   cram schools, 129
   critical pedagogy in, 12, 33, 115, 117–20, 124, 132–33
   critical theories and, 3–4, 7, 116–17
   cultural stereotypes/bias in, 120, 134
   de-schooling, 101–2, 128–29, 132–33
   financing of, 129, 130–31
   generalizability, 214
   graduated guardianship, 125
   hands-on learning in, 120
   hegemony in, 116, 118, 122–23, 125–26, 131–32
   historical background, 17–18, 125–27
   as indentured servitude, 129, 130–31
   Indigenous spirituality/ways of knowing in, 117–19, 185–88, 192–200
   of law students, 107–8

education, training (*cont.*)
   learning environment, 120–23
   learning *vs.* teaching, 127–28, 130
   libertarian model, 124–25
   limitations of, 18–19
   mentorships, 121
   neoliberal influence on, 19, 123, 128, 132
   power relationships, 114–15, 116–17, 118–19, 121–22, 124
   privilege in, 117–18, 130–31, 132
   purpose/function of, 114–15
   social control via, 116, 119, 125–28, 129–30, 131–32, 151, 210
   social work generally, 115, 134
   standardized tests, 129–30
   student evaluations, 121–22
   student *vs.* faculty expectations, 121–22
   totalizing institutions, 116–17
   truth/morality, 124–25
   utilitarianism in, 118
Eiler, E. C., 171–72
elite panic, 139, 164–65, 215
employment. *See* supported employment
End of Social Work, The (Burkhardt), 183, 211
enlightenment, 116
Enlightenment (historical period), 86–87, 126
entrance exam war, 129
environmental justice/sustainability, 58–60
environmental movement, 18
environmental refugee status, 62–63
environment in human development, 57–63
Erickson, C. L., 59–60
Essential Law for Social Work Practice in Canada (Regehr/Kanani), 103–4
essential services, 11, 19, 30, 47–48
Estes, N., 89–90
Ethiopia, 60

Fabian socialism, 146
Fanon, F., 154, 198
fascism, 31, 66, 99–100, 150, 156, 205–7
fast food, 71

Faure, S., 124–25
FEMA, 161–62
Ferrell, J., 25, 98–99
Ferrer, F., 124
Finn, M., 142–43
First Nations, 5, 87–88. *See also* Indigenous peoples
Firth, R., 148–49, 153, 156–57, 160–63, 176
Fortier, C., 185–87, 204–5
Foucault, M., 12, 20, 85, 86, 114, 116, 118–19, 191
free trade agreements, 149
Freire, P., 114, 117–18
Fry, E., 87

Gelderloos, P., 91–92, 93, 94–95
genealogy, 119
Genovese, K., 140–42
German Romanticism, 64
Gilbert, M. S., 211, 215–16
Giroux, H., 132–33
Gitterman, A., 174
Giwa, S., 104–5
globalization, 30, 81, 116
Global North, 60, 158
Global South, 30
Godwin, W., 23, 24, 66–67, 95–96, 127
Goffman, E., 42, 116
Goldman, E., 124, 188–89, 190
Goodchild, A., 103–4
Goodman, P., 143–44
Gordon, U., 32–33, 186–87
Gouldner, A. W., 20, 21–22, 23, 40–41, 44–45
Graeber, D., 26, 37–38, 42, 155–58, 175, 186–87, 195, 198
Graham, R., 22–23, 150
Gramsci, A., 89–90
Gramsci is Dead (Day), 187
great man theory, 4
green social work
   affinity groups, 70
   biodiversity, 59–60, 65
   class divisions, 67
   climate change, 57–63, 69, 71, 73–75, 207

complementarity, 70
consumer culture, 71
degrowth, 72–73
disaster relief, 62
dispossession of resources, 61–62
eco-communities, 65
eco-fascism, 73–74
eco-technology, 64–65, 68–69, 70
environmental impact assessments, 60–61
environmental justice/sustainability, 58–60
environmental refugee status, 62–63
environment in human development, 57–63
ethical consumption, 71
green movements, 71–72
irreducible minimum, 70
liberal hegemony, challenging, 70–71, 72–73
overpopulation, 66–67, 74
ownership as fiction, 12
pollution, 58, 65–66, 71
power relationships, 66–67, 75
primitivism, 68–69
social ecology, 65
state's view of nature, 67–69, 74, 207
urban heat islands, 62
usufruct, 70
victim blaming, 66–67, 74
Grubacic, A., 155–57, 158, 175

Hackett, C., 83, 101
Hasankeyf, 60–61
Hassan, S., 109–10
heat deaths, 62
Heckert, J., 191
Heenan, D., 120
Heller, C., 71–72
Hern, M., 126–27
Hick, S., 4
Hobbes, T., 21, 140–41
Holmes, O. W., 93
housing, 43–44, 101
Howard, J., 87
humanism, 105–6, 160
humanitarianism, 91

Hurricane Katrina, 165
Hurricane Sandy, 161–62
hydroelectric dams, 60–61

identity
  core identity groups, 148
  employment as, 36–38, 40–42, 48–49
  social work roles, 181–88
Idle No More, 89, 194
Ilisu Dam, 60–61
Illich, I., 102, 128–29
immigrants, 149
Inconvenient Indian, The (King), 89–90
Indians Wear Red, 88
Indigenous Action, 195–96
Indigenous peoples
  activism/resurgence by, 197–99, 201–3
  assimilation of, 195–96, 204–5
  climate change impacts, 73–75
  colonial legacies, 202
  governance models, 200
  mass incarceration/killing of, 80, 87–90
  mutual aid practice by, 149, 153, 154
  prefiguration and, 202–3
  private property views, 5
  race as social construction, 196–97
  reconciliation with, 192–97
  self-determination, 196–97, 202
  settler literature regarding, 200–5
  sovereignty, 186–87, 198, 202–3, 204–5
  spirituality/ways of knowing, 117–19, 185–88, 192–200
  voluntary association with, 201–4
individualism, 149, 162
industrialization, 45, 63, 114, 116, 185
Industrial Workers of the World (Woblies), 98
in-group vs. out-group phenomena, 140, 148, 166–67, 207
instrumentalism, 65
Insurgent-S, 196
intentional communities, 73
internationalism, 197–99
invisible hand theory, 4–5
Israel, 32

Japanese occupation of Korea, 143

Jarvis, D., 57–58
Jun, N., 158–60

Kaba, M., 148
Kanani, K., 107–8
Kaslow, F., 105–6
Kenney, J., 85–86
Kenya, 60
Kim, H. C., 29
King, T., 89–90
Kinna, R., 188, 190
Kirst-Ashman, K. K., 205–6
Klein, N., 6, 69, 185–86
Kletsan, P., 103
Klito, 189
Knuttila, M., 20, 21, 40
Kondiaronk, 155–56
Kravetz, D., 107–8
Kropotkin, P., 63, 91, 142–43, 149, 155–57, 169, 171–72, 173, 176, 187

labor unions, 71
Lance, M., 158–60
Laursen, E., 148–49
law enforcement. *See* carceral system; policing
law of population, 66–67
LeFrancois, B., 207–8, 209–11
Lenin, V., 27, 157
Levin, T., 205–6
Levine, B. E., 208–9
Lewis, A. G., 201–2
LGBT+ in social work, 191
liberalism, 21–22
libertarian communitarianism, 209
libertarianism, 22–28
Lincoln, P., 91–92, 93, 94–95
Lind, K., 174–75
Lindström, V., 36–37
Living in Indigenous Sovereignty (Carlson-Manthara), 203
Lloyd, V., 86–87
Locke, J., 21
Loewenberg, F. M., 205–6
Luxembourg, R., 184
Lyons, M. N., 206

Maligait, 200

Malm, A., 207
Marshall, P., 1, 22–24, 49, 71–72
Martin, B., 96
Marx, K., 10–11, 39–40, 63–64, 68–69, 116, 157, 168–69, 187, 191, 202
Massachusetts schools, 127
Mauss, M., 157
May, T., 191–92
Maynard, R., 81–83, 84, 87–88, 89, 92–93
McKay, I., 67, 68–69, 70
mercantilism, 20, 21
Meyer, M., 120
Milgram Study, 140–41
Mill, J. S., 21–22
Mino-Pimatisiwin, 185
misinformation, 165
Modern School, 124
Monaghan, J., 88, 89
monarchies/feudal state, 20, 45, 46–47
Mood Disorders Society of Canada, 51
Moore, S., 73–74, 207
Morales, E., 148–49
Mullaly, B., 8–9, 58–59, 166, 168–69
Mulroney, B., 84
Muskat, B., 169
mutual aid
  all-in-the-same boat phenomenon, 166–67, 174–75
  anarchist principles of, 142–43, 176–77
  bystander indifference, 141–42
  challenges to, 141–42, 176
  charity *vs.*, 143, 150–51, 153, 162
  collective morality and, 141, 145–46, 161
  colonial legacies, 150, 171
  community building via, 143, 145–46, 148–49, 150–51, 152, 158–63, 170–71
  concepts, definitions, 144, 147, 148, 149, 151, 159, 169
  consciousness raising in, 152, 168
  context, 140–41
  core identity groups, 148
  COVID-19 pandemic, 143, 148, 158–63

development/internalization of, 139
elite panic and, 139, 164–65, 215
funding/resources, 152
gift economies, 157–58
group work, 139, 165–69, 173–74
harm reduction by, 154–55, 162–63
health benefits, 169–70, 210–11
hegemony of capital and, 155–56
Indigenous frameworks, 149, 153, 154
in-group *vs.* out-group phenomena, 140, 148, 166–67, 207
as innate human capacity, 138–39, 145, 147, 155–58, 159–60, 165–66, 175
localism in, 160, 161–63, 172–73
loyalty to state opposed to, 145–46
managerial revolutions, 146
Marxist–Leninist model, 157–58
neoliberal influences, 149, 153, 162, 171–72
origins of historically, 198
prefiguration and, 143, 144
racism and, 140, 150
resistance to warfare state via, 143–45, 147
social work role in, 165–76
state subversion of, 146–50, 155–56, 160–61
as trauma healing, 174
Ubuntu framework, 170–71
unpredictability of, 148
white supremacy and, 156
Mutual Aid (Kropotkin), 142–43, 149
Myers. C., 121–22

NAACP, 17–18
National Association of Social Workers (NASW), 79–80
nationalism, 24
natural selection, 66–67
Nazis, 74, 207
Negri, A., 39–40
Newman, S., 99
New York Times, 142
Nishnaabekwe, M. S. (Nahnebahnwequay), 198
Noakes, S., 107–8
Noble, C., 133

Noir et Rouge, 146–47
non-governmental organizations (NGOs), 152, 161–62
No One Is Illegal, 149

Occupy movements, 201
Occupy Sandy, 163
Occupy Wall Street, 161–62
Ostergaard, G., 146

Palestine, 32
Palmater, P., 88–89, 199–200
Pandemic Pedagogy, 132
Paradise Built in Hell, A (Solnit), 139
paternalism, 32
patriotism, 25–26
penitentiary. *See* carceral system
Person in Environment (PIE) perspective, 57–58
Piaget, J., 139
Pickerill, J., 203–4
Picket, K., 216
Pinsky, H., 98
policing. *See also* carceral system
    abolition/defunding, 79–80, 82
    crime and, 81–91
    killings by police, 89–90, 94
    as violence, 160
positivism, 118
power relationships
    capitalism, 66–67, 118
    carceral system, 86–87, 97–98
    education/training, 114–15, 116–17, 118–19, 121–22, 124
    empowerment, 213–17
    gender equality, 189
    green social work, 66–67, 75
    in patriarchy generally, 188–90
    rights-based approaches, 199–200
    in social work, 183, 188–90
    supported employment, 39–40, 41, 44–45, 48–49, 52–53
Price, J., 200
Prilleltensky, I., 208
Prince, J., 147
Prinsloo, R. C. E., 107
prison industrial complex, 81, 107. *See also* carceral system

private property rights, 5, 12, 23, 27–28, 66, 70–71, 91, 155–56
privilege
　anarchists position of, 202
　carceral system and, 80, 84
　in education/training, 117–18, 130–31, 132
　Eurocentric position of, 203–4
Program for Assertive Community Treatment (PACT), 37, 39
Project SITKA, 89
Proudhon, J. P., 5, 63, 91, 188
psychosis, 207–9
PTSD, 174

Quakers, 198

racism, 6, 38n.1, 132, 140, 150, 214
Rappoport, C., 31
Rasenberger, J., 142
Read, H., 147
Reagan, R., 84
reciprocity, 21–22, 28
Reddy, S. K., 101–2, 128–29
Red Nation, 89–90
refugees, 60, 140, 149
Regehr, C., 107–8
Reisch, M., 29
Research and Destroy, 128
residential schools, 80
Richmond, M., 17–18, 57–58
Rise of Ecofascism, The (Moore/Roberts), 207
Ritter, A., 23, 24, 28
Roberts, A., 73–74, 207
Rogowski, S., 106
Romande Anarchist Federation, 143
Roosevelt, Theodore, 17–18
Rosenwald, M., 174
Royal Canadian Mounted Police (RCMP), 79–80
Russell, B., 45–47, 49

Samimi, C., 107
Saskatchewan Commission on First Nations and Metis Peoples and Justice Reform, 88–89
Schmid, A., 85

Schulman, L., 174
Schutzstaffel (SS), 74
second state environmentalism, 59–60
Seifert, A., 74
self-determination, 25, 28, 48, 202
Selkirk Mental Health Centre (SMHC), 37, 43–45
Serve Your Youth, 158–59
settlement house movement, 17–18
settler literature, 200–5
Shulman, L., 165–66, 168, 169
Silent Spring (Carson), 59–60
Simpson, L. B., 197–99, 204–5
slavery, 48–49, 81, 82–83
Sliva, S. M., 107
Smith, A., 155–56
Smith, L. H., 132
social control
　mutual aid and, 151, 157, 157
　social work as agents of, 58–59
　via education/training, 116, 119, 125–28, 129–30, 131–32
　work as, 45, 47–48
social Darwinism, 142–43, 175
socialism, 47–48, 187
social work
　advocacy/social justice role, 29, 32, 56, 103–8, 205–7, 211–15
　as agents of social control, 58–59
　anarchism's relationship to, 7–10, 32–33, 181–88, 209–11
　anti-capitalist approach, 185
　critical, 39, 44
　economic theories in, 4
　empowerment, 213–17
　as enablement of oppression, 6–7, 185, 210–13
　feminist, 2–3, 47–48, 131, 160–61, 188–90
　identity/roles of, 181–88
　international, 30
　LGBT+ in, 191
　Marxist-influenced, 39–40, 44, 160–61, 191, 209–11
　neoliberal influences on, 3, 9, 10–11, 19, 29, 39–40, 212–13
　police social workers, 103–8

policy making role, 4, 184
political context, 3–13
postmodern anarchism in, 191–92
power relationships in, 183, 188–90
rural, 59
social reform, 30, 33, 184–85
social world relationships, 1–2
structural, 168–69
theories of, 2–3
two-spirit people in, 191
Solnit, R., 139, 163–65
Solomon, B. B., 213–14
Somalia, 60
S.O.S. Alternatives to Capitalism (Swift), 8
sovereignty, 5, 186–87, 194–95, 198, 202, 204–5
Spain, 62
Spirit Level, The (Wilkinson/Picket), 216
squatting movements, 146
Stanford Prison Experiment, 140–41
state. *See* welfare state
state-primacy theory, 27
Steinberg, D. M., 172–73
Structural Social Work theory, 131
suffragette movement, 188–89
supported employment
    abolition of, 47–48
    anarchist principles of, 45–50
    autonomy, 41, 43–44, 48–49
    bullshit jobs, 37–38, 42
    capitalism/commodification, 37–39, 38n.1, 40, 42, 46, 48, 49–50, 52
    collective self-interest, 49
    deinstitutionalization, 42, 43
    elderly, 36–37
    employment as identity, 38, 40–42, 48–49
    empowerment/equality, 51
    false consciousness, 51
    free creative spirit and, 50
    government contract, 37–38
    idleness/leisure, 45–48, 49–50
    morality of work/work ethic, 45–47, 52
    occupational stress, 41, 50–51
    power relationships, 39–40, 41, 44–45, 48–49, 52–53
    psychiatric rehabilitation, 11, 36–40, 42, 43–45, 50–51
    useless men/citizens, 41, 44
    vocational rehabilitation, 38–39
    work and mental health, 43–45
    work as life purpose, 37–40
    work as social control, 45, 47–48
    work role in society, 40–42
survival of the fittest, 142–43, 155–56
sustainability, 30

Tanenbaum, J., 189–90
Tawinikay, 192–95
terrorism, 89
Thatcher, M., 5, 160–61
"The Abolition of Work," 47
there is no alternative (TINA), 5
"The Shock Doctrine," 69
Tolstoy, L., 26, 96–97, 148–49
Toronto Anti-Violence Intervention Strategy (TAVIS), 104
totalitarianism, 162–63, 206–7
training. *See* education, training
Trudeau, J., 79–80
Turk, B., 83, 101
Turkey, 60–61
Turtle Island, 185–86, 193, 194, 198, 201
2SLGBTQIA+, 191
two-spirit people in social work, 191
tyranny of the majority, 4–5, 23–24

Ubuntu, 170–71
Umbutu (humanity), 107
unitary moral self, 208
unsettling the commons, 204–5
Unsettling the Commons (Fortier), 186–87
urban heat islands, 62
utilitarianism
    carceral system, 87
    education, training, 118
    in employment/as identity, 38, 40–42, 48–49
    historical origins, 20–22

vagrancy laws, 83
van Breda, A. D., 170–71
Van Wormer, K., 59–60
victim blaming, 66–67, 74, 184

vocational rehabilitation. *See* supported employment
Volin, 26, 27–28
voting, 24, 94, 199–200
Vsevolod Mikhailovich Eikhenbaum. *See* Volin
Vygotsky, L., 139

Walia, H., 90, 99, 102, 140, 149, 186–87
Walter, N., 147
wealth accumulation
  carceral system and, 95–96, 102
  mutual aid and, 155–56, 157–58
  by the welfare state, 23, 26, 27
welfare state
  anarchist/libertarian thoughts about, 22–28, 209–11
  austerity reforms, 18–20
  boundaries, national interests, 25–26, 28, 89, 90, 150, 186–87
  capitalism relationship to, 8–9
  creation of in Germany, 156–57
  domination/hierarchy patterns in, 63–64, 69
  economy/politics relationships, 26–28
  legitimacy of, 23–24, 140
  maintenance of authority, 24–25, 67–68
  as organized violence, 24–26, 160–61
  political context, 19–20
  social relationships mediation, 23
  social work in origins of, 17–20, 29
  state as social worker employer, 18–19
  state's roles/responsibilities, 16–17, 21–22
  taxation, 28
  theories of, 20–22
  war as condition of, 26
  wealth accumulation, 23, 26, 27
Wengrow, D., 186–87, 198
Werner, S., 105–6
West, J., 8–9
Wet'suwet'en protests, 5
white supremacy
  carceral system and, 82–84, 101
  Indigenous people subjugation by, 193, 203
  mutual aid and, 156
  totalitarianism and, 162–63, 206–7
Wieck, D. T., 147, 149
Wilkinson, R., 216
Williams, K., 81
Wolf, R., 23–24
work. *See* supported employment
Wu Zhihui, 125

Yellow Bird, M., 140

Zapf, M. K., 59
Zastrow, C. H., 205–6
Zetkin Collective, 207